Authority, Autonomy, and the Archaeology of a Mississippian Community

Florida Museum of Natural History: Ripley P. Bullen Series

FLORIDA MUSEUM

Authority, Autonomy, and the Archaeology of a Mississippian Community

ERIN S. NELSON

University of Florida Press

Gainesville

First cloth printing, 2020
First paperback printing, 2024

29 28 27 26 25 24   6 5 4 3 2 1

The Library of Congress has cataloged the printed edition as follows:
Names: Nelson, Erin S., author.
Title: Authority, autonomy, and the archaeology of a Mississippian community
 / Erin S. Nelson.
Description: Gainesville : University of Florida Press, 2020. | Series:
 Florida Museum of Natural History: Ripley P. Bullen series | Includes
 bibliographical references and index. |
Identifiers: LCCN 2019015769 (print) | LCCN 2019018344 (ebook) | ISBN
 9781683401230 (ePDF) | ISBN 9781683401124 (cloth) | ISBN 9781683404347 (pbk.)
Subjects: LCSH: Mississippian culture—Mississippi—Delta (Region) | Indians
 of North America—Mississippi—Delta (Region)—Antiquities. | Delta (Miss.
 : Region)—Antiquities.
Classification: LCC E99.M6815 (ebook) | LCC E99.M6815 N45 2020 (print) | DDC
 976.2/4—dc23
LC record available at https://lccn.loc.gov/2019015769

University of Florida Press
2046 NE Waldo Road
UF PRESS   Suite 2100
Gainesville, FL 32609
UNIVERSITY   http://upress.ufl.edu
OF FLORIDA

Contents

Figures

Tables

Acknowledgments

I have so many people to thank I barely know where to start. Ray Wood introduced me to archaeology the summer after my sophomore year at the University of Missouri and for that I am exceptionally grateful. He was also the first person to tell me I was good at it, something I might not have known had he not said it. Jay Johnson introduced me to the best bookstore in the South, the wonder that is the Mississippi Delta, and Parchman Place, a site I've spent more than a decade thinking about. Thank you for that. Vin Steponaitis has set an example as an archaeologist, a teacher, and a mentor that I can only aspire to. Margie Scarry has been a role model in more ways than one. My deepest thanks to you both.

I'd also like to acknowledge my fellow travelers in archaeology. First, my cohort (more or less) from the Ole Miss days at Parchman, especially Matt Reynolds, Bryan Haley, Kelsey Lowe, Aaron Fogel, Glenn Strickland, Jessica Kowalski, and Lorrie Jerome. Though there was no beating the heat, poison ivy, and mosquitos, you all made it so much better. Matt, Kelsey, and Glenn helped me track down photographs, field records, and samples that were otherwise scattered. Special thanks to Bryan and to Ed Henry for technical assistance with geophysics and GIS. John Connaway taught me much and more about dirt archaeology in the Delta. No one will ever be as dedicated to Mississippi Delta archaeology as John.

UNC's Research Labs of Archaeology was my home as I worked to turn field notes and bits of pottery into this book. Thank you to Steve Davis and Brett Riggs for all your assistance over the years. Your commitment to students and to scholarship in archaeology is inspiring. To my wonderful cohort of archaeologists at UNC, thank you. I owe a wealth of gratitude in particular to Meg Kassabaum for an exceptionally memorable Memorial Day weekend involving bikers, baling twine, poison ivy, and chiggers. Anna Semon kept me going during a rough patch of fieldwork. David

Cranford showed up with beer AND popsicles. I'm so grateful to many others for their assistance during the fieldwork part of this project, especially Mary Beth Fitts, Ben Shields, Rebecca Shellenberger, Dee O'Brien, Stephen Harris, Rosie Crow, Melissa Litschi, Natty DeMasi, Anna Morton, and Mike Goldstein.

Ashley Peles and Mallory Melton analyzed the faunal and botanical assemblages from Parchman Place, respectively. I look forward to many future food-focused collaborations! Many thanks to Rosie Crow and Jenny Holder for wrestling with surface collections and GIS. Zoe Jenkins and Abigail Dupree assisted with illustrations and photography. Emily Ann Guhde taught me everything I know about Excel. Without my writing buddies, this book would not exist. Thank you Caela O'Parks, Martha King, Claire Novotny, Marc Howlett, Bill Westermeyer, Tomás Gallareta-Cervera, Anna Krome-Lukens, Emily Ditto, Andrew Ofstehage, Krista Mehari, and Charlene Dadzie. Thanks also to George for cinnamon rolls at Bread and Butter, to Rudi for the Room of Requirement, and to Martha for the use of her kitchen table.

This work has benefitted from funding and logistical support at all stages. Funding was generously provided by the National Science Foundation (DDIG 1036363), the Center for Study of the American South, the Timothy P. Mooney Fellowship, and the UNC Graduate School. Brenda Moore and Lisa-Jean Michienzi helped me navigate UNC's bureaucracy. Joe Noe graciously allowed me to work on the portion of Parchman Place that is privately owned, and the Archaeological Conservancy granted permission to excavate on the portion in their trust. Jessica Crawford and George Lowry of the Archaeological Conservancy provided logistical support as well as frog pots, watermelon, and backfilling. The University of Mississippi's Center for Archaeological Research lent me their magnetometer and their expertise in processing geophysical datasets. Coleman Allen's hunting camp made for a field house well appointed in wildlife.

Several people were instrumental in the research design, execution, and writing of this book. Special thanks to Vin Steponaitis, Margie Scarry, Jay Johnson, Brett Riggs, Tricia McAnany, Valerie Lambert, and Silvia Tomášková for the many ideas, questions, and suggestions that challenged me to think more deeply about my writing and interpretations. Greg Waselkov has become a valued mentor, and I thank him for his support and for his willingness to provide great feedback on last-minute drafts. Chris Rodning and Maureen Meyers provided invaluable suggestions for improving the manuscript. Judith Knight and the folks at University of Florida Press helped bring this project to fruition.

Finally, I'd like to thank my parents, David and Laura Stevens, for their unwavering support throughout the years, and Sheri Nelson, for her equally unwavering if more recent support. David Nelson, I have no words. Thank you for everything.

1

Mississippian Communities in the Northern Yazoo Basin

The nature of Mississippian communities has been a subject of considerable interest to archaeologists for decades, with research centering around questions of social complexity, the nature of leadership, forms of social organization, economic relationships, identity, and ideology. Never before, however, have archaeologists had so many sources of information about Mississippian communities upon which to base their interpretations. The ever-increasing resolution of spatial patterns in the archaeological record has led to a recognition of the astounding diversity in the physical organization of residences, sites, and regions. This diversity indicates considerable variability in how Mississippian people conceived of and experienced everyday life within their households and communities and in their interactions with people from outside their communities. Old and new approaches to understanding kin-based social organization and worldview among Mississippian people allow us to glimpse how they may have understood their relationships with neighbors and strangers; with the plants, animals, and landscape features that coexist in the physical realm; and with beings and phenomena located in the unseen spiritual realm. Theoretical approaches to understanding the nature of human action and structural constraints on that action provide a framework for considering persistence and change within communities, and recent consideration of non-Western ontologies allows us to envision a worldview in which both human and non-human agents can act in social realms. These disparate sources of information converge in ways that have the potential to enrich our interpretations of Mississippian communities to an extent that previous generations of archaeologists could hardly imagine.

Drawing on these perspectives as well as new archaeological data from Parchman Place (22CO511), this book takes the position that community-building by Mississippian people was a process of placemaking that involved repeated re-creations of a distinct worldview in a particular place (or places). This worldview largely rested on kin-based social organization and a belief that humans bore responsibility for maintaining the balance, and thus the overall health, of their communities, the physical world they inhabited, and the broader cosmos. Much evidence points toward the tendency for Mississippian social relations to be strongly hierarchical. And yet, archaeological data from Parchman Place and elsewhere suggest that different Mississippian people or groups of people practiced placemaking and world creation in different ways, through different media, and to achieve different goals. Consequently, despite the very visible outcomes of actions taken by powerful people (mound-top residences, palisades, some forms of community spatial organization and feasting refuse), community-building was decidedly *not* the exclusive purview of elite members of Mississippian communities. Rather, leadership was routinely checked by those who wished to emphasize kin group autonomy and those who valued the maintenance of balance among distinct social groups. In what follows, I outline an approach to thinking about Mississippian communities that emphasizes the multiple ways that people created community in place, both through the physical organization of community spaces, and through depositional practices that emphasized particular, if conflicting, values. In interrogating these conflicts, it becomes clear that negotiation was a constant feature of Mississippian community-building, that heterarchical social organization (sensu Crumley 1995, 2005) was valued and closely guarded, and that hierarchical tendencies were counteracted by acts of deposition grounded in a particularly Mississippian worldview.

Situating Mississippian Communities

Archaeologists have always recognized placemaking as a tangible form of community-building, though our understandings have evolved as our grasp of spatial patterns, built landscapes, and Mississippian worldviews have expanded. Culture-historians constructed archaeological cultures or phases based on recurring similarities among artifact assemblages located in close spatial proximity to one another (Mainfort 2005; Phillips 1970; Phillips et al. 1951; Willey and Phillips 1958), an approach that has been criticized for its tendency to conceive of past communities as "natural," conservative, unchanging entities bounded in time and space (Jones 1997; Murdock 1949; O'Brien and Lyman 1998). The critique is valid, although close reading of the work of culture historians, such as Phillips (1970:23), reveals a more complicated view of past peoples and our reconstructions of their cultures. As Dunnell (1985) pointed out, early investigators working in the Lower Mississippi Valley were aware of limitations in their methods of regional survey, surface collection, and ceramic seriation, and considered their work preliminary to the task of reconstructing the lifeways and relationships of the ancient people of that region.

Responding to critiques of the descriptive nature of culture-historical approaches, many scholars began to investigate how Mississippian socio-political systems functioned in regional contexts (e.g., Anderson 1994; Blitz 1993a; Hally 1993; King 2003; Steponaitis 1978). Through spatial analysis of settlement patterns and monumental architecture, these studies initially emphasized the largest Mississippian sites and the actions of elite members of society who were thought to have dominated their development. This emphasis on social hierarchy and elite mechanisms of control has remained influential in Mississippian studies (e.g., Blitz 2010; Cobb 2003), even as these same studies drew attention to the incredible diversity of Mississippian social forms. Furthermore, these large-scale studies focused on chiefdoms or polities rarely considered the nature of local communities except in terms of their form and function within regional systems (Yaeger and Canuto 2000:4). In my view, this omission is largely a matter of scale; studies of social organization and culture change can be productively adapted to investigate local communities.

Site-specific investigations contribute to our more recent understanding that Mississippian communities were organizationally diverse and that particular spatial organizations establish, communicate, and reinforce particular understandings of social organization (Blitz 1999; Boudreaux 2007; Dye and Cox 1990; Hally 2008; King 2006; Knight 1998; Knight and Steponaitis 1998; Lewis and Stout 1998; Marcoux 2008; Pauketat 2007; Pauketat and Alt 2003; Rogers and Smith 1995). Knight (1998) has shown that Moundville, for instance, was organized as a sociogram, materializing social relations among the main corporate kin groups making up Moundville society in the 13th century (see also Knight 2010, 2016; Wilson

2008). Like Moundville, the spatial layout of well-excavated Mississippian sites like Town Creek, King, and Cahokia also consists of discrete clusters of architecture interpreted as the residential areas of corporate kin groups (Boudreaux 2007: 93–94; Hally 2008:272–290; Pauketat 2003:43; Wilson 2008:87–92).

More recently, our understanding of spatial patterns at Mississippian communities has been facilitated by near-surface geophysical exploration, particularly magnetic gradiometry, which, given the right conditions, is particularly useful for revealing buried architectural features. Geophysical applications have been productively combined with principles of landscape archaeology (Ashmore and Knapp 1999; David and Thomas 2008; Snead et al. 2009), to consider how past societies were organized socially (Conyers 2010; Conyers and Leckebusch 2010; Nelson 2014), how cultural ideas about the use of space have persisted (or not) over time (Nelson 2014; Thompson et al. 2011), and how human groups have interacted with the broader landscape (Dalan et al. 2003; Kvamme 2003). In line with landscape approaches in archaeology, these studies recognize that geophysical methods are well suited to identifying built features such as domestic or monumental architecture, but also the negative spaces defined by the built environment (see, for example, articles in a special issue of *Archaeological Prospection* edited by Thompson [2014]). I draw on geophysical data from Parchman Place collected since 2002 to explore the ways Mississippian people used the built environment as well as empty spaces to establish social order within their community, how they experienced everyday interactions with their kin and neighbors, and how relationships among kin groups changed over time as people shifted their living spaces to align with monumental architecture.

While spatial patterns in the archaeological record can tell us much about social organization within communities, archaeologists have also looked to ethnographic accounts of the social organization and belief systems of later southeastern Native groups to see if they can shed light on those of their Mississippian ancestors. Despite local variation and change over time (Urban and Jackson 2004), many of the principles guiding kin-based social organization were broadly shared among colonial period Indian groups. The Muskogean-speaking peoples (including the Chickasaws, Choctaws, Creeks, and others) historically located near the study area held many aspects of social organization in common, including matrilineal descent and matrilocal residence as well as organizing structures such as clans and moieties. Members of these social entities were distributed in towns in similar ways, and individual towns likewise interacted with other towns in similar ways (Hudson 1976; Knight 1990, 2018; Speck 1907; Swanton 1928a, 1931, 1946; Urban and Jackson 2004). These widespread similarities, the late date of the Parchman phase, and archaeological evidence (presented herein) suggest that some of these shared principles of social organization are relevant for understanding the nature of community at Parchman Place and other Mississippian sites.

Knight (1990:2) has attempted to reconstruct "the nature of basic kin groups and their relationship to the political system" of Mississippian societies from contact period accounts of several southeastern Indian groups, including the Timucuas, Chickasaws, and Natchez. He began with the common observation that clans in the southeastern United States were generally exogamous social categories based on filial descent through matrilines (though some were patrilineal). Clans were affiliated with one of two major social divisions (sometimes called moieties) that were both contrasting and complementary in nature. Within these major divisions or moieties, clans were ranked, and the two moieties were also ranked with respect to one another. Members of clans did not constitute localized groups, but were dispersed among many different towns.

Local manifestations of clans frequently took the form of small-scale, corporate lineages or sub-clan groups, such as the "house-groups" of the Chickasaws (Brightman and Wallace 2004; Knight 1990, 2010; Speck 1907; Swanton 1928a) and Choctaws (Galloway and Kidwell 2004; Swanton 1931; Urban and Jackson 2004), and the *hûti* of the Creeks (Knight 2018; Swanton 1928c). These groups, composed of related women and their husbands and children, resided together and were tied to estates that included houses, shared communal space, and agricultural fields. Chickasaw estates were named and their members were thought to share particular characteristics of personality and custom. I suggest in the following chapters that residential neighborhoods at Parchman Place, particularly those centered around courtyard groups, represent the living arrangements of local clan-based lineages similar in character to house-groups, an argument Wilson (2008:17, 75) has made for multi-household groups at early Moundville (cf. Knight 2016; Scarry and Steponaitis 2016).

On a larger scale, multiple lineages or house-groups resided together in towns, referred to by the Creeks as *talwas* (Ethridge 2003; Knight 1994; Swanton 1946) and by the Choctaws as *oklas* (Galloway and Kidwell 2004).

Towns were autonomous, considered by Urban and Jackson (2004:703) to be the "minimally self-sufficient units of Muskogean social organization." Often, they were associated with shared ceremonial facilities, perhaps including a square ground, ball ground, and council house (Lewis et al. 1998). Town members shared a ceremonial fire and were referred to as being of the same "fire." Though towns had a physical presence on the landscape, physicality was not their defining feature. In fact, towns could be nucleated or dispersed across the landscape, and could move locations entirely while retaining their essential character. The members and their shared ceremonial practice constituted a town, much in the way we think of congregants and their shared religious practice as constituting a church (Scarry and Steponaitis 2016). In later chapters of this work, I present evidence that people living at Parchman Place in the 14th and 15th centuries arranged their living spaces in ways analogous to Choctaw and Chickasaw towns (see also Nelson 2020).

While ethnographic analogy is useful for understanding social organization and worldview in broad strokes, temporal distance and culture change pose some limits on their usefulness for interpreting Mississippian contexts. Interdisciplinary efforts to decipher Mississippian iconographic motifs, however, have recently shed much light on a worldview that is distinctly Mississippian (King 2007; Knight 2013; Lankford et al. 2011; Reilly and Garber 2007; Townsend and Sharp 2004). Based on these efforts, we know that beliefs about the geography of the cosmos were broadly shared among Native North American people (Hudson 1976; Knight 2013; Lankford et al. 2011; Pauketat and Emerson 2001; Reilly and Garber 2007; Townsend and Sharp 2004). Generally speaking, this geography consisted of three realms connected at their centers by an *axis mundi*. The Above World was multilayered and had associations with "structure, expectableness, boundaries, . . . order, stability, and past time" (Hudson 1976:128). The sun resided here, as did other supernaturals (the sun was considered the "chief deity" [Swanton 1928d] or "Creator" [Jackson 2003]). The Beneath World, composed of water, was also multilayered. Categorically opposed to the Above World, it was associated with "inversions, . . . invention, fertility, disorder, change [and] future time" (Hudson 1976:128), and was inhabited by underworld beings, notably the "underwater panther." Between the Above and Beneath Worlds was *this* world, the Middle World, inhabited by humans, plants and animals, powers associated with the four winds, and *fire*, the earthly representation of the sun. Balance between the worlds was of utmost importance and it was the responsibility of humans to actively maintain that balance (Hudson 1976; Lankford 2007).

Mississippian and other southeastern Indian people carried out this responsibility in various ways. They mapped their vision of the cosmos on portable objects (e.g., Lankford 2004, 2007; Pauketat and Emerson 1991) and inscribed it in various ways on the landscape (Baires and Baltus 2017; Baltus 2016; Charles et al. 2004; Diaz-Granados et al. 2018; Knight 1981, 1986; Pauketat 2008; Swanton 1928b). Indeed, many Indian people continue to re-create this world in modern ceremonial dance and mound-building practices (e.g., Jackson 2003; Miller 2015). Residents of Parchman Place incorporated this practice in various ways and at particular key moments. The material traces of these activities can tell us much about social negotiations that took place as community members acted in accordance with their beliefs about the kind of community they wanted to live in.

Significantly, placemaking at Parchman Place and other Mississippian sites involved a number of interactions between people and particular substances, including ash, clay, and shell. These practices suggest that approaches focusing on the symmetrical and relational aspects of human/other-than-human interactions resonate with Mississippian understandings of the ways that humans and non-humans coexist in the world (e.g., Baltus and Baires 2016; Bennett 2010; Buchanan and Skousen 2015; Fowler 2013; Harrison-Buck and Hendon 2018; Ingold 2007; Latour 1993, 2005; Pauketat 2008, 2013a, 2013b; Pauketat and Alt 2005; Skousen 2012; C. Watts 2013; V. Watts 2013). In particular, I consider the meaningful nature of *assemblages* (e.g., Bennett 2010; Fowler 2013; Harris 2013, 2014; Mills 2008; Pauketat 2013a, 2013b; Pollard 2008) to be useful in thinking about how Mississippian people created community in place.

As groupings of material substances and objects, assemblages are important "in that their ability to make something happen . . . is distinct from the sum of the vital force of each materiality considered alone" (Bennett 2010:24). Therefore, an assemblage can be created to achieve a form of agency that exceeds its constituent parts. This phenomenon has been discussed in the archaeological literature of North America as *bundling* (Brown 2010; Pauketat 2013a, 2013b; Zedeño 2008, 2013), a practice in which humans gathered together powerful objects or substances to concentrate their power in a specific location or container (e.g., a cache, mound, pit, or ceramic vessel; see Baltus 2016; Pauketat 2013b). When considered in this light, depositional practices from Parchman Place can be understood as part of a worldview in which particular substances are animate and can act in ways that are social. These assemblages play a role in community-building.

In line with other studies that rethink the concept of community as a "natural" social unit (Díaz-Andreu et al. 2005; Harris 2014; Pauketat 2007; Stark 1998; Yaeger and Canuto 2000), this book focuses on the processes by which community identity is created, maintained, and transformed. I consider past communities to be dynamic forms of social organization that are continually constructed through various forms of practice (Barth 1969; Bourdieu 1977; Canuto and Yaeger 2000; Diaz-Andreu et al. 2005; Giddens 1979, 1984; Harris 2013; Jones 1997; Lucy 2005; Marcus 2000; Pauketat 2007; Pauketat and Alt 2003; Vermeulen and Govers 1994). Emphasizing *what people did* shifts archaeological attention away from static settlement patterns and ceramic assemblages to matters of daily routine and more intentional acts meant to communicate social messages (Dobres 2000; Marcoux 2008; Pauketat 2007:2). Along with a viewpoint that emphasizes practice, I also seek to understand that practice within a Mississippian worldview. Ethnographic analogy and iconographic studies move us further in that direction, as do theoretical approaches that seek to de-emphasize a largely Western, anthropocentric view of community and community-building, instead emphasizing the places, substances, things, animals, and other non-humans that play a role within indigenous concepts of community.

In the chapters that follow, I document a number of moments when Mississippian people in the northern Yazoo Basin took active responsibility for the creation and continued maintenance of their community. They did this in many ways, a great number of which involved the emplacement of materials such as soils, shell, ash, the remains of meals, and so forth, in ways that amplified the ability of those materials to influence the social and historical trajectory of the community. While some of these actions align well with the hierarchical tendencies we often associate with Mississippian societies, others reflect the desire of some community members to balance authority with values that emphasized autonomy and non-hierarchical (heterarchical) relationships. These findings suggest the need to interrogate how community-building takes place across the Mississippian world and who (and what) plays a role in that process.

The Late Mississippi Period in the Northern Yazoo Basin

The Yazoo Basin is described by Phillips et al. (1951:16) as the area, approximately 60 miles (97 km) across at its widest point, between the Mississippi and Yazoo Rivers and extending for approximately 200 miles (322 km) between Memphis, Tennessee, and Vicksburg, Mississippi (Figure 1.1). It is characterized by a complex network of basins and ridges resulting from multiple abandoned river channels and meander scars of the Mississippi, Ohio, Deer Creek, Sunflower, and Yazoo Rivers. These meandering rivers created natural levees ideal for intensive cultivation of maize and other native cultigens. It is no surprise, therefore, that the northern Yazoo Basin was densely occupied during the late Mississippi period (AD 1300–1550). Archaeological remnants of these Mississippian communities include dozens of sites, typically with one or more earthen platform mounds, plazas, and residential areas.

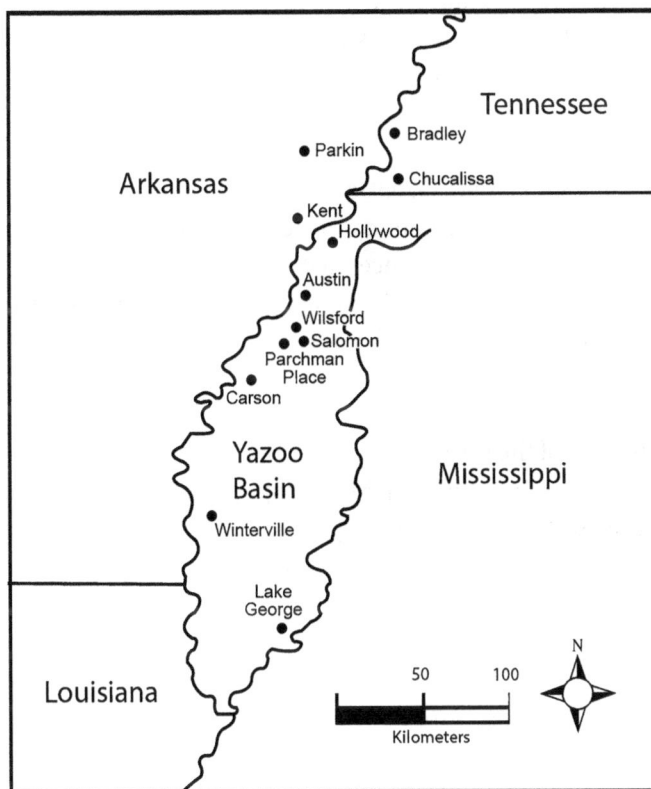

Figure 1.1. The Yazoo Basin with location of Parchman Place (22CO511) and selected Mississippian sites mentioned in the text.

Philip Phillips (1970:924) organized late Mississippi period sites in the region into a "bewildering array of phases" on the basis of geographical proximity and minor differences in frequencies of surface-collected ceramics, expressing frustration all the while about the difficulties of assigning chronological placements to assemblages that consisted of almost entirely undecorated shell-tempered pottery. This work focuses on Parchman Place, the type site for the Parchman phase, which represents the late Mississippi period occupation in the northern half of present-day Coahoma County and adjacent portions of Tunica and Quitman Counties, Mississippi. Based on surface collections from Parchman Place, as well as the Carson (22CO505), Salomon (22CO504), Dundee (22TU501), and West (22TU520) sites, Phillips (1970:938) described the Parchman phase as "ill-defined" and "unusually tentative." This situation is little improved today, despite efforts of subsequent researchers, notably Mary Evelyn Starr (1984), who examined surface collections from several sites conducted by the Mississippi Archaeological Survey (MAS) and Mississippi Department of Archives and History (MDAH) (see also Brain 1988; Brown 2008; Lansdell 2009; McNutt 1996b; Stevens 2008). Nearby contemporaneous phases include the Hollywood phase to the north (sites east of the Mississippi River formerly included in Phillips' Kent phase), and the Hushpuckena-Oliver and Quitman phases to the south and southeast (McNutt 1996b:180; Phillips 1970:938–942). None of these phases is well understood and some are dubious constructions at best. Phillips says about Hushpuckena-Oliver, for instance, that he was forced to combine two phases for which John Belmont (1961) had previously demonstrated "a clear typological separation" simply because "our 1941 counts and their simple typology afford no possibility of using [Belmont's] more sensitive criteria" (Phillips 1970:941).

The culture history of the early and middle Mississippi periods is even murkier. Phillips did not propose any Mississippi period phases earlier than the ones previously mentioned, despite a temporal gap following his Peabody phase, representing Late Woodland traditions in the region. Notably, Phillips was quick to add that the Peabody phase "is *particularly* open to question" (Phillips 1970:917, emphasis in original). Elizabeth Hunt (2017) recently reported that the Austin site (22TU549) spans the Late Woodland to Mississippian transition in the region, and proposed the Austin phase to designate the early Mississippian occupation. So far Austin is the only known site in the northern Yazoo that transitions from a Peabody phase component to an early Mississippian one. Brent Lansdell (2009) also had some success in determining early Mississippian ceramic markers from Carson collections. Carson lacks a Peabody phase component. Clearly, more culture-historical work, however maligned as inadequate, is needed before we can begin to address more nuanced questions about the lives and communities of Mississippian people in this region.

Further afield, we know quite a bit about the late Mississippi period occupation in northwest Mississippi and northeast Arkansas, including the Kent, Parkin, Nodena, and Walls phases (House 1991, 1993; McNutt 1996a:178–180, 1996b, 2008; Phillips 1970:930–939; Smith 1990; cf. Mainfort 1999, 2003, 2005). The Kent phase, located on the Lower St. Francis River, is characterized by a complex series of occupations and abandonments that correspond with periods of population dispersion and nucleation (House 1991, 1993, 1996). John House thinks that the Kent site became a regional paramount center between AD 1350–1450, but sees a lack of compelling evidence for well-developed political hierarchy after AD 1450. Further north, on the Middle St. Francis River, Phyllis Morse (1981, 1990) also documented population nucleation at late Parkin phase sites, interpreting this as a response to encroachment by other Mississippian peoples in the vicinity of Memphis. Fortifications at Parkin phase sites are cited as additional evidence of this (late Kent phase sites are also fortified). The Nodena phase, located in Arkansas along the Mississippi River north of Memphis, appears to have a settlement pattern similar to that of the Parkin phase; Dan Morse considered the Bradley site to be a paramount center and chiefdom capital in the late Mississippi period (D. Morse 1990:78–80). Finally, the Walls phase, in the vicinity of present-day Memphis, Tennessee, and the far northwest corner of Mississippi, includes the major bluff-top site of Chucalissa, as well as a number of single-mound sites located in the bottomlands in the far northern reaches of the Yazoo Basin (Lumb and McNutt 1988; McNutt 1996b; Smith 1990).

Of interest here is the interpretation of several researchers that the Walls, Parkin, and Nodena phases correspond to the Soto-era provinces of Quizquiz, Aquixo, and Pacaha respectively (Dye 1993; Hudson et al. 1990; Hudson 1997; McNutt 1996b; Mitchem 1996; D. Morse 1990; P. Morse 1990; Morse and Morse 1983). The Spaniards relate that the province of Quizquiz (Walls phase, east of the Mississippi River) was subordinate to the powerful province of Pacaha, west of the Mississippi. When the Spaniards crossed the river, they encountered the people of Aquixo

(Parkin phase), who were at war with the more powerful Pacaha (Nodena phase people) to the north. This may explain the nucleated, fortified settlements of the Parkin and Nodena phases. Perhaps Mississippian people living at Kent phase sites were buffered somewhat by the fact that the Parkin phase was geographically between Kent and Nodena, but Kent phase settlements were nucleated and fortified just the same.

It is unclear how and to what extent Parchman phase people were drawn into these regional sociopolitical maneuverings, but what is clear is the existence of powerful and vertically integrated polities a short distance to the north. Similar polities with powerful leaders may have existed in the southern Yazoo Basin, generally defined as the region south of "Phillips' Green Line," that is, the imaginary line running between present-day Greenwood and Greenville, Mississippi (Kidder 1998:147; Phillips et al. 1951:5–35; Phillips 1970; Riser 2009). The Winterville (22WS500) and Lake George (22YZ557) sites each boasted over 20 earthen mounds and were regional administrative centers for Plaquemine Mississippian populations between AD 1200–1350 (Brain 1978, 1989; Williams and Brain 1983). However, these centers did not have large residential populations. Instead they seem to follow the Coles Creek pattern in which large sites functioned as gathering places for dispersed populations (Brain 1989; Kowalski 2019). After AD 1350, their use declined. There are no known sites of comparable proportions during the late Mississippi period, when Parchman phase sites were occupied. Despite the common observation that southern and northern Yazoo Basin cultures show markedly different developmental trajectories, there are a handful of ceramics from early deposits from Parchman Place that demonstrate contact between the two regions. Ongoing work at Carson may also shed light on this relationship.

In addition to Parchman Place, a small number of sites with Parchman phase components have been investigated further. These include Barbee (22CO510; Walling and Chapman 1999); Carson (Butz 2015; Carpenter 2013; Connaway n.d.; James 2010, 2015; Johnson and Connaway 2019; Lansdell 2009; McLeod 2015; Mehta 2015; Mehta et al. 2012, 2017); Salomon (Connaway 1983; Johnson et al. 2016); West (Buchner 1996, 2002; Dye and Buchner 1998); and Wilsford (22CO516; Connaway 1984a). Of these sites, all but Carson are fairly modest, with one to five earthen mounds and associated village areas. Wilsford is notable for a series of unusual structures built on raised platforms, excavated by John Connaway

(1984a). Similar structures recently excavated by Connaway and Jay Johnson at Carson have been interpreted as mortuary structures (James 2010, 2015).

By far the largest site in the region, Carson stretches for more than a mile. When first mapped by William Henry Holmes (Thomas 1894), the site had 7 large and 80 small mounds as well as an earthen embankment. Recent work indicates that mound building began circa AD 1200 (Butz 2015; Carpenter 2013; Mehta 2015; Mehta et al. 2012, 2017). At that time, the people of Carson were interacting with Cahokian Mississippian people from the American Bottom. Evidence of this contact includes stone tools identical in material and manufacturing techniques to those from Cahokia, as well as pottery and architectural styles similar to those of Cahokia but unknown elsewhere in the northern Yazoo Basin (Butz 2015; Johnson 1987; Johnson and Connaway 2019; Lansdell 2009; McLeod 2015; see also Williams and Brain 1983:375–376, 409–412). This contact sparked significant social change in the region that would have affected nearby communities as well as the people who lived at Carson.

What we know of other Parchman phase sites underlines the critical need for chronological refinement within the phase. Located mere kilometers from one another, Parchman phase sites appear to lack fortifications, unlike their better-known contemporaries to the north and northwest. Some sites, including Parchman Place, lack Woodland and early Mississippi period components altogether. Others, such as Carson, Austin, and Salomon have early Mississippi period ceramics. Only Austin has both Late Woodland and early Mississippian components (Hunt 2017; Johnson et al. 2016:68; Lansdell 2009). Complicating matters, we have yet to formulate a cohesive sense of what Middle Mississippian looks like in the region. These problems must be addressed if we are to understand how Mississippian communities developed and related to one another. Fortunately, we can work toward refining chronology while also addressing compelling questions about the ways in which Mississippian people practiced community-making in the Yazoo Basin.

Parchman Place (22CO511)

Parchman Place is located in present-day Coahoma County, Mississippi, just west of the small town of Coahoma, between Mill Creek, a tributary of the Sunflower River, and a smaller unnamed drainage to the east. The natural levee and ridge and swale topography that characterizes the site was created by the flooding action of two successive Mississippi River channels (Fisk's [1944] channels 10 and 11; Saucier's [1994] meander belt stages 2 and 3; see also Lowe 2006). Levee sands underlying Parchman Place were deposited by one or both of these major channels, which were abandoned well before the site was occupied, leaving behind a stable land-form not subject to routine flooding (Stout-Evans 2011a). The siltier soils overlying coarse levee sands were deposited by smaller, less active creeks that reclaimed portions of the older channels. Presently, Mill Creek has partially recaptured Fisk's channel 10, the earlier of the two major chan-nels in Parchman Place's vicinity, while the unnamed drainage to the east corresponds to Fisk's channel "J" (Stout-Evans 2011a; see also Lowe 2006).

Early archaeologists to visit Parchman Place include Cyrus Thomas, who called the site Roselle (Weinstein et al. 1985), and Calvin Brown, who described it as "a mound . . . on the Roselle Place two miles southwest of Coahoma" (Brown 1926:107; Phillips et al. 1951:51). The first significant work at Parchman Place, however, occurred in April 1940, when James Ford and James Griffin of the Lower Mississippi Survey (LMS) made surface collections and surveyed and mapped the site, which, they noted "exhibits a well-defined plaza arrangement dominated by a large platform mound of uncertain shape, about 60 m in diameter at the base and 6 or 7 meters high" (Phillips et al. 1951:372; Steponaitis et al. 2002). Their site map also depicts four smaller platform mounds ranging in height from 1.5 to 3 m and labeled in Figure 1.2a as Mounds B through E. According to John Connaway and Samuel McGahey (1970), Mound B was bulldozed in 1970 to a height of approximately 8 feet (2.4 m), although originally recorded by the LMS as 6 feet (1.8 m) tall. Mound B was damaged again in 1984, when a backhoe removed a small portion of the southeast edge for fill. The backhoe cut exposed a burned Mississippian structure approxi-mately 1 m above the base of the mound (Connaway 1985). The remaining platform mounds are more or less intact, having been acquired by the Archaeological Conservancy in 2002 (Crawford 2015; Finger 2003).

The original LMS map depicts eight small rises or "house mounds," ranging from 0.3 to 2 m in height. Six of them define the boundaries of a large plaza to the east, south, and west. The remaining two are lo-cated away from the plaza, one between Mounds B and D in the north-eastern quadrant of the site and the other well to the south of the plaza.

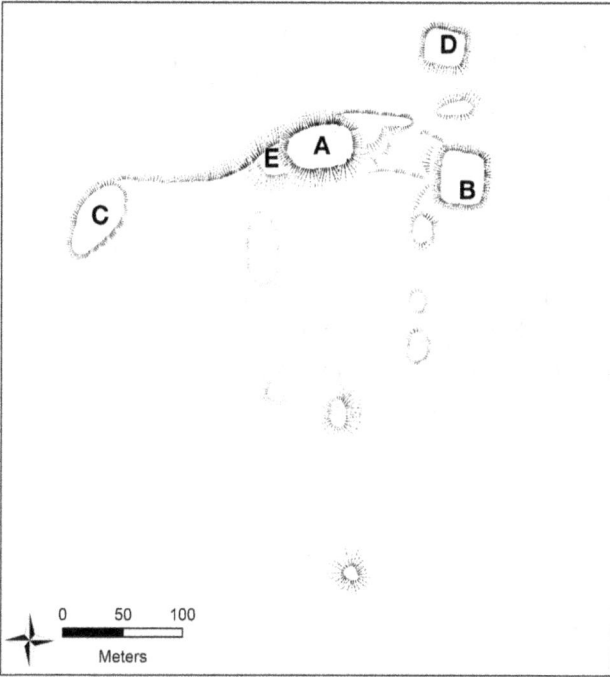

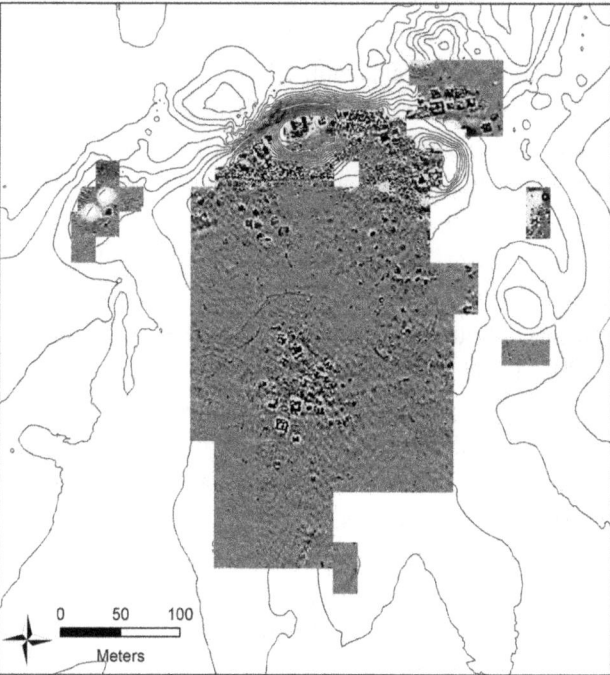

Figure 1.2. Parchman Place (22CO511), Coahoma County, Mississippi. (*a*) Site features including platform mounds (*A–E*), plaza, and house mounds. Adapted from Ford and Griffin's 1940 plane table map (Steponaitis et al. 2002). (*b*) Center for Archaeological Research topographic map (50 cm contour interval) with overlay of magnetic gradiometer results.

Subsequent field maps, including those by William Haag (1950) and Ian Brown (1978), also show house mounds surrounding the plaza. Haag recorded two on the western edge of the plaza and as many as four more, while Brown's map confirms the two recorded by Haag and indicates up to three more. None of the house mounds are currently visible, and one objective of the current research was to ascertain through coring whether anything remained of them below the current surface.

In 2002, Jay Johnson initiated the modern era of archaeological investigations at Parchman Place, holding University of Mississippi field schools there until 2006, after which point he began work at Carson in response to a portion of that site's imminent destruction by land levelling. Johnson's work focused primarily on mapping, near-surface geophysical survey, and ground-truthing of geophysical anomalies in mound and residential areas of the site. Subsequent to Johnson's work, I directed fieldwork from 2009 to 2011, during which I expanded the geophysical and excavation coverage, cored platform and house mounds, and conducted controlled surface collections (Nelson 2016). While much of this recent work is treated in detail in the following chapters, here I briefly outline findings from geophysical survey, controlled surface collections, and GIS reconstruction of daub scatters mapped by MDAH in order to establish what is currently known about Parchman Place's physical layout.

Magnetic gradiometry surveys have led to the identification of more than 40 burned Mississippian structures at Parchman Place, including confirmed buildings on the summits of Mounds A, D, and E and in four discrete residential areas of the site (Figure 1.2b; Fogel 2005; Johnson and Haley 2006; Lowe and Fogel 2007a, 2007b; Nelson 2014). Three of the residential areas or "neighborhoods" identified via geophysical survey correspond with the locations of house mounds mapped by the LMS in 1940 that are no longer visible. These include Neighborhood 1, located at the northwest perimeter of the plaza; Neighborhood 2, located at the southern end of the plaza; and Neighborhood 3, located in the northeastern portion of the site, in the triangular area delineated by Mounds A, B, and D (Figure 1.3). The fourth residential area is located in the swale between Mounds A and B. Superficially, this fourth area looks as though it could be part of Neighborhood 3. However, structures in the A-B swale were built on an artificially raised platform and predate Neighborhood 3, hence their separation.

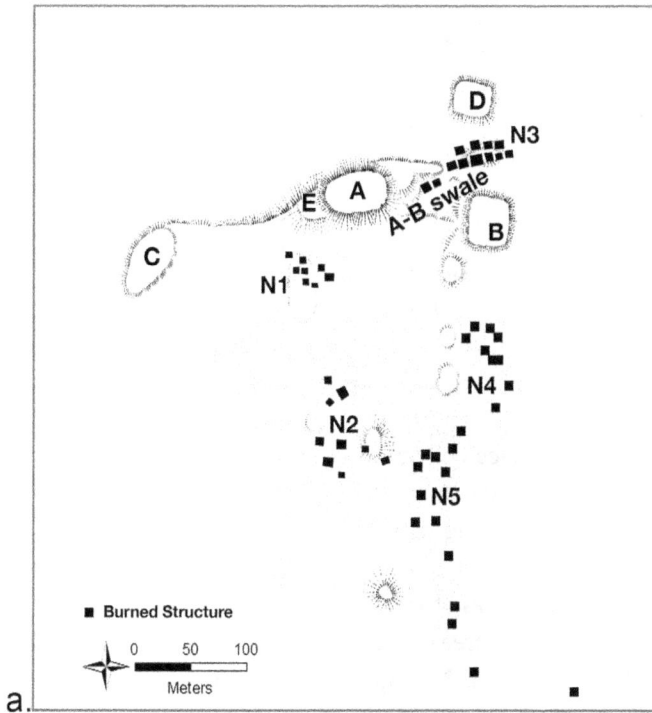

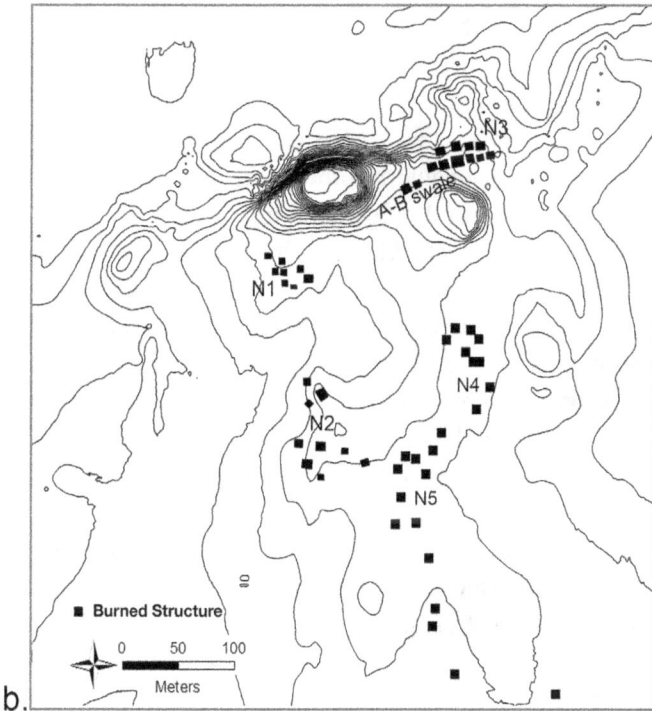

Figure 1.3. Mississippian structures identified at Parchman Place (22CO511) overlaid on (a) 1940 LMS map and (b) modern topographic map. Features in Neighborhoods 1, 2, 3, and the A-B swale are plotted to scale. Features in Neighborhoods 4 and 5 are not to scale. Mound summit structures are not shown.

Although the LMS map shows a series of three house mounds defining the eastern edge of the plaza, gradiometer results in this area were not easily interpreted. Connaway (1984b) and colleagues, however, recorded more than 20 burned structures revealed by plowing in the 1980s, the locations of which I have reconstructed in ArcGIS. The results of the reconstruction show that the daub concentrations fall into two more or less discrete clusters (Figure 1.3). The first (Neighborhood 4) is located along the southeastern perimeter of the plaza just east of two of the house mounds recorded by the LMS. The second (Neighborhood 5) is located along the southern perimeter of the plaza and continues in a diffuse "tail" toward the south.

Results of a controlled surface collection in 2010 indicate that areas of high surface artifact density correspond well with the residential areas located using geophysical techniques and the recorded daub outcrops just described, while the plaza area had low artifact densities. We also encountered high artifact densities at the northeastern plaza perimeter, just west of the northernmost of three house mounds mapped by the LMS along the eastern edge of the plaza. Magnetic patterning in this location is unclear, but surface artifact density very probably indicates an as-yet-uninvestigated residential area in this location.

All told, then, we know that Parchman Place consists of one large and four smaller earthen platform mounds arranged along a natural levee overlooking Mill Creek. Mound A is by far the largest of the mounds, originally recorded at 6 or 7 m in height; the others range in height from 1 to more than 3 m. Prior to destruction by modern plowing, eight low house mounds were also present, six of which were built along the perimeter of a roughly 1.5 hectare plaza located south of the main mound group. These six house mounds, as well as a seventh to the northeast, correspond well with discrete residential areas or neighborhoods detected via magnetic gradiometry and confirmed by excavation (Figure 1.3).

While excavations in residential and mound contexts are treated in detail in later chapters, I give brief descriptions of analysis units associated with each excavation area in Table 1.1. These form the basic units for the ceramic analyses presented in Chapters 2 and 3 and are discussed in detail in Chapters 4 and 5, which focus on mound and off-mound excavations, respectively. In most cases, I defined analysis units as fill episodes bounded by interfaces that represent living surfaces. For mound contexts, therefore, analysis units typically correspond to discrete episodes

Table 1.1. Analysis units for excavated contexts from Parchman Place (22CO511)

Excavation area	Analysis unit	Description of deposit or interface	C14 (cal BP)
Mound E Base (MEbase)	B	Lensed and basket-loaded mound fill; loose topsoil	
	–	Fired floor with wall trench; daub and thatch	
	A	Lensed and basket-loaded mound fill	597 ± 38 BP
Mound E SW Slope (MEsw)	D	Mound fill; white ash/kaolin; loose topsoil	
	–	Surface with bowl; daub rubble	
	C	Mound fill	
	–	Structure with post holes; daub rubble and thatch	500 ± 38 BP
	B	Mound fill	
	–	Mound surface; daub rubble and thatch; mussel shell	587 ± 38 BP
	A	Basket-loaded mound fill	
Mound E Summit (MEsum)	E	Mound fill	
	–	Fired floor [Floor 1] with wall trench and post	
	E	Mound fill	
	–	Fired floor [Floor 2] with wall trenches and posts	
	D	Mound fill	
	–	Fired floor [Floor 3] with possible wall trench; daub rubble and thatch	390 ± 40 BP
	C	Clean mound fill	
	–	Fired floor [Floor 4] with wall trenches and posts; daub rubble	
	B	Mound fill	
	–	Floor? ["missing floor"] with wall trench and pit	
	A	Mound fill	
	–	Truncation event	
	–	Fired floor [Floor 5] with double wall trench and posts	

(continued)

Table 1.1—*Continued*

Excavation area	Analysis unit	Description of deposit or interface	C14 (cal BP)
Mound E Summit, cont.	A	Mound fill; white mantles (kaolin, ash, mussel shell)	
	–	Fired floor [Floor 6] with wall trench; daub rubble and thatch	470 ± 40 BP
	A	Mound fill	
Mound A Summit (MAsum)	A	Mound fill; disturbed topsoil	
	–	Floor surface? [Structure 1] with wall trench	350 ± 30 BP
	A	Mound fill	
	–	Fired floor [Structure 2]; Daub rubble and thatch	
Mound D Summit (MD)	A	Mound fill; disturbed plow zone	
	–	Surface [Structure 1] with wall trench	478 ± 38 BP
	A	Mound fill	
	–	Surface [Structure 2] with wall trenches	
Neighborhood 1 (N1)	D	Fill; disturbed plow zone	
	–	Surface?; pot sherds	482 ± 38 BP
	D	Clay cap; fill	
	–	Surface indicated by pit	
	C	Clay cap	
	–	Surface with wall trench and pit	
	B	Fill; ash layers	
	A	Original surface; ceramics and faunal remains	640 ± 30 BP
Neighborhood 2	B	Fill; disturbed plow zone	
	–	Fired floor [Floor 2] with wall trench and posts; daub rubble	
	A	Fill	
	–	Fired floor with wall trench, posts and hearth [Floor 1]; daub rubble, roof beams, cane matting	547 ± 38 BP

Excavation area	Analysis unit	Description of deposit or interface	C14 (cal BP)
Neighborhood 3 (Unit 10-4)	A	Zoned fill	
	–	Surface or floor with wall trench	
	A	Zoned fill	
	–	Floor with posts; daub rubble	
	A	Zoned fill	
	–	Surface or floor	
	A	Zoned fill	
	–	Surface or floor	
	A	Fill	
	–	Surface with posts; thatch	
	A	Subsoil mixed with ash	505 ± 38 BP
Neighborhood 3 (Unit 11-13)	A	Disturbed plow zone	
	–	Surface with pot break; thatch	
	A	Mottled fill	446 ± 38 BP
	–	Surface or floor with post	
	A	Mottled fill; daub rubble	
Neighborhood 4	A	Disturbed plow zone	
	–	Fired floor with wall trench and pit	
	A	Clean fill	
	–	Fired floor with wall trench; fired wall fragment; burned beam	
A-B Swale (AB)	C	Disturbed plow zone	
	–	Fired floor; post with clay reinforcement; jar; daub rubble	570 ± 60 BP
	B	Mottled fill	
	–	Structure?	
	A	Striated fill with ash, mussel shell, and ceramics	
	A	Clayey fill; possible midden	609 ± 39 BP

of mound construction separated by structure floors. In some cases, difficulties in excavating complicated mound stratigraphy meant that artifacts belonging to multiple mound construction stages were mixed during collection. In these cases, a single analysis unit may represent multiple construction stages, as in the case of Analysis Unit A from the Mound E Summit excavation (see Table 1.1). I followed the same principles in assigning analysis units for excavations in residential areas.

The chapters that follow explore community-building activities employed by people living at Parchman Place during the 14th and 15th centuries through the lens of several different material practices, including the production of pottery, as it relates to both chronology and foodways; mound building and other depositional practices; and the organization of community space. The need for improvements in chronology should be apparent from the foregoing discussion. To address this need, I combined traditional type-variety, attribute, and functional analyses of stratified ceramics assemblages with radiocarbon dates (Table 1.2; Figure 1.4) to differentiate early (14th century) and late (15th century) sub-assemblages. Correspondence analyses confirm temporal differences in both decorative attributes and in vessel shapes.

Functional analyses of pottery vessels had the additional goal of identifying food-related activities at Parchman Place. Foodways are an important means by which people express individual and group identities, and food-related activities can be used to create community ties or, alternatively, to make social distinctions among people. In other words, they are an important and multivalent aspect of community-making. Using correspondence analysis, I identified two distinct functional assemblages that occur at Parchman Place: a domestic assemblage of cooking, serving, and storage vessels suitable for everyday use; and a serving assemblage containing both very large and very small vessels. The depositional contexts of serving assemblages indicate their use in feasting events related to the founding of the Parchman Place community and provides one of the earliest examples of how Mississippian people at Parchman used depositional practices to create community in place. Later, the remains of inclusive eating events were specially deposited along with large quantities of ash in Neighborhood 1. I interpret these remains as the result of one or more community-renewal and world-renewal events similar in character to maize harvest ceremonies performed by later Muskogean and other southeastern Indian communities.

Table 1.2. Radiocarbon dates for Parchman Place (22CO511)

Context/Analysis Unit (AU)	Material Dated	Uncal C14 Age (BP)	1 σ cal Date Range	2 σ cal Date Range	Lab #
Md B structure	Thatch	340 ± 95	AD 1466–1642 (68.2%)	AD 1408–1688 (86.2%) AD 1730–1809 (7.0%) AD 1926– . . . [a] (2.3%)	UGa-5286
Md A summit structure (Mound A summit, AU A)	Post	350 ± 30	AD 1480–1522 (29.4%) AD 1572–1630 (38.8%)	AD 1458–1530 (41.3%) AD 1538–1635 (54.1%)	Beta-418054
Md E post-truncation structure (Mound E summit, AU C/D)	Thatch	390 ± 40	AD 1445–1516 (53.6%) AD 1596–1618 (14.6%)	AD 1436–1528 (60.8%) AD 1544–1634 (34.6%)	Beta-215212
N3 late pot break (Unit 11-13, AU A)	Corn	446 ± 38	AD 1424–1465 (68.2%)	AD 1410–1512 (91.8%) AD 1600–1616 (3.6%)	X26166A
Md E pre-truncation structure (Mound E summit, AU A)	Thatch	470 ± 40	AD 1416–1450 (68.2%)	AD 1330–1339 (1.0%) AD 1396–1489 (93.9%) AD 1603–1608 (0.6%)	Beta-215215
Md D late structure (Mound D, AU A)	Hickory Shell	478 ± 38	AD 1417–1446 (68.2%)	AD 1330–1340 (1.3%) AD 1396–1474 (94.1%)	X26161A
N1 between structures 2 & 3 (Neighborhood 1, AU A)	Cane	482 ± 38	AD 1415–1445 (68.2%)	AD 1328–1341 (2.0%) AD 1396–1469 (93.4%)	X26163A
Md E SW structure (Mound E SW, AU B/C)	Cane	500 ± 38	AD 1410–1440 (68.2%)	AD 1322–1346 (7.5%) AD 1392–1453 (87.9%)	X26159A

(continued)

Table 1.2—*Continued*

Context/Analysis Unit (AU)	Material Dated	Uncal C14 Age (BP)	1 σ cal Date Range	2 σ cal Date Range	Lab #
N3 early structure (Unit 10-4, AU A)	Thatch	505 ± 38	AD 1407–1440 (68.2%)	AD 1320–1349 (10.0%) AD 1391–1452 (85.4%)	X26165A
N2 early structure (Neighborhood 2, AU A)	Corn	547 ± 38	AD 1324–1346 (25.0%) AD 1393–1425 (43.2%)	AD 1306–1364 (41.9%) AD 1384–1438 (53.5%)	X26164A
A-B Swale late structure (A-B Swale, AU B/C)	Post	570 ± 60	AD 1308–1362 (41.8%) AD 1386–1419 (26.4%)	AD 1292–1436 (95.4%)	Beta-219713
Md E top of first mound stage (Mound E SW, AU A/B)	Thatch	580 ± 40	AD 1310–1360 (48.9%) AD 1386–1407 (19.3%)	AD 1296–1417 (95.4%)	Beta-223031
Md E basal midden (Mound E base, AU A)	Cane	597 ± 38	AD 1308–1362 (53.1%) AD 1386–1402 (15.1%)	AD 1296–1412 (95.4%)	X26160A
A-B Swale basal midden (A-B Swale, AU A)	Pecan Shell	609 ± 39	AD 1301–1331 (27.1%) AD 1338–1368 (27.1%) AD 1382–1398 (14.0%)	AD 1291–1409 (95.4%)	X26167A
N1 original surface (Neighborhood 1, AU A)	Thatch	640 ± 30	AD 1292–1316 (27.0%) AD 1355–1388 (40.7%)	AD 1282–1329 (41.0%) AD 1340–1396 (54.4%)	Beta-418055

Note: Results were calibrated using OxCal v4.2.3 (Bronk Ramsay 2013) and r:5 IntCal 13 atmospheric curve (Reimer et al. 2013). Late 16th- and early 17th-century dates are considered implausible based on ceramic evidence.

[a] Date extends out of range.

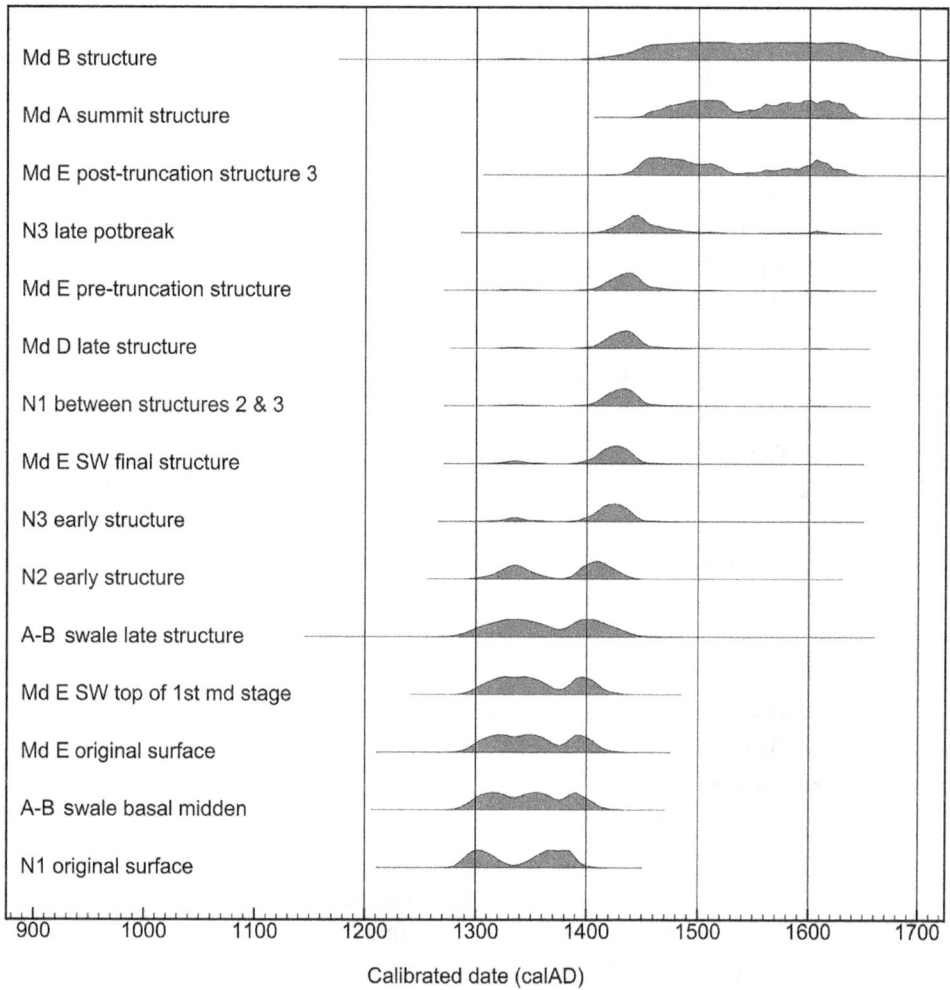

Figure 1.4. Calibrated radiocarbon dates from Parchman Place (22CO511). OxCal v4.2.4 Bronk Ramsey (2013); r:5 IntCal13 atmospheric curve (Reimer et al. 2013). See also Table 1.2.

Mound building can also be understood as an action that anchors a community to a particular place. Archaeological evidence indicates that mound building and the activities associated with it were important components of the founding of the Mississippian community at Parchman Place. Mounds A and E have been the subject of the most intensive excavations at Parchman Place and form the basis for a history of mound building at the site, supplemented by radiocarbon dates (Table 1.2; Figure 1.4) and limited information available from other mound investigations. Detailed reconstructions of mound stratigraphy reveal a complicated social and political history for Parchman Place that is directly tied to conventional practices associated with mound building as well as disruptions of those practices. Evidence for feasting, mantle construction, building and dismantling of summit structures, and use of specific sediments and substances as well as acts of truncation, expansion, and incorporation combine to reveal the ways that leadership and authority were intertwined with community values in the northern Yazoo Basin.

To further explore the nature of Mississippian communities, I also consider residential areas of Parchman Place, incorporating data from historic maps, geophysical survey, excavation, coring, GIS reconstruction of mapped surface features, and controlled surface collections. Based primarily on geophysical results, I discuss the spatial organization of these neighborhoods with special attention to the empty spaces that organized surrounding architecture and the social activities and relationships these features promoted. Excavations and coring data in residential areas, along with radiocarbon dates (Table 1.2; Figure 1.4), provide the basis for a reconstruction of residential history. These lines of evidence indicate ways the people living at Parchman Place identified themselves with one another and with their community as a whole, and how they drew social distinctions among themselves at various times. Of particular interest is a reorganization of neighborhood space sometime in the 15th century that physically aligned one portion of the population with the largest platform mound at the site. Atypical mound-building practices that accompany this reorganization of space indicate that this action on the part of some members of the community was contested by others.

In short, this book explores several related questions. What constituted a Mississippian community in the northern Yazoo Basin? More importantly, *how* were these communities created, maintained, and transformed through practice? Mound building, the organization of community space, and food-related activities such as pottery production, daily food consumption, and communal eating events all speak to issues of identity formation and intra-group social relations that took place at scales ranging from households and neighborhoods, to entire sites and regions, to the Mississippian world as a whole. In bringing a range of material practices to bear on questions about Mississippian social organization in the Yazoo Basin, this book provides a framework for considering how Mississippian people negotiated authority and autonomy within their communities.

2

Ceramics, Chronology, and Community

As "objects brought forth out of earth, water, and fire," pottery vessels "were simultaneously products and facilitators of important social relationships" (Baltus 2018:66). In other words, they were meaningful assemblages of materials brought together by potters to *do things*—prepare and serve food, carry sacred fire, communicate messages about social belonging or exclusion. This chapter focuses on the meaningful decisions Mississippian potters made in choosing materials, forming, firing, and decorating their pottery. These choices were simultaneously technological, ideological, and social. Tempering a clay vessel with crushed mussel shell, for instance, increased the pot's ability to withstand thermal shock, while also drawing the power of the Beneath World into the vessel walls (Baltus 2018; Steponaitis 1984). Shell-tempered pottery was an integral part of the maize-based foodway that nourished the bodies of Mississippian people and influenced the rhythms of their daily lives and their yearly ceremonial cycle (Briggs 2016; VanDerwarker et al. 2013; Witthoft 1949).

The choices potters made in terms of clay, tempering agents, and decorative techniques also afford archaeologists a way of organizing material culture in space and time, and so this chapter is also concerned with describing the results of Mississippian potters' choices with an eye toward refining site-specific and regional chronology. This goal is broadly aligned with a long-standing attempt by archaeologists in the Lower Mississippi Valley (LMV) to figure out what happened, when and where: "until a certain amount of order has been achieved in respect to time-space relations on a regional scale, it may be questioned whether satisfactory cultural inferences can be drawn from any archaeological materials" (Phillips et al. 1951:61). As discussed in Chapter 1, the northern Yazoo was densely occupied during the late Mississippi period, and we still have a very limited understanding of how these late period sites are related to one another. Refining the ceramic chronology is a critical step in determining whether Parchman phase sites were contemporary, or whether they only appear to be so because our ability to date them is unrefined. Furthermore, since pottery played an integral role in cooking, eating, and other activities that mediated social relationships among community members, understanding the potters' choices and how those choices persisted or changed provides a valuable window into the history of Mississippian communities.

Prior to 2002, surface-collected ceramics were the only materials available from Parchman Place and most other sites in the northern Yazoo Basin (Brown 1978, 2008; Phillips et al. 1951; Phillips 1970). An important objective of the work described here was to recover a sample of ceramics for which we have stratigraphic control to see if there are significant changes in the ceramics assemblage over time. Since 2002, a sample consisting of 25,808 ceramic body and rim sherds greater than one quarter inch has been recovered from surface collections and excavations in mound and residential contexts at Parchman Place. With the goal of chronological refinement in mind, I classified each sherd to type and (where possible) variety, on the basis of criteria described by Phillips (1970) and refined by a number of others (particularly Brain 1988, 1989; Brain et al. 1995; Williams and Brain 1983; Table 2.1). I refer readers to those sources for descriptions of the types and varieties employed here (see also appendices in Nelson 2016).

To capture potentially meaningful temporal variation not encompassed in the type-variety system, I also recorded attributes that cross-cut types and varieties, including information on rim form, lip treatment, and presence and type of appendages such as handles, nodes, and lugs (House 1991, 1993; Lansdell 2009; Lumb and McNutt 1988; Mainfort 1999, 2003, 2004, 2005; McNutt 2008; Nelson 2016 Appendix 2; Phillips 1970; Smith 1969; Williams and Brain 1983; Tables 2.2, 2.3, and 2.4). These analyses are aided by a suite of radiocarbon dates from both mound and residential contexts (Table 1.2; Figure 1.4) as well as a correspondence analysis of ceramic types and varieties recovered by excavation. Based on these analyses, I propose two divisions of the Parchman phase: Parchman I, corresponding to the 14th-century occupation of Parchman Place, and

Table 2.1. Types and varieties recovered from surface collections and excavated contexts at Parchman Place (22CO511)

Type and variety	Surface (ct)	Excavated (ct)	Total (ct)	% of total assemblage
Avenue Polychrome *var. Avenue*	40	57	97	0.38%
Barton Incised *var. Barton*	442	409	851	3.30%
Barton Incised *var. Estill*	9	8	17	0.07%
Barton Incised *var. Midnight*	2	3	5	0.02%
Barton Incised *var. Togo*	4	2	6	0.02%
Barton Incised *var. unspecified*	24	4	28	0.11%
Baytown Plain *var. Baytown*	323	132	455	1.76%
Bell Plain *var. Bell*	665	979	1644	6.37%
Carson Red on Buff *var. Carson*	28	25	53	0.21%
Grace Brushed *var. Grace*	1	1	2	0.01%
Hollywood White *var. Hollywood*	181	62	243	0.94%
Kimmswick Fabric Impressed *var. Kimmswick*	0	1	1	0.00%
Kinlock Simple Stamped *var. Kinlock*	2	0	2	0.01%
L'Eau Noire Incised *var. unspecified*	0	2	2	0.01%
Larto Red *var. Larto*	11	2	13	0.05%
Leland Incised *var. unspecified*	5	8	13	0.05%
Mississippi Plain *var. Neeley's Ferry*	5,644	10,374	16,018	62.07%
Mississippi Plain *var. unspecified*	3,897	22	3,919	15.19%
Mulberry Creek Cordmarked *var. unspecified*	34	16	50	0.19%
Nodena Red and White *var. Nodena*	66	22	88	0.34%
O'Byam Incised *var. unspecified*	0	1	1	0.00%
Old Town Red *var. Beaverdam*	270	87	357	1.38%
Old Town Red *var. Old Town*	47	13	60	0.23%
Parkin Punctated *var. Parkin*	49	115	164	0.64%
Parkin Punctated *var. unspecified*	11	7	18	0.07%
Pouncey Pinched *var. Pouncey*	2	1	3	0.01%
Rhodes Incised *var. Horn Lake*	6	2	8	0.03%
Salomon Brushed *var. Salomon*	0	1	1	0.00%
Unidentified Brushed	1	0	1	0.00%
Unidentified Engraved	3	12	15	0.06%
Unidentified Fabric Impressed	1	0	1	0.00%

Type and variety	Surface (ct)	Excavated (ct)	Total (ct)	% of total assemblage
Unidentified Incised	64	71	135	0.52%
Unidentified Painted	3	1	4	0.02%
Unidentified Plain	1,150	270	1,420	5.50%
Unidentified Punctated	0	1	1	0.00%
Walls Engraved var. Hull	17	18	35	0.14%
Walls Engraved var. Walls	1	6	7	0.03%
Winterville Incised var. unspecified	2	5	7	0.03%
Winterville Incised var. Winterville	32	31	63	0.24%
Total	13,037	12,771	25,808	100.00%

Table 2.2. Rim form and lip treatment for ceramic vessels from Parchman Place (22CO511)

Rim/Lip	Surface (ct)	Excavated (ct)	Total (ct)	% of Total Rim Assemblage
Simple (97.09%)				
Rounded	316	358	674	50.34%
Flattened	189	287	476	35.55%
Intermediate	100	50	150	11.20%
Folded (1.12%)				
Rounded	3	4	7	0.52%
Flattened	–	6	6	0.45%
Intermediate	–	2	2	0.15%
Thinned (0.90%)				
Rounded	2	7	9	0.67%
Flattened	2	–	2	0.15%
Intermediate	–	1	1	0.07%
Thickened (0.52%)				
Rounded	3	3	6	0.45%
Flattened	1	–	1	0.07%
Beveled (0.30%)	–	4	4	0.30%
Tiered (0.07%)	–	1	1	0.07%
Total	616	723	1,339	100%

Table 2.3. Decorative embellishment for ceramic vessels from Parchman Place (22CO511)

Decorative Embellishment	Surface (ct)	Excavated (ct)	Total (ct)	% of Total Attribute Assemblage
Scalloped (39.08%)				
Gently undulating rounded rim	7	18	25	28.74%
Large rounded notches	2	7	9	10.34%
Incised (20.69%)				
Vertical/perpendicular incisions exterior lip	2	2	4	4.60%
Vertical/perpendicular incisions interior lip	–	3	3	3.45%
Vertical/perpendicular incisions top of lip	1	1	2	2.30%
Horizontal/parallel incision exterior lip	1	–	1	1.15%
Horizontal/parallel incision interior lip	–	1	1	1.15%
Horizontal/parallel incision interior and exterior lip	–	1	1	1.15%
Horizontal/parallel incision top of lip	2	1	3	3.45%
Diagonal incisions top of lip	1	2	3	3.45%
Notched (12.64%)				
Notched exterior lip	1	1	2	2.30%
Notched exterior lip (short, wide)	–	1	1	1.15%
Notched interior lip	–	1	1	1.15%
Notched top of lip	–	1	1	1.15%
Notched interior to exterior lip	1	1	2	2.30%
Triangular notches interior to exterior	–	4	4	4.60%
Punctated (4.60%)				
Circular punctations top of lip	2	–	2	2.30%
Thumbnail punctations below exterior lip	1	–	1	1.15%
Thumbnail punctations exterior lip	1	–	1	1.15%
Other (22.99%)				
Burnished	–	13	13	14.94%
Node	1	5	6	6.90%
Stepped incision/etching on interior of bowl	–	1	1	1.15%
Total	23	64	87	100%

Table 2.4. Handles associated with ceramic vessels from Parchman Place (22CO511)

Handles	Surface (ct)	Excavated (ct)	Total (ct)	% of total rim assemblage
Lug (71.13%)				
Oval Lug	4	20	24	24.74%
Oval Lug Below Lip	–	1	1	1.03%
Downturning Oval Lug	–	5	5	5.15%
Fat Lug	–	1	1	1.03%
Elongated Oval Lug	–	6	6	6.19%
Downturning Elongated Oval Lug	–	2	2	2.06%
Triangular Lug	–	2	2	2.06%
Indeterminate Lug	12	15	27	27.84%
Indeterminate Lug Below Rim	–	1	1	1.03%
Loop Series (16.49%)				
Loop	1	1	2	2.06%
Intermediate Loop/Strap	–	1	1	1.03%
Strap	1	8	9	9.28%
Tube	–	3	3	3.09%
Zoomorphic	–	1	1	1.03%
Unspecified (12.37%)				
Broken Or Missing	1	7	8	8.25%
Not Recorded	2	2	4	4.12%
Total	21	76	97	100%

Parchman II, corresponding to the 15th-century occupation. In the chapters that follow, I outline a series of community actions and social changes that occurred at Parchman Place throughout the 14th and 15th centuries using the refined ceramic chronology as a temporal framework. A more detailed understanding of the ceramic sequence not only has demonstrated utility in understanding the occupational and social history of Parchman Place, but has potential for underwriting similar analyses at Parchman phase sites within the region where occupational history is still poorly understood (e.g. Connaway n.d.; Johnson et al. 2016; Lansdell 2009; Mehta et al. 2017; Nelson 2020).

In Phillips' (1970:939–940) original formulation, the Parchman phase was described as having "approximately even proportions of Mississippi Plain, *var. Neeley's Ferry* and Bell Plain (rim counts)," these being the most common coarse and fine shell-tempered undecorated or "plain" wares in the region respectively. Among decorated coarse shell-tempered wares, Phillips reports "a marked predominance of Barton Incised over Parkin Punctated" (Phillips 1970:939). Walls Engraved *var. Hull* was consistently present, and Old Town Red and other painted types were also well represented, all of these being shell-tempered fine wares. The phase was also marked by the presence of southern types, including Owens Punctated and Leland Incised (Phillips 1970:939–940). Though "ill-defined" and "unusually tentative" (Phillips 1970:938, 940), Phillips considered the Parchman phase to be late Mississippian in age (Phillips et al. 1951:372), an interpretation since confirmed by others (Brown 1978, 2008; McNutt 1996b; Nelson 2014, 2016; Starr 1984; cf. Brain 1988).

The Lower Mississippi Survey (Brown 1978, 2008) and the Mississippi Archaeological Survey (MAS) (Starr 1984) conducted additional surface collections at Parchman Place in 1977 and 1984 respectively, and in 2010 and 2011 I conducted a controlled surface collection of the entire site, resulting in a 25% sample of surface material. All three previous surface collections from Parchman Place (Starr 1984: Table 31) as well as my own (Table 2.1) are overwhelmingly dominated by Mississippi Plain sherds, but the samples differ considerably in proportions (Figure 2.1). Phillips found that the 1940s LMS collections contained a 2:1 ratio of Mississippi Plain (57.66%) to Bell Plain (31.45%), while surveys conducted by Brown and members of MAS found approximately the same proportion of Mississippi Plain (59.84% and 62.24% of their respective samples) but differed from Phillips in the proportion of Bell Plain (12.6% and 15.99% respectively). My controlled surface collections resulted in 73.18% Mississippi Plain and 5.10% Bell Plain, an approximate ratio of 14:1. This is a serious discrepancy, but one that can be explained by differing survey strategies as well as site formation processes.

The three surface collections conducted prior to my work in 2010 and 2011 were opportunistic surveys where collection areas were chosen for the quantity and/or quality of ceramics to obtain large samples and diagnostic types, whereas my survey used timed intervals and collection squares of uniform size to collect samples from the entire site. While this method results in a more representative sample, my survey suffers from a disadvantage in that modern plowing and differential breakage rates of coarse versus fine earthenware vessels likely result in an overrepresentation of Mississippi Plain (coarse shell-tempered ware) relative to Bell Plain (fine shell-tempered ware) sherds compared to earlier surveys. That

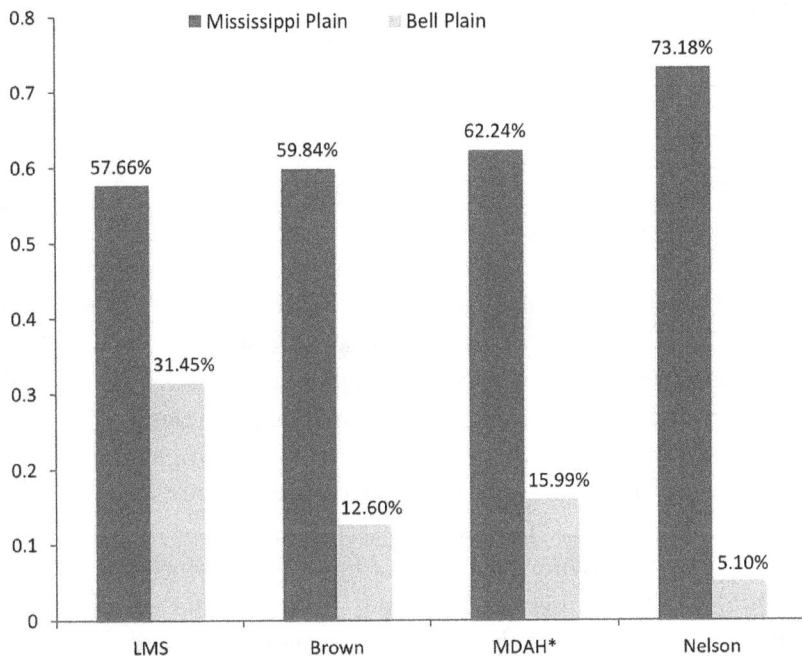

Figure 2.1. Histogram of Mississippi Plain and Bell Plain ceramics from four surface collections: Lower Mississippi Survey (LMS), 1940; Ian Brown, 1977; Mississippi Department of Archives and History (MDAH), 1980s; and Erin Nelson, 2010–11 (shown as percentages of the respective assemblages). *MDAH counts for Bell Plain include sherds types as Bell Plain and Addis Plain.

my sample should differ most from the LMS sample, while the other two are intermediate, is not surprising.

Other discrepancies also exist among the four samples. Phillips, for instance, finds much lower proportions of the painted types Old Town Red and Nodena Red and White in the LMS collection than do other researchers. For such a small sample (127 sherds), Brown's survey resulted in a relatively high diversity of types, including several that were not present in the LMS or MDAH samples: Pouncey Pinched, Grace Brushed, Mound Place Incised, and Anna Incised. Brown also has higher proportions of Barton varieties and Walls Engraved *var. Hull*, though this is potentially a result of sample bias. The only other surprise is the relative lack of Parkin Punctated in any of the early samples; only one specimen was found in all three early surveys, as compared to my sample, where it is well represented (though difficulties in sorting Parkin sherds that lack rim portions are well established). I also have slightly less Barton Incised in my surface collection than others (just over 3% compared with 6–13%). Finally, I collected types that were not encountered by any of the previous surveys, including Winterville Incised and Mulberry Creek Cord Marked, which occurred in moderate numbers in my sample, and Larto Red and Rhodes Incised *var. Horn Lake*, which were minority types.

Given differences in collection strategies and sorting conventions, as well as the effects of site formation processes, the ceramic assemblage recovered from recent surface collections at Parchman Place accords fairly well with Phillips,' Brown's, and Starr's descriptions of Parchman phase ceramics, with exceptions as noted previously. It is worth mentioning here that Brain has also attempted to refine the Parchman phase as part of his reconstruction of late prehistoric-protohistoric Tunica movements (Brain 1988). Brain deviates from previous researchers in recognizing two ceramic components at Parchman Place: the Hushpuckena I (sub)phase, dating to the 14th century, and the Parchman phase, which Brain claims is protohistoric (AD 1541–1673) in date. (Hushpuckena I was previously subsumed in Phillips' combined Hushpuckena-Oliver phase, a formulation even Phillips considered dubious).

Ceramics that delineate Hushpuckena I correspond to what Williams and Brain (1983) term the Yazoo 5 subset and include Owens Punctated (*vars. Menard, Poor Joe*, and *Widow Creek*) and Winterville Incised *var. Ranch*, as well as the painted types Avenue Polychrome and Nodena Red and White (Brain 1988:266; Williams and Brain 1983:324). For Brain, the Parchman phase proper is characterized by the Yazoo 8 subset, including Barton Incised *vars. Davion* and *Portland*, Owens Punctated *var. Redwood*, and Winterville Incised *var. Tunica* (Brain 1988: 393). Thus, Brain suggests that Parchman Place was occupied at least as early as the 14th century, as evidenced by a slightly different (and earlier) ceramic assemblage than the one originally described by Phillips. The earliest radiocarbon dates from Parchman Place fall in the 14th century (Table 1.2; Figure 1.4), though my own type-variety classification of ceramics from Parchman Place do not indicate the presence of the Yazoo 5 and Yazoo 8 subsets described by Williams and Brain. Echoing Brown's observation, I find that "the markers that Brain put forth really do not seem to be very common in the region" (Brown 2008:382). However, my analysis supports Brain's assertion that two ceramic components can be distinguished at Parchman Place.

While classification of surface-collected ceramics provides a solid beginning, we can refine our understanding of ceramic chronology by incorporating samples from stratified and/or dated contexts and by considering vessel attributes that are not encompassed within the regional type-variety classification system. In the following section I characterize the entire sample of 25,808 ceramic rim and body sherds recovered since 2002 by type and variety. Furthermore, I report rim form, lip treatment, and handle and node characteristics for 1,339 rim sherds. Correspondence analysis of the type-variety results as well as presence/absence data of ceramic types and attributes for securely dated contexts suggests temporal variation among Parchman Place sub-assemblages.

Undecorated or plain wares make up nearly 91% of the Parchman Place ceramic assemblage recovered since 2002 (Table 2.1). Mississippi Plain *vars. Neeley's Ferry* and *unspecified* make up the overwhelming majority of the sample at 77.25%. Bell Plain *var. Bell* comes in at a distant second, at 6.37% of the total assemblage. This finding is in stark contradiction to Phillips' expectation (based on rim sherds only) that Parchman phase assemblages will have roughly even proportions of Mississippi and Bell Plain varieties (see also Brown 1978, Starr 1984). Two other plain ware categories were recorded. The grog-tempered ware, Baytown Plain (n = 455) makes up 1.76% of the overall sample, while unidentified plain wares (n = 1420) make up 5.5%.

Decorated sherds, consisting mainly of incised, punctated, engraved, and painted types make up just under 9% of the Parchman Place sample. Not surprisingly, Barton Incised varieties (Figures 2.2 and 2.3) make up the largest proportion of decorated sherds in the sample, with the majority classified as *var. Barton*, though *vars. Estill, Midnight, Togo*, and *unidentified* were also present. Parkin Punctated *vars. Parkin* and *unspecified* (Figure 2.4) make up less than 1% of the overall sample; the proportion of Barton to Parkin varieties is roughly 5:1. Winterville Incised (Figure 2.3), the more southerly, curvilinear counterpart to Barton, also makes up less than 1% of the sample.

Painted wares (Figure 2.5) make up a relatively large proportion of decorated types, equaling Barton Incised varieties in contribution. Old Town Red *var. Beaverdam* is the most numerous of the shell-tempered painted types, comprising 15.17% of all decorated types. Hollywood White and Nodena Red and White examples are also well-represented, together making up 14.06% of decorated wares. Avenue Polychrome makes up an

Figure 2.2. Examples of Barton Incised *var. Barton* from Parchman Place (22CO511).

Figure 2.3. Examples of Barton Incised *var. Midnight* (*a, b, c*); Barton Incised *var. Estill* (*d*); Barton Incised *var. Togo* (*e, f, k*); and Winterville Incised *var. Winterville* (*g, h, i, j, l, m, n, o*) from Parchman Place (22CO511).

Figure 2.4. Examples of Parkin Punctated *var. Parkin* (*a, b, c, d, e, f, g*); Parkin Punctated *var. unspecified* (*h, i, j, m, n, o, p*); and Kinlock Simple Stamped (*k, l*) from Parchman Place (22CO511).

additional 4.12% of the decorated sample, significant because of their presumed very late chronological position in the ceramic sequence. Finally, Old Town Red *var. Old Town* and Carson Red on Buff make up 2.55% and 2.25% of the decorated assemblage respectively.

Two other types exist in significant numbers in the sample (Figure 2.6). Mulberry Creek Cord Marked makes up 2.12% of the decorated sample, while Walls Engraved *var. Hull* (n = 35) makes up 1.49%. Minority types and varieties include Larto Red, Leland Incised, Rhodes Incised *var. Horn Lake*, Walls Engraved *var. Walls*, Pouncey Pinched *var. Pouncey*, Grace Brushed *var. Grace*, Kinlock Simple Stamped *var. Kinlock*, L'Eau Noire Incised *var. unspecified*, Kimmswick Simple Stamped *var. Kimmswick*, O'Byam Incised *var. unspecified*, and Salomon Brushed *var. Salomon*. Also present are various unidentified varieties exhibiting incised, engraved, painted, punctated, brushed, and fabric impressed surface treatments.

As noted previously, vessel attributes that crosscut types and varieties may have much potential for making finer-grained chronological

Figure 2.5. Examples of Old Town Red *var. Beaverdam* (*a, b*); Nodena Red and White *var. Nodena* (*c, d*); Hollywood White *var. Hollywood* (*e, f*); Avenue Polychrome *var. Avenue* (*g, h, i, j, k, l.*); Old Town Red *var. Old Town* (*m, n*); and Carson Red on Buff *var. Carson* (*o, p, q*) from Parchman Place (22CO511).

distinctions among ceramic components that otherwise look quite similar. To this end, I recorded rim and lip attributes related to form, finish, and decorative embellishment for 1,339 rim sherds (Tables 2.2 and 2.3). Although sometimes used interchangeably, I follow Phillips et al. (1951) and others in distinguishing between rim and lip portions in my analysis and the two were recorded separately. By rim form, I refer to the form of the uppermost portion of the vessel (above the neck and shoulder), including the lip and immediately adjacent regions. Lip treatment refers exclusively to the finishing of the vessel opening or orifice.

Simple rims are by far the most common rim form, occurring on all vessel types in the assemblage. When further subdivided by lip treatment, simple rounded rims were the most common, followed by simple flattened. Simple intermediate rims, falling somewhere between rounded

Figure 2.6. Examples of Mulberry Creek Cord Marked *var. unspecified* (*a, b*); Walls Engraved *var. Hull* (*c, d, e, f, g*); Leland Incised *var. unspecified* (*h, i*); Rhodes Incised *var. Horn Lake* (*j, k*); Walls Engraved *var. Walls* (*l, m*); Pouncey Pinched *var. Pouncey* (*n, o*); Larto Red *var. Larto* (*p, q*); Grace Brushed *var. Grace* (*r, s*); L'Eau Noire Incised *var. L'Eau Noire* (*t*); Yates Net Impressed (*u*); and Withers Fabric Marked (*v*) from Parchman Place (22CO511).

and flattened, are also common. The remaining rim forms are very rare. Folded rims occur on 15 vessels, including jars and bowls. Most folded rims were then rounded or flattened to finish. Twelve rims in the sample were thinned. Of these, nine were rounded, two were flattened, and one was intermediate. Thinned rims occur primarily on coarse ware jars, bowls, and bottles, though one fine ware jar had a thinned rim. Seven rims in the sample were thickened, a treatment confined to bowls of either coarse or fine ware. Four vessels had beveled rims. The beveled form, sometimes called the "Memphis Rim Mode" (House 1993:27) is primarily associated with jars at Parchman Place. Finally, one vessel (a coarse ware jar) has an unusual rim form made by pinching up the clay of the rim into a peak, then flattening a portion of it so that the rim appears to be "tiered."

Decorative embellishments on the rim or lip were recorded separately from rim finishes and consist of decorative motifs that were added to the lip after it was finished by rounding, flattening, etc. Generally speaking, they consist of various types of scalloping, incision, notching, and punctation. Other decorative embellishments occur on or in the vessel body and include burnishing, addition of nodes, and in one case, a cut-away design on the interior of a bowl that is reminiscent of bas-relief. Eighty-seven vessels in the assemblage had some form of embellishment not encompassed by the type and variety classification.

Among the 87 vessels included in the attribute sample, scalloping was the most common rim treatment and includes both gently undulating rounded rims (Lansdell 2009:54) and rims with large rounded notches removed. Both of these are a fairly common treatment for serving bowls at Parchman Place, occurring on fine and coarse ware varieties of flaring rim and wide shallow bowls (Nelson 2016: Figure 2.12). Following scalloping, fine line incision is the next most common form of decorative attribute, occurring on 20.69% of the attribute sample (Nelson 2016: Figure 2.13). Three types of incision are distinguishable: (1) continuous line incision that is horizontal or parallel to the vessel rim, (2) multiple vertical incisions that are perpendicular to the vessel rim, and (3) multiple diagonal incisions occurring on the top of the vessel lip. Horizontal or parallel incision is associated with bowl forms and can occur on the top of the lip, on the exterior of the vessel just below the lip, or on the interior of the vessel just below the lip. One example has horizontal incision on both the interior and exterior vessel rim. Likewise, vertical or perpendicular incision can occur on the top of the lip, on the vessel exterior, and on the vessel interior. This treatment is primarily associated with bowls, though one coarse ware jar has exterior vertical incision. Diagonal incision can occur on bowls and jars and is always found on the top of the lip.

Notching sometimes occurs on the exterior vessel lip, on the interior vessel lip, and on the top of the lip. In these placements, the notching is typically small, shallow, and rectangular in shape. Two additional types of notching were achieved by cutting away or otherwise completely removing clay from the vessel wall, resulting in a crenellated effect. These notches extend from the interior to the exterior of the vessel walls and can be rectangular or triangular in shape. In two examples, triangular notches were ground out of the vessel wall subsequent to firing. Notching is most commonly found on bowl forms, but at least one coarse ware jar has triangular notches that were ground out after the vessel was fired.

Four vessels exhibit punctations as a lip treatment (Nelson 2016: Figure 2.13), including circular punctations on the top of the lip and thumbnail punctations on or below the exterior lip. Both vessels with circular lip punctations were bowls, while one jar had thumbnail punctations 2 cm below the exterior lip. The other vessel is of indeterminate shape.

Decorative attributes that are not associated with vessel rims include the addition of nodes, overall burnishing, and decorative embellishment on the vessel interior. Nodes are uncommon, occurring six times in the sample. In two cases, nodes were located on the shoulders of jars. Two other jars had nodes on their handles, a treatment considered by Smith to be early in the Mississippian sequence at Chucalissa (Smith 1969:4). Though fine ware vessels are common at Parchman Place, burnishing is not a common surface treatment, occurring on only 13 vessels for which shape could be determined. Though rare, burnishing is found on jars, bowls, and bottles of various types. Finally, one fine ware flaring rim bowl has an unusual interior decoration, consisting of a stepped geometric design that was made by cutting away clay to leave behind a raised design in the manner of bas-relief (Figure 2.7). Since neither the design, the technique used to make it, nor the paste and temper combination is typical for Parchman Place, this bowl is likely nonlocal in manufacture.

Handles of various types are fairly rare in the sample, but are most often associated with jars, 72 of which had some type of handle appended. Four bowls also had handles, as well as 21 vessels of indeterminate shape for a total of 97 handles in the sample. Handles, including lugs as well as those making up the loop-form handle series (Smith 1969) are tabulated in Table 2.4 (see illustrations in Figure 2.8). Handles in the loop-form series include loop, intermediate loop-strap, strap, tube or wide strap, and zoomorphic forms.

Though referred to here as handles, it is unclear whether lugs were always functional or sometimes merely decorative. If they functioned as handles, they could have been used to pick up and transport vessels (e.g., in and out of cooking fires), as appendages to which vessel covers could have been lashed, or even to suspend vessels as over a cooking fire. Lug handles as a group make up the majority of handles observed in the sample, with most of those being oval in shape. Oval lugs were appended to

Figure 2.7. Flaring rim bowl with stepped interior design from Parchman Place (22CO511).

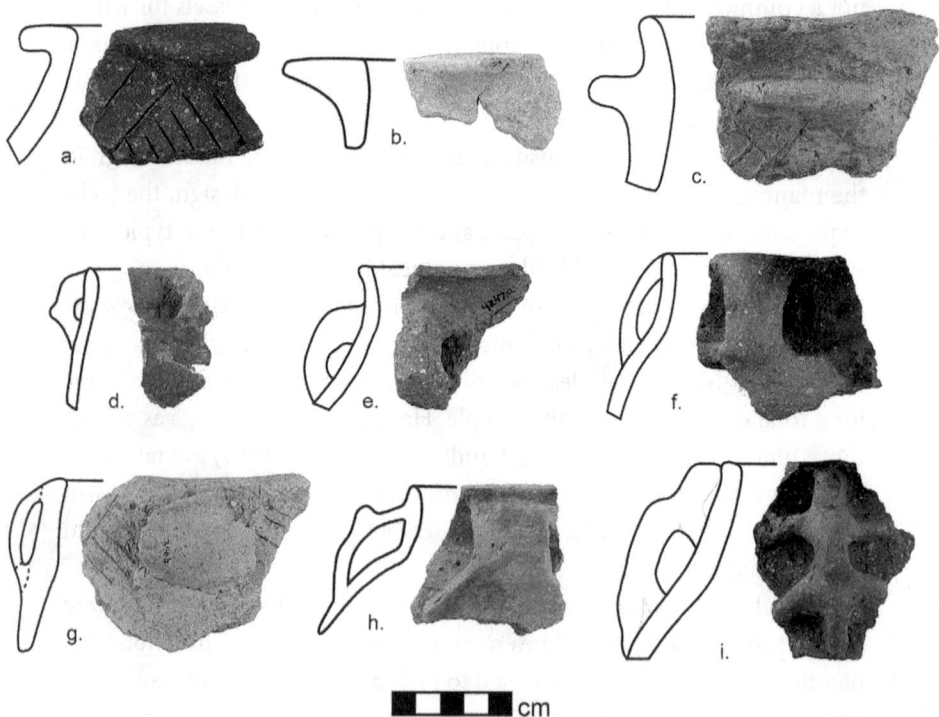

Figure 2.8. Handles from Parchman Place (22CO511), including oval lug (*a*); triangular lug (*b*); oval lug below lip (*c*); loop with nodes (*d*); intermediate loop-strap (*e*); strap (*f*); tube or wide strap (*g*); strap with nodes and "legs" (*h*); and zoomorphic (*i*).

both jars and bowls. In one case, oval lugs were attached about 2 cm below the rim of the jar; all others formed part of the vessel rim. Five oval lugs associated with jars were downturning rather than flat. One jar lug was "fat," termed a "Hushpuckena lug" by Belmont (1961) and considered by him to be an early variant of a thinner and later Oliver phase lug (Lansdell 2009:57; Phillips 1970:941). Eight elongated oval lugs were recorded in the sample, all associated with jar forms. Two elongated jar lugs were also downturning. Two lug handles were roughly triangular in shape. One of these was attached to a bowl, while the other was attached to a vessel of indeterminate shape.

Loop-form series handles make up 16.49% of the handles recorded in the sample. True loop handles are rare in the Parchman Place sample, occurring just twice—both times on jars. One of these has two nodes at its base and is attached to a very small jar of indeterminate ware. One handle in the sample appears to be intermediate between that of a loop and a strap handle. It is attached to a small jar of indeterminate ware. Strap handles are the most common of the loop-form series handles, occurring nine times, typically in association with jars. One strap handle associated with a small coarse ware jar was attached at the shoulder of the vessel by two "legs" and has one node visible on the upper portion, though there were probably originally two. Three examples of tube handles were identified in the Parchman Place assemblage, one on a medium-sized coarse ware jar, the other two on vessels of indeterminate shape. One of the latter was embellished with vertical incisions at the base of the handle. One complete zoomorphic handle was found during excavations at Parchman Place. The handle was formed into the shape of a four-legged animal with a long tail, perhaps a feline or lizard form. Unfortunately, very little of the vessel to which it was attached was recovered. However, it appears to have been a coarse ware jar of indeterminate size.

In summary, the only attributes that occurred with any frequency in the vessel assemblage were simple rounded/simple flattened rims (all vessel types), gently undulating rounded rims (bowls), rims with large rounded notches removed (bowls), and various types of lug handles (mostly jars). The following section details the results of a correspondence analysis focusing on types and varieties from excavated contexts at Parchman Place. Because of the very rare occurrence of vessel attributes, however, multivariate statistical methods were unsuccessful at detecting meaningful patterned differences in attribute frequencies among excavated contexts.

Considering presence/absence in excavated contexts suggests that chronological differences in attribute frequencies may exist that are obscured by small sample sizes. These are also discussed in the following section.

Following the type-variety analysis, correspondence analysis was used to determine whether there was significant variation within the sample and whether that variation could be attributed to temporal differences in the makeup of sub-assemblages from different parts of the site. The resulting graph (Figure 2.9a) plots ceramic types and varieties against excavated contexts in two-dimensional space. Spatial proximity indicates the degree of similarity or correspondence of ceramic assemblages among contexts.

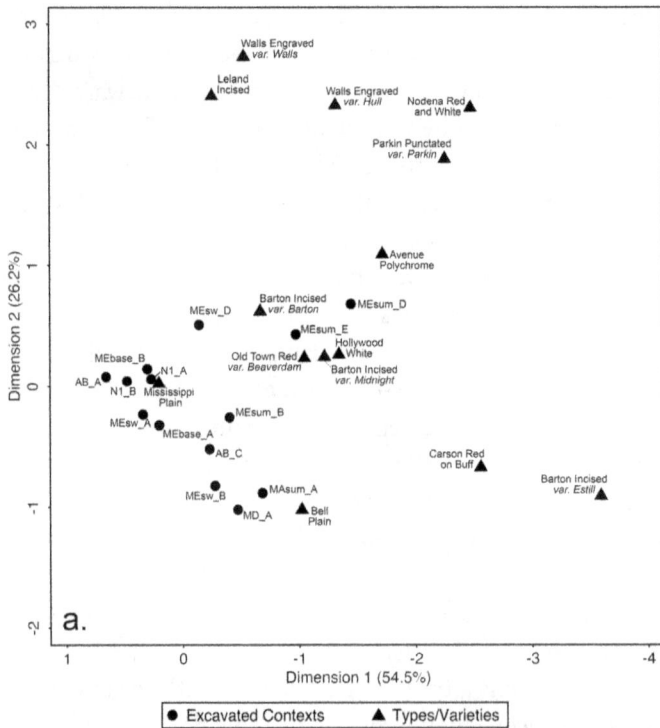

Figure 2.9. Correspondence analysis (CA) biplot showing (*a*) correspondence among ceramic types/varieties and excavated contexts. (*b*) The same biplot highlighting two distinct clusters along the first dimension. Dimension one separates contexts based on the presence (right cluster) or absence (left cluster) of fine, painted wares. (*c*) The same biplot highlighting two distinct clusters along the second dimension. Dimension two separates contexts based on their frequencies of plain (lower cluster) versus decorated (upper cluster) fine wares. Variables plotted in light gray are not well captured by the first (*b*) and second (*c*) dimensions. A key to context abbreviations can be found in Table 1.1.

Figure 2.9—*continued*

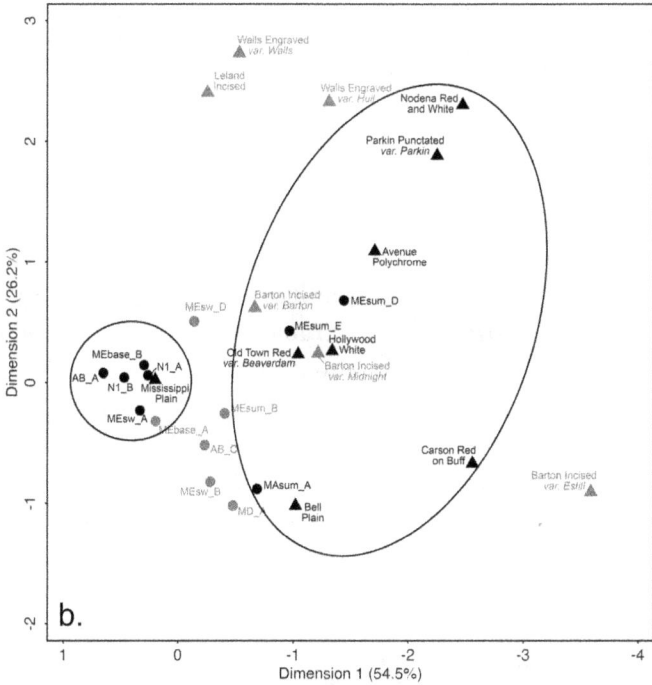

b.

● Excavated Contexts   ▲ Types/Varieties

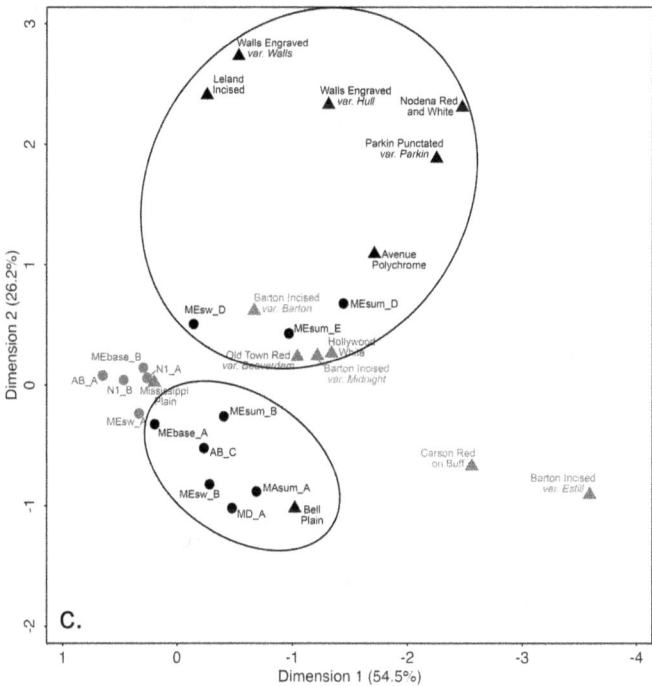

c.

● Excavated Contexts   ▲ Types/Varieties

Dimension 1 accounts for 54.5% of the total variation within the sample and is overwhelmingly controlled by Mississippi Plain *var. Neeley's Ferry*, the dominant plain ware in the assemblage (Figure 2.9b). This type forms a cluster with a number of excavated contexts near the origin of the graph. To the right of the origin is a more dispersed group that includes the types (in order of their influence on the analysis as measured by squared correlation) Parkin Punctated *var. Parkin*, Avenue Polychrome *var. Avenue*, Carson Red on Buff *var. Carson*, Bell Plain *var. Bell*, Hollywood White *var. Hollywood*, Old Town Red *var. Old Town*, and Nodena Red and White *var. Nodena*. These types pull three contexts toward the right side of the graph, while several others are not well captured by the first dimension as evidenced by their low squared correlation and contribution scores. Because Mississippi Plain *var. Neeley's Ferry* occurs in high proportions in every excavated context, Dimension 1 appears to separate contexts based on the relative presence and/or abundance of fine and especially painted wares. Additionally, the coarse ware type Parkin Punctated pulls away from Barton Incised, the more common decorated coarse ware, which plots more closely to Mississippi Plain.

These results support the interpretation that two temporally distinct sub-assemblages can be distinguished in the Parchman Place sample. Radiocarbon data (Table 1.2; Figure 1.4) and stratigraphy confirm this interpretation. Excavated contexts that plot in a cluster with Mississippi Plain *var. Neeley's Ferry* all returned 14th-century dates (see Table 1.1 for analysis units and associated C14 dates). These contexts include deposits from the lower levels of Mounds A and E and from residential areas in Neighborhood 1 and the swale between Mounds A and B. Contexts that plot closer to the right side of the graph along with painted and fine wares are from Mounds A and E and have returned 15th-century dates. One context (MEsum_B) also returned a 15th-century date, but as it falls stratigraphically between the earlier and later contexts, its intermediate position in the biplot is unsurprising.

The second dimension accounts for an additional 26.2% of variation and appears to separate contexts based on differing frequencies of plain versus decorated fine wares, particularly rare engraved and incised varieties (Figure 2.9c). Toward the bottom of the graph, a number of contexts cluster with Bell Plain *var. Bell*. Plotting near the top at the opposite end of the graph from Bell are (in order of their squared correlation value) Walls

Engraved *var.* Hull, Leland Incised, Nodena Red and White, Parkin Punctated, and Walls Engraved *var. Walls*. Avenue Polychrome and Barton Incised *var. Barton* are also pulled in this direction, though Barton's overall quality is low. These varieties appear to pull three contexts from Mound E away from the group that clusters with Bell. Interestingly, the varieties pulled out by the second dimension are not only rare, but some are nonlocal as well—Leland Incised is considered a southern type, while Walls Engraved *var. Walls* is more commonly found in the Memphis subregion. The pattern expressed along Dimension 2 may also be chronological to some extent as decorated fine wares correspond well with 15th-century contexts, while contexts corresponding well with Bell are chronologically mixed. The possibility that these patterns can be explained by contexts of use instead of or in addition to change over time is explored in the next chapter.

In some ways, temporal patterns in the correspondence analysis are not surprising. We know from Phillips et al. (1951:448–49), for instance, that painted and finely decorated types are more common among Late Mississippi period assemblages than earlier ones. Brain (1988) also inferred two temporally distinct components at Parchman Place, although my analysis demonstrates that occupation of the site was continuous rather than punctuated, as Brain supposed. However, the fact that two distinct ceramic assemblages at Parchman Place can be separated using multivariate statistics is significant in terms of our ability to refine chronology based on ceramic phases in the northern Yazoo and lends confidence to trait lists generated from stratified and dated contexts.

The majority of ceramic types, varieties, and rim and handle attributes occur in contexts spanning Parchman Place's occupation; others are associated with 14th- *or* 15th-century contexts, but not both. Tables 2.5 and 2.6 list ceramic traits identified at Parchman Place by time period. Though vessel forms are not discussed in detail until Chapter 3, they are included in Table 2.6 because some attributes occur on different vessel forms at different times. For example, folded rims are associated with bowl forms in the 14th century but do not appear on jar forms until the 15th century.

The results of the analyses presented here indicate that we are now in a position to subdivide the Parchman phase in a way that may prove more useful for making chronological assessments at a finer scale at Parchman Place and within the region, a necessary first step for understanding the

Table 2.5. Types and varieties associated with excavated ceramics from 14th- and 15th-century contexts at Parchman Place (22CO511)

14th Century	14th/15th Century	15th Century
L'Eau Noire Incised var. L'Eau Noire	Avenue Polychrome var. Avenue[a]	Barton Incised var. Estill
Salomon Brushed var. Salomon	Barton Incised var. Barton	Barton Incised var. Midnight
	Baytown Plain var. Baytown	Barton Incised var. Togo
	Bell Plain var. Bell	Carson Red on Buff var. Carson
	Hollywood White var. Hollywood	Grace Brushed var. Grace
	Larto Red var. Larto	Pouncey Pinched var. Pouncey
	Leland Incised var. unspecified	Rhodes Incised var. Horn Lake
	Mississippi Plain var. Neeley's Ferry	Walls Engraved var. Walls
	Mulberry Creek Cord Marked var. unspecified	
	Nodena Red and White var. Nodena[b]	
	Old Town Red var. Beaverdam	
	Old Town Red var. Old Town[a]	
	Parkin Punctated var. Parkin[a]	
	Walls Engraved var. Hull[b]	
	Winterville Incised var. Winterville	

[a] Present only in late 14th-century contexts.
[b] Present in very small numbers in the 14th century.

Table 2.6. Attributes associated with excavated ceramics from 14th- and 15th-century contexts at Parchman Place (22CO511)

14th Century	14th/15th Century	15th Century
triangular incisions on top of lip (jar)	simple rim (jar, bowl, bottle)	beveled rim (jar)
lug below lip (jar)	oval lug (jar)	folded rim (jar)
folded rim (bowl)	elongated oval lug (jar)	peaked rim (jar)
notched exterior lip (bowl)	strap handle (jar)	thinned rim (jar)
notched interior lip (bowl)	burnishing (jar, bottle)	incision perpendicular to rim on exterior lip (jar)
triangular lug (bowl)	thickened rim (bowl)	downturning oval lug (jar)
	thinned rim (bowl)	downturning elongated oval lug (jar)
	gently undulating rounded rim (bowl)	fat lug (jar)
	large rounded notches (bowl)	loop handle (jar)
		intermediate loop/strap handle (jar)
		tube handle (jar)
		zoomorphic handle (jar)
		incision parallel to rim on interior, exterior, or top of lip (bowl)
		incision perpendicular to rim on interior or exterior lip (bowl)
		oval lug (bowl)
		stepped bas-relief design on interior of body (bowl)
		burnishing (bowl)

Table 2.7. Ceramic types, varieties, and attributes present in proposed Parchman I subphase

Types and Varieties	Attributes
Barton Incised *var. Barton*	simple rim (jar, bowl, bottle)
Baytown Plain *var. Baytown*	oval lug (jar)
Bell Plain *var. Bell*	elongated oval lug (jar)
Hollywood White *var. Hollywood*	strap handle (jar)
L'Eau Noire Incised *var. unspecified*	**triangular incisions on top of lip (jar)**
Larto Red *var. Larto*	**lug below lip (jar)**
Leland Incised *var. unspecified*	burnishing (jar, bottle)
Mississippi Plain *var. Neeley's Ferry*	thickened rim (bowl)
Mulberry Creek Cord Marked *var. unspecified*	thinned rim (bowl)
Old Town Red *var. Old Town*	gently undulating rounded rim (bowl)
Salomon Brushed *var. Salomon*	large rounded notches (bowl)
Winterville Incised *var. Winterville*	**folded rim (bowl)**
	notched exterior lip (bowl)
	notched interior lip (bowl)
	triangular lug (bowl)

Note: Bold type indicates exclusive presence in subphase.

social relationships among people within and among the communities that lived and interacted here. To that end, I propose the following subdivisions, with trait lists shown in Tables 2.7 and 2.8.

The Parchman I Subphase

Parchman I roughly corresponds to the 14th century. In addition to the plain ware "supertypes" Mississippi Plain, Bell Plain, and Baytown Plain, Parchman I also contains Barton Incised *var. Barton* and its more southerly counterpart, Winterville Incised *var. Winterville*. Clay-tempered types are well represented—in addition to Baytown, these include Larto Red, Mulberry Creek Cord Marked, and Salomon Brushed *var. Salomon*. Less common incised varieties include L'Eau Noire Incised *var. unspecified* and Leland Incised *var. unspecified*, both shell-tempered, though L'Eau Noire is more typically found on clay-tempered paste. Painted wares in addition to Larto include Hollywood White *var. Hollywood* and Old Town Red *var. Old Town*, both shell-tempered.

Table 2.8. Ceramic types, varieties, and attributes present in proposed Parchman II subphase

Types and Varieties	Attributes
Avenue Polychrome *var. Avenue*[a]	simple rim (jar, bowl, bottle)
Barton Incised *var. Barton*	oval lug (jar)
Barton Incised var. Estill	elongated oval lug (jar)
Barton Incised var. Midnight	strap handle (jar)
Barton Incised var. Togo	**beveled rim (jar)**
Baytown Plain *var. Baytown*	**folded rim (jar)**
Bell Plain *var. Bell*	**peaked rim (jar)**
Carson Red on Buff var. Carson	**thinned rim (jar)**
Grace Brushed var. Grace	**incision perpendicular to rim on exterior lip (jar)**
Hollywood White *var. Hollywood*	**downturning oval lug (jar)**
Larto Red *var. Unspecified*	**downturning elongated oval lug (jar)**
Leland Incised *var. Unspecified*	**fat lug (jar)**
Mississippi Plain *var. Neeley's Ferry*	**loop handle (jar)**
Mulberry Creek Cord Marked *var. Unspecified*	**intermediate loop/strap handle (jar)**
Nodena Red and White *var. Nodena*[b]	**tube handle (jar)**
Noe Perforated *var. Noe*	**zoomorphic handle (jar)**
Old Town Red *var. Beaverdam*[a]	burnishing (jar, bottle)
Old Town Red *var. Old Town*	thickened rim (bowl)
Parkin Punctated *var. Parkin*[a]	thinned rim (bowl)
Pouncey Pinched var. Pouncey	gently undulating rounded rim (bowl)
Rhodes Incised var. Horn Lake	large rounded notches (bowl)
Walls Engraved *var. Hull*	**incision parallel to rim on interior, exterior, or top of lip (bowl)**
Walls Engraved var. Walls	**incision perpendicular to rim on interior or exterior lip (bowl)**
Winterville Incised *var. Winterville*	**oval lug (bowl)**
	stepped bas-relief design on interior of body (bowl)
	burnishing (bowl)

Note: Bold type indicates exclusive presence in subphase.
[a] Type/variety present in late 14th-century contexts.
[b] Type/variety present in very small numbers in 14th century.

Information on vessel attributes associated with the Parchman I subphase comes from 87 jars, 47 bowls, and 11 bottles from excavated contexts dating to the 14th century. Parchman I jar and bottle forms have simple flattened or simple rounded rims. Bowl rims are more variable, including simple flattened, simple rounded, thickened, thinned, and folded forms. Additional rim embellishment on jars is very uncommon, but triangular incision on the top of the lip has been observed. Bowls not uncommonly have scalloped rims, either of the gently undulating rounded variety or with scallops achieved by the removal of large rounded notches. Bowls can also have notching on the interior or exterior lip. Burnishing is uncommon, occasionally occurring on jars and bottles but not bowls. Handles are also uncommon, but include oval and elongated oval lugs attached at or below the lip of jars, and triangular lugs on bowls. Strap handles are sometimes found on jars. Types, varieties, and attributes that are found *exclusively* in Parchman I include L'Eau Noire Incised *var. unspecified,* Salomon Brushed *var. Salomon,* folded bowl rims, triangular incisions on jar lips, interior and exterior notched bowl lips, lugs attached below the rim, and triangular bowl lugs.

The Parchman II Subphase

Parchman II corresponds roughly to the 15th century. With the exception of the traits just listed as exclusively related to the Parchman I subphase, the core of the Parchman II assemblage looks similar. However, it is marked by a proliferation of ceramic types, varieties, and attributes not found in the earlier time period. Varieties of Barton Incised, including *Estill, Midnight,* and *Togo* appear in Parchman II, though all are significantly less common than *var. Barton,* the dominant decorated coarse ware in both assemblages. Parkin Punctated *var. Parkin,* which does occur in late 14th-century contexts, is more frequently associated with the later subphase. Additionally, the coarse ware varieties Pouncey Pinched *var. Pouncey* and Grace Brushed *var. Grace* make their first appearance. However, it is the increase in the frequency of fine ware vessels, especially those with painted and finely engraved or incised surface decorations, that really marks this subphase as distinct from what came before. Painted types such as Avenue Polychrome *var. Avenue,* Old Town Red *var. Beaverdam,* and Nodena Red and White first occur in the late 14th century, but are found in greater numbers during the 15th century. Carson Red on

Buff appears only in the 15th century. Finally, Rhodes Incised *var. Horn Lake,* and Walls Engraved *vars. Walls* and *Hull* mark the Parchman II subphase.

There is also an explosion of decorative attributes associated with the Parchman II subphase, as well as a number of attributes that drop out of favor. These observations are based on a sample of 171 jars, 56 bowls, and 29 bottles from excavated contexts dating to the 15th century. Jar rims, which were almost never elaborated in the earlier subphase now include beveled, thinned, peaked, and folded forms, as well as the more common simple rounded or simple flattened finishes. Jar rims are not typically further elaborated, but perpendicular incision on the exterior rim does exist (see also Mainfort 2003 on exterior notching). Perpendicular incision occurs on interior and exterior bowl rims in the Parchman II subphase, as does parallel incision on the interior, exterior, or top of bowl rims. None of these occur prior to Parchman II.

Handle forms also occur more frequently and in greater variety. On jar forms, both oval and elongated oval lugs are sometimes downturning, a trait not seen before Parchman II. One example of a "fat" lug also occurs on a jar form. Other handle forms for jars include loop, intermediate loop/strap, strap, tube, and zoomorphic, while only strap handles were observed in the preceding subphase. Notably, the results of the handle analysis (excluding lugs) do not conform to expectations of changes in handle shape over time that are prevalent in the Memphis subregion (e.g., Smith 1969). The entire series of loop-form handles (loop, intermediate, strap, tube, zoomorphic) is associated with 15th-century contexts at Parchman Place. The only handle also occurring in the 14th century (though with less frequency than in the 15th) is the strap handle, thought by others to occur later in Mississippian assemblages than loop and intermediate handles.

Bowls are also sometimes associated with oval lugs. Burnishing of bowls is also in evidence (not observed in Parchman I, though burnishing was previously used to treat jars and bottles). One unusual bowl has a stepped interior design that was created by cutting away the clay around it to leave a raised design. The atypical design and method of decoration, as well as the paste of the vessel suggest that it is nonlocal in origin.

There are two simultaneous trends apparent in the choices Mississippian potters made at Parchman Place. On the one hand, their decisions about materials, methods of manufacture, and even decorative techniques were essentially conservative, with the core of their pottery assemblage remaining consistent throughout the 14th and 15th centuries. This indicates strong continuity in how Mississippian potters understood the role/s of pottery in social life and how best to imbue their pots with desired characteristics by combining clay, shell, water, and fire in particular ways. On the other hand, there was a trend toward increased experimentation and the incorporation of new decorative techniques over time. These techniques, particularly painting and engraving, were most often associated with fine shell-tempered serving wares, indicating that potters put increasingly more effort into the outward appearance of vessels used for eating and perhaps for ceremonial occasions. As the coming chapters will demonstrate, there is much evidence for social negotiation among community members at Parchman Place in the early 15th century, coincident with the beginning of the Parchman II subphase, as people used atypical mound-building practices and rearranged neighborhood space to promote particular values. When viewed alongside these other material practices, an increased emphasis on finely decorated pottery may be understood as an expression of increasing social negotiation in the late period. In other words, people began to use pottery to emphasize social distinctions among themselves in ways they had not done when the community was first founded.

It is worth pointing out here that many of these trends in decorating fine serving wares are thought to have their origins to the north of the Parchman phase area. Types including Parkin Punctated, Walls Engraved, Rhodes Incised, Nodena Red and White, and other painted types are all more prevalent in the Walls, Parkin, and Nodena phases, now understood to be the archaeological remnants of the Soto-era provinces of Quizquiz, Aquixo, and Pacaha (Dye 1993; Hudson et al. 1990; Hudson 1997; McNutt 1996b; Mitchem 1996; D. Morse 1990; P. Morse 1990; Morse and Morse 1983). These more northerly provinces related to one another through open warfare and relations of political dominance and subordination (at least as interpreted through Spanish eyes). The increasing prevalence of northern pottery types in Parchman phase assemblages may indicate that Parchman phase people were increasingly drawn into regional Mississippian politics, though there is no obvious evidence of hostilities with neighboring groups. In any case, it is a possibility that requires further investigation. Refinements to the ceramic chronology described in this chapter provide a much-needed framework for continuing this line of inquiry among Parchman phase sites and for reconstructing the social history of particular communities.

3

Ceramics and Foodways
at Parchman Place

Food and foodways are salient indicators of individual and group identity, and food-focused events are frequently involved in community building activities aimed at fostering social cohesion, emphasizing social difference, or both (Appadurai 1981; Blitz 1993b; Briggs 2015, 2016; Dietler and Hayden 2001; Kassabaum 2014:314–325; Knight 2001; Scarry and Steponaitis 1997; Twiss 2007; Van der Veen 2003; Welch and Scarry 1995). Throughout this book, I use ceramics data in combination with other archaeological evidence to consider how people living at Parchman Place used foodways to promote particular relationships among community members and to rebalance and re-create a world that was distinctly Mississippian. In this chapter, I identify distinct vessel categories manufactured by Parchman Place potters based on characteristics such as size, shape, paste and temper composition, use wear, and other attributes that have been shown to relate to vessel function and use in Mississippian contexts (Braun 1980, 1983; Hally 1983a, 1983b, 1984, 1986; Pauketat 1987; Shepard 1956; Steponaitis 1984; Wilson and Rodning 2002). I also address temporal trends in the manufacture of specific vessel classes. Furthermore, I conducted a correspondence analysis that demonstrates the presence of functionally distinct ceramic assemblages at Parchman Place. These include a baseline domestic assemblage as well as a special-use assemblage that I argue is related to large-scale communal eating events that mark the founding of the Parchman Place community and establish social relationships among founding members that are reinforced, contested, and transformed in various ways in the decades that follow.

In his comprehensive review of the relationships among Mississippian ceramic vessel types and their performance characteristics, Hally (1984, 1986) drew upon ethnohistoric literature regarding the food storage, preparation, and consumption habits of southeastern Indian groups to hypothesize about the intended use of vessel categories identified in Barnett phase assemblages from northwest Georgia. He found that domestic vessel assemblages tended to consist of various vessel shapes that occurred in multiple sizes, which could be correlated with ethnographically observed food-related activities (see also Briggs 2015, 2016; Pauketat 1987; Wilson and Rodning 2002).

While whole vessel assemblages are needed to do the kind of extensive analyses of which Hally provides an example (e.g., Brown 2005; Childress 1992; Cruciotti et al. 2006; Hally 1986; Pauketat 1987; Steponaitis 1983), the Parchman Place ceramics sample consists of fragmentary rim and body sherds and includes only a small number of vessels that could be partially reconstructed. Basic vessel shape, however, could be identified for rim sherds of sufficient size, especially when more than one portion of the vessel (lip, neck, shoulder, body, or base) was represented. I identified basic shape categories (jar, bowl, bottle) for rim sherds by visual inspection, with reference to illustrated whole vessel and rim profiles recovered from the northern Yazoo and adjacent regions (Brown 2005; Childress 1992; Cruciotti et al. 2006; Hally 1972; House 1991; Lansdell 2009; Phillips 1970; Steponaitis et al. 2002). In some cases, I was able to assign sherds to secondary shape categories. For jars, these include simple and standard forms. Five subcategories of bowl could be identified: simple, flaring rim, wide shallow, carinated, and restricted. Bottles were subdivided into standard neck, narrow neck, and wide neck forms. To determine size classes, I measured vessel orifice diameter by comparing the arc of rim sherds representing 5% or more of the total rim diameter of the parent vessel with a standard rim diameter and percentage chart. Orifice diameter has been shown to correlate well with volume estimates for certain vessel classes, including jars and some bowl forms, but not bottles (Childress 1992:39; Hally 1983a; Pauketat 1987:113–114; Whallon 1969). Though rarely evident, I recorded use alteration in the form of sooting residues; I did not observe any unequivocal examples of wear or abrasion related to vessel use. These additional analyses, combined with paste characteristics and rim and handle attributes already recorded form the basis of the discussion on vessel function and use.

The following discussion of Parchman Place vessel forms is organized by basic shape (jars, bowls, and bottles) and further subdivided by size (jars) and shape (bowls and bottles). Of the 1,369 rim sherds recovered from the sample, basic vessel shape could be determined for 716. An additional 23 body sherds contained sufficient portions of the vessel to determine basic shape categories in the absence of the rim portion, bringing the total number of sherds for which basic vessel shape could be determined to 739. This number includes 513 jar forms, 168 bowls, and 58 bottles.

Jar Forms

Two basic jar forms were identified in the Parchman Place sample (Figure 3.1; Table 3.1). "Standard" jars (n = 67) were chiefly defined on the basis of an outsloping rim portion (Phillips et al. 1951:105), while "simple" jars (n = 233) had vertical or slightly insloping rim portions, the latter being equivalent to Steponaitis' (1983:69) "neckless" jar. Given the fragmentary nature of the ceramic assemblage, it was not possible to determine how rim form

Table 3.1. Types, varieties, and shapes for ceramic jars from Parchman Place (22CO511)

Jars	Simple	Standard	Indet. or Not Recorded	Jar Total
Mississippi Plain *var. Neeley's Ferry*	97	26	76	199
Mississippi Plain *var. unspecified*	4	1	1	6
Barton Incised *var. Barton*	118	25	84	227
Barton Incised *var. Estill*	1	–	4	5
Barton Incised *var. unspecified*	2	2	6	10
Winterville Incised *var. Winterville*	3	2	2	7
Winterville Incised *var. unspecified*	1	1	1	3
Parkin Punctated *var. Parkin*	1	1	4	6
Parkin Punctated *var. unspecified*	–	1	–	1
Pouncey Pinched *var. Pouncey*	–	–	1	1
Bell Plain *var. Bell*	2	1	16	19
Old Town Red *var. Beaverdam*	–	–	1	1
Unidentified Plain	2	4	14	20
Unidentified Incised	2	3	3	8
Total	233	67	213	513

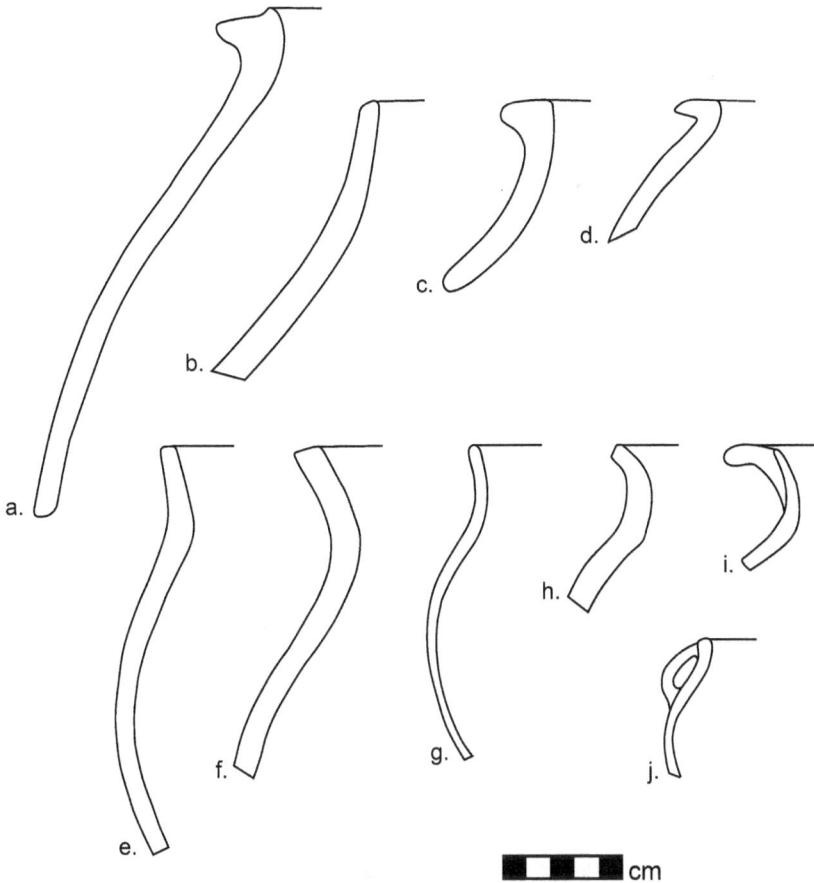

Figure 3.1. Examples of jar forms from Parchman Place (22CO511), including simple jars (*a, b, c, d*) and standard jars (*e, f, g, h, i, j*).

relates to body shape in this sample, though the more complete standard jar profiles indicate squat, globular bodies as a general rule. Whether simple jar profiles were of similar proportions is unknown, though Mississippian assemblages frequently have more than one jar form (e.g., Hally 1984, Steponaitis 1983; Wilson 2008). In any case, and despite initial expectations, secondary shape did not have any discernible relationship to size or to presence or location of sooting—simple and standard jars are present in all size classes and exhibit sooting at approximately the same rate. As both shape categories were utilized primarily for cooking, simple and standard jars are grouped together in the discussion that follows.

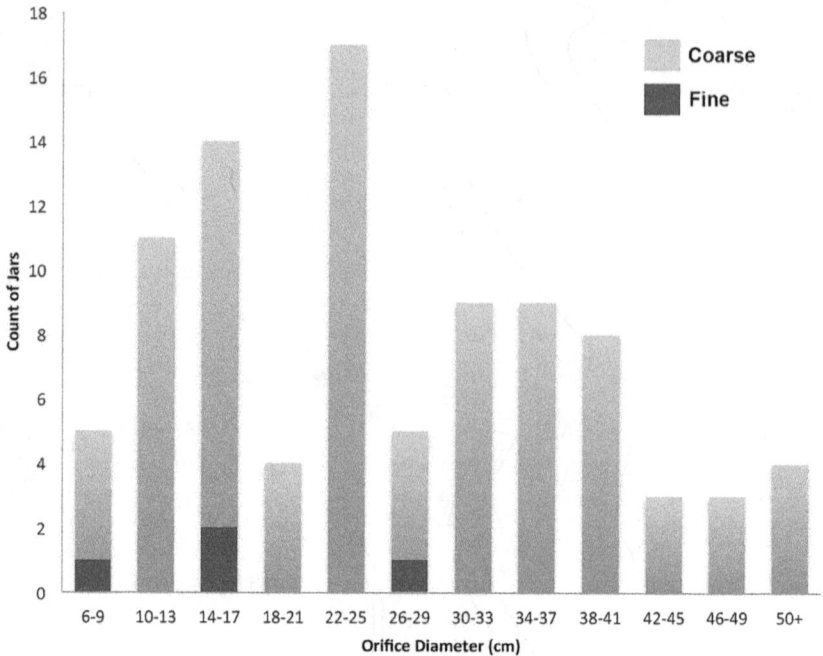

Figure 3.2. Frequency histogram of jar sizes distinguishing coarse ware (n = 88) and fine ware (n = 4) jars from Parchman Place (22CO511).

One hundred jars in the sample had rim sherds of sufficient size to determine orifice diameter. Orifice diameters range from 7 to greater than 50 cm, with the majority falling between 10 and 40 cm. A frequency histogram of the results indicates three mid-range size classes where most of the data fall, as well as a few examples on either end of the distribution, for five total size classes (Figure 3.2). Although the overwhelming majority of jars of all sizes were manufactured on coarse shell-tempered paste, reflecting their function as utilitarian cooking vessels, the three smallest size classes were occasionally also made on a fine shell-tempered paste. The following section summarizes the characteristics of these jar classes and offers some hypotheses for their intended use.

Very Small Jars

Very small jars (n = 5) had orifice diameters of 6–9 cm. The majority were of coarse shell-tempered or indeterminate ware, though there was one example of a very small Bell Plain jar with a burnished exterior surface (one coarse ware jar was also burnished). Very small jars were made in both simple and standard shapes and both lug and strap handles were observed, though there was no evidence of sooting for jars of this size class. Despite low numbers, very small jars were fairly widely distributed at the site, occurring in the 14th and 15th centuries, and in mound and neighborhood contexts. The rare occurrence of these jars at Parchman Place suggests a specialized, non-everyday use. Further, their small size and orifice as well as their easily covered shape may have rendered them suitable for holding rare, valuable, or perishable goods. Some possibilities include prepared condiments or various herbs used for flavoring food or for medicinal or ritual use (Hally 1986:271). They also could have contained small amounts of nonfood products such as pigments. The lack of evidence for sooting indicates that these vessels were probably not placed directly in fires, though the coarse shell-tempered jars could have withstood some degree of thermal shock (Hally 1983b; Steponaitis 1984). Burnishing on two examples further suggests the "special" nature of their contents, contexts of use, or both. Burnishing may also have made these jars more suitable for holding liquids as the burnishing would prevent evaporation through the vessel walls (Henrickson and McDonald 1983:633).

Small Jars

Small jars (n = 30) measured from 10–18 cm in orifice diameter. The majority are of coarse ware, though two examples were made on Bell Plain paste (Figure 3.3). Small jars were made in both simple and standard shapes, and both lug and strap handles were observed. Five coarse ware jars had sooting on the exterior neck and shoulder portions. None of the jars were burnished. Small coarse ware jars were used as small cooking vessels, as sooting on the exterior neck and shoulders indicates they were used directly over fire (Hally 1983b). Both simple and standard coarse ware jars would have been efficient at absorbing and retaining heat and reducing evaporation, and both would also have been resistant to thermal shock. Handles would allow them to be moved while hot and also could have been used to secure coverings; strap handles may have been used to suspend jars over a flame. More specifically, small coarse ware jars were suitable for boiling or parboiling small quantities of things that do not keep well after cooking or that are available or eaten only in small quantities

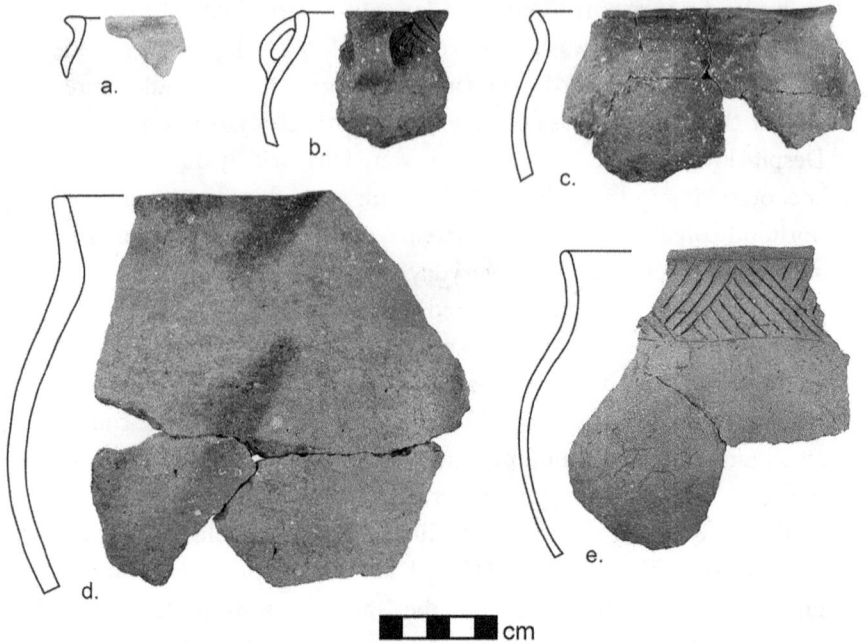

Figure 3.3. Examples of small (*a, b, c*) and medium (*d, e*) jars from Parchman Place (22CO511). Example *a* is manufactured on a fine Bell Plain paste, while the others are of coarse ware paste equivalent to Mississippi Plain *var. Neeley's Ferry*.

(e.g., beans, squash, greens, ramps, mushrooms, or small mammals; Hally 1986:287). Small cooking jars also may have been used to prepare small quantities of individual ingredients that were later added to a larger cooking pot to make a stew or comparable dish (Hally 1986:269–271). Small fine ware jars were probably not used for cooking, since they never show sooting and their resistance to thermal shock would be less than optimal. The most likely use for these vessels was short-term storage or serving of small amounts of prepared food. Small coarse ware jars were ubiquitous in excavated contexts at Parchman Place and occurred throughout the 14th and 15th centuries, while the extreme rarity of small fine ware jars indicate that they were not in common use.

Medium Jars

Medium jars had orifice diameters of 20–28 cm. I identified one example of a medium fine ware jar in the Parchman Place sample, though the majority (n = 22) are of coarse ware (Figure 3.3). As with small jars, medium jars were made in simple and standard shapes, and had handles of various types, including lug handles and one example of a tube or wide strap handle. Four coarse ware examples were sooted on the exterior neck and/or shoulder portions, indicating use as cooking vessels. The fine ware example was burnished on the exterior.

Aside from their larger capacity, medium-sized jars had similar mechanical performance characteristics to small jars and (excepting the single fine ware example) can be interpreted as medium-sized general purpose cooking vessels. In addition to their primary role in preparing large quantities of food such as maize and beans by boiling, medium jars were suitable for soaking foods as a preliminary step in the processing sequence, as when foods that were stored in a dried state (parched maize, hominy, beans, starchy seeds) were rehydrated prior to consumption or further processing. Soaking can also change the nature of the food, as in nixtamalization, a process that increases the nutritional value of maize and makes it easier to grind (Briggs 2015, 2016). These jars could also have been used in the short term to store/serve prepared food such as fermented corn soup or *sofkee* for intermittent consumption (Hally 1986:269, 286). Medium coarse ware jars occurred with near ubiquity in mound and neighborhood contexts dating to the 14th and 15th centuries. Though exceedingly rare in the sample, medium fine ware jars were probably used for short-term storage or for serving, especially considering that burnishing would inhibit evaporation.

Large Coarse Ware Jars

Large jars had orifice diameters of 30–40 cm. All 26 large jars identified in the sample were manufactured on coarse shell-tempered paste. Both simple and standard jar shapes were represented and a handful of lug handles were observed. Only one large jar had evidence of sooting on the exterior neck and shoulder. Despite similarities with medium coarse ware jars in overall body shape, proportions, paste and temper, and other attributes, the large size and weight of these vessels when filled would make moving them difficult. Like the large pinched rim jars of the Barnett phase (Hally 1986:285–6), large coarse ware jars from Parchman Place were probably used primarily for storage of various foodstuffs, such as parched whole maize and hominy (whole kernel or ground), and other foods such as nuts, oily and starchy seeds, and beans that may have been stored in their dried form. Even highly perishable foods such as fruits, meats, and shell-fish could have been preserved by drying or smoking and stored for later consumption. Ethnographic accounts furthermore suggest that oil, water, and corn soup were stored in large jars (Hally 1986:285). They were also used to cook large quantities of food as the occasion required. They were ubiquitous in mound and neighborhood contexts and occurred through-out the 14th and 15th centuries.

Very Large Coarse Ware Jars

Very large jars ranged from 45 to 50 cm in orifice diameter. Ten examples of very large coarse shell-tempered jars were present in the sample. Four jars had lug handles and one had evidence of sooting on the shoulder. As with large jars, very large jars would have functioned as long-term stor-age vessels for large quantities of liquids and solid foods. With their very large capacity, they would have been difficult to move when full, but their restricted but still rather wide orifices would minimize spilling, while also facilitating removal of contents through scooping. Additionally, covers could be secured on standard jars or jars with handles. Sooting on one example indicates that they were at least occasionally used for cooking or heating contents. Very large coarse ware jars were used throughout the 14th and 15th centuries and occur in mound and neighborhood contexts.

Bowl Forms

Bowls in the Parchman Place sample were more variable than jars when shape, size, and paste combinations were considered. Of 168 bowls identi-fied, 116 could be assigned to five secondary shape categories, including simple, wide shallow, flaring rim, carinated, and restricted profiles (Figure 3.4; Table 3.2). Forty-seven bowl rims were sufficiently large to measure orifice diameter. When graphed in a frequency histogram (Figure 3.5), the resulting distribution of orifice diameters indicates the presence of four size modes. As described later, some shapes/sizes were manufactured on both coarse and fine wares, while others were manufactured on one or the other.

In addition to shape and size, the main considerations for determin-ing bowl function are ware and presence of sooting, though decorative

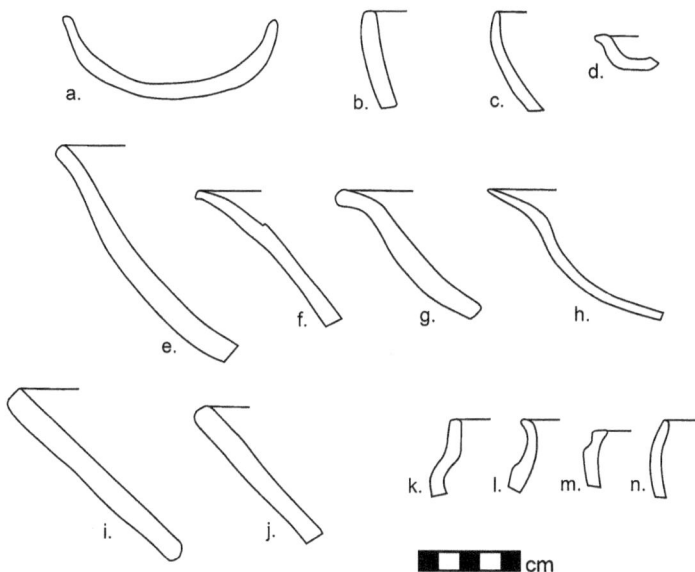

Figure 3.4. Profile drawings of bowls from Parchman Place (22CO511), including simple (a, b, c, d [with lug]); flaring rim (e, f, g, h); wide shallow (i, j); carinated (k, l, m); and restricted (n).

Table 3.2. Types, varieties, and shapes for ceramic bowls at Parchman Place (22CO511)

Bowls	Simple	Wide Shallow	Flaring Rim	Carinated	Restricted	Indet. or Not Recorded	Bowl Total
Mississippi Plain *var.*							
Neeley's Ferry	15	14	15	–	–	11	55
Mississippi Plain *var.*							
unspecified	3	2	3	–	–	1	9
Old Town Red *var.*							
Old Town	–	–	2	–	–	–	2
Bell Plain *var. Bell*	7	2	15	3	1	14	42
L'Eau Noire Incised							
var. unspecified	–	–	–	–	1	1	2
Old Town Red *var.*							
Beaverdam	–	–	1	–	–	–	1
Walls Engraved *var.*							
Hull	2	–	5	1	–	3	11
Baytown Plain *var.*							
Baytown	1	–	–	–	–	–	1
Unidentified Plain	13	–	8	1	1	21	44
Unidentified Incised	–	–	–	–	–	1	1
Total	41	18	49	5	3	52	168

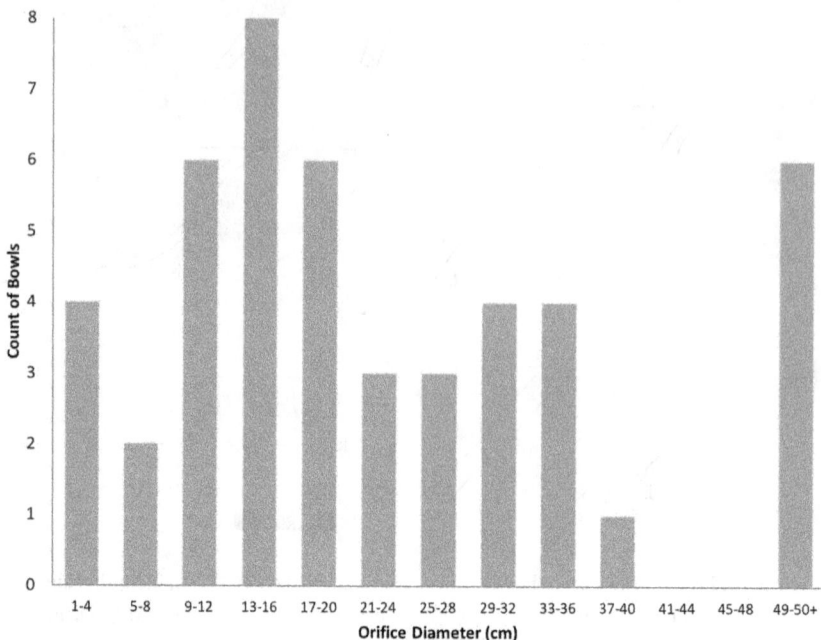

Figure 3.5. Frequency histogram of ceramic bowls from Parchman Place (22CO511) for which orifice diameter could be measured, indicating four size classes: very small (2–7 cm), small (10–23 cm), medium (25–38 cm), and large (~50 cm).

embellishments may also indicate vessels used for special purposes. Certainly, the prevalence of rim and lip embellishment suggests that many bowls were used in contexts where they were particularly visible, such as the serving of prepared foods to groups of various size and composition. The following discussion of bowls is organized primarily by shape.

Simple Bowls

Simple bowls were more or less hemispherical in shape with no inflection points from base to rim. Forty-one examples of simple bowls were present in the sample, making up 35.3% of the sample for which secondary shape could be determined. Simple bowls were manufactured on a coarse shell-tempered ware equivalent to Mississippi Plain *var. Neeley's Ferry* in three different sizes: small, medium, and large; and on a fine shell-tempered ware equivalent to Bell Plain *var. Bell* in two sizes: small and medium. Additionally, five very small (miniature) simple pinch bowls were identified—all typed as unidentified plain.

Simple bowls were the only bowl forms in the sample that had lug handles, though they were rare, occurring on two coarse ware bowls and one fine ware bowl, as well as one miniature pinch bowl. Furthermore, the rims of simple bowls were rarely embellished, though horizontal and vertical incisions were observed on two fine ware examples. There was no evidence of sooting on simple bowls, though coarse shell-tempered examples had potential for cooking or heating because their paste composition and rounded contours would have made them resistant to thermal shock. Instead, simple bowls were more likely used as utilitarian food preparation and serving vessels as their unrestricted orifice and general stability would have facilitated the manipulation of contents by mixing, stirring, or grinding, and contents could easily be scooped or ladled.

Though their overall body proportions and mechanical performance characteristics were similar, simple bowls would have varied in function according to their size. Small simple bowls (10–23 cm in diameter) may have been used as individual or small group serving dishes or to serve foods prepared in small quantities such as condiments or dipping sauces. Medium simple bowls (25–38 cm in diameter) were likely used to prepare or serve larger quantities of food. One example of a large (~50 cm in diameter) simple coarse ware bowl was identified in the sample. As with the smaller sizes, the wide orifice would facilitate manipulation and scooping of the vessel contents, however, the large size and capacity may have prevented moving the vessel when full. This bowl could have been used to serve large amounts of prepared foods or for various steps in the preparation of certain foods. Soaking, for instance, was a preliminary step in the preparation of maize, which was likely processed in large quantities. Parching of maize or other foodstuffs is another possibility. Bowls would also be well suited for mixing wet and dry ingredients to make dough for bread, dumplings, or fritters (Hally 1986:289).

Wide Shallow Bowls

I consider wide shallow bowls to be a subset of simple bowls in that they do not have inflection points. However, they are truncated so as to be shallower than simple (hemispherical) bowls. They are substantially more wide than deep, with a lower center of gravity and a larger orifice relative to height. There were 18 examples of wide shallow bowls in the sample, making up 15.5% of bowls for which secondary shape could be determined. The great majority were manufactured of coarse shell-tem-pered (Mississippi Plain) ware; sizes include small (n = 1), medium (n = 3), and large (n = 5). The remaining coarse ware (n = 7) and fine ware (n = 2) wide shallow bowls were of indeterminate size.

Wide shallow bowls typically had thick ("chunky") vessel walls and undecorated rims, though five coarse and one fine wide shallow bowl had gently undulating rounded rims. Generally, the thicker the vessel wall, the lower its thermal conductivity and resistance to thermal shock, but the greater its flexural strength or breakage load (Braun 1983: 118). Although the thick vessel walls might argue against cooking as a primary function, two wide shallow bowls showed direct evidence of use over fire. One of the medium-sized bowls has exterior sooting, while one of the large ex-amples has sooting on the interior. As with simple bowls, wide shallow bowls would have had a range of uses that was dependent on size.

Given their similar mechanical performance characteristics, the uses of small coarse ware wide shallow bowls were probably similar to that of small simple bowls. That is, they were probably multipurpose bowls used for mixing and serving small amounts of solid or viscous food. Like small simple bowls, they were uncommon in the sample, the only example was recovered from an early domestic context. Medium coarse ware wide shallow bowls ranged in size from 32–38 cm in orifice diameter. Except-ing their rather thick vessel walls, they had similar mechanical perfor-mance characteristics to medium-sized simple bowls. These bowls were likely used for food preparation such as mixing of prepared ingredients and for serving of solid and semisolid foods. Exterior sooting on one ex-ample suggests that they were also sometimes used for cooking or heating food or perhaps for parching maize or nuts. Another possibility is that these bowls could be used upside down in the manner of an oven and that the sooting could result from hot coals heaped on the outside (Hally 1986:269). Other food preparation activities such as soaking of maize or leaching of tannins from acorns could have been performed in wide shal-low bowls. Medium coarse ware wide shallow bowls were uncommon in the Parchman Place sample. Two examples were recovered from residen-tial contexts, while a third was associated with an intermediate construc-tion stage of Mound E.

Five of the nine measurable coarse wide shallow bowls had rim diam-eters of approximately 50 cm. This suggests a special function for these large coarse vessels that has to do with the processing or preparation of

large amounts of food or for serving large groups of people. Interior sooting on one of the examples could indicate that the bowl was used to carry
fire or perhaps turned upside down over a fire to trap heat in the manner of an oven. Therefore, this class of vessels may have been used in
the manner of large simple bowls, that is, for manipulating, serving, and
sometimes heating or reheating large amounts of food. However, due to
their compromised thermal properties, they were probably not used for
cooking at high temperatures such as those required for boiling foods like
maize or beans for long periods of time. One possibility is that they were
used for parching, a common way of preparing large quantities of maize,
nuts, and other foods for storage and consumption (Hally 1986:269).
Parching maize, for instance, requires cooking dried kernels slowly at low
temperatures, a process that may have been well suited to thick-walled
wide shallow bowls. Large wide shallow bowls were considerably more
prevalent in early contexts at Parchman Place, with four of five examples
recovered from 14th-century contexts. The fifth is of unknown date.

Flaring Rim Bowls

Flaring rim bowls were the most numerous bowl type, with 49 examples
identified (42.2% of bowls for which secondary shape could be determined). Flaring rim bowls have a simple body with an outflaring rim
where the inflection point between the body and rim can be either smooth
or sharp. On vessels that are large enough to tell, the bases of flaring rim
bowls appear flattened. Though deep flaring rim bowls are known for
some Mississippian assemblages (e.g., Childress 1992:37, Hally 1984:55),
the flaring rim bowls from Parchman Place are uniformly shallow. Flaring
rim bowls were manufactured in small (ranging from 20–23 cm diameter)
and medium (ranging from 28–36 cm diameter) sizes in roughly equal
numbers on coarse and fine shell-tempered paste. Several examples fall
somewhere between the coarse shell-tempered paste indicative of Mississippi Plain *var. Neeley's Ferry* and the fine shell-tempered paste indicative
of Bell Plain *var. Bell*.

Both coarse and fine ware bowls were frequently decorated. Some of
the decoration is captured by the type-variety classification, including
painting (e.g., Old Town Red *vars. Old Town* and *Beaverdam*) and fine line
incision (e.g., Walls Engraved *var. Hull*). However, flaring rim bowls of all
types had rim embellishments, most commonly scalloping achieved by a

Figure 3.6. Medium Mississippi Plain flaring rim bowl from Parchman Place (22CO511) with scalloped and incised rim and interior sooting.

gently undulating rounded rim or the removal of large rounded notches. Other rim embellishments include linear incision, triangular linear ticking, and notching on the flared portion of the interior lip. Figure 3.6 depicts a nearly complete coarse flaring rim bowl with a scalloped rim as well as linear incisions on the rim. A flaring rim bowl with an unusual, probably nonlocal, paste (Figure 2.7) has a stepped design on the interior body portion produced by cutting away the surrounding clay to leave a raised design. Finally, allover burnishing occurs on two fine ware examples. Both fine and coarse ware flaring rim bowls are common in 14th- and 15th-century residential and mound contexts, though fine ware examples are more common during the 15th century.

Thus, flaring rim bowls had stable bases, easy access to contents, and were frequently decorated on the outflaring portion of the rim and elsewhere. These characteristics as well as their ubiquity suggest that the flaring rim bowl was commonly used as a serving bowl by the residents of Parchman Place. However, sooting on two coarse ware examples suggests that some of these bowls were also occasionally used for cooking or heating food or for carrying fire. A small coarse ware wide shallow bowl was sooted on the exterior where the rim started to flare, indicating its use over direct heat. A medium coarse wide shallow bowl (illustrated in Figure 3.6) had sooting or blackening on the interior, suggesting that this vessel may have been used to carry fire, coals, or ashes from one location to another.

Carinated and Restricted Bowls

Carinated bowls and restricted bowls are both minority types in the sample, with five examples of carinated and three examples of restricted bowls. Carinated bowls are identified by the presence of a carina, a more or less abrupt angle on the exterior (usually shoulder portion) of the bowl, resulting in orifice constriction. As in carinated bowls, the rim portions of restricted bowls narrow toward the top of the vessel. However, restricted bowls are "simple" in profile in that they do not have a sharp angle separating body from rim. In all three examples from Parchman Place, orifice constriction was slight (as was constriction in the carinated bowls). All measurable carinated and restricted bowls fell into the "small" category, restricted bowls measuring 12–13 cm in rim diameter and carinated bowls measuring 14–15 cm in rim diameter. Neither carinated nor restricted bowls occurred on coarse shell-tempered wares but were associated with Bell Plain paste as well as an unidentified paste that resembles descriptions of Addis Plain (e.g., Brain 1989:70, Phillips 1970:48–49). Decorative techniques included incising and engraving (e.g., Walls Engraved *var. Hull* and L'Eau Noire Incised *var. unspecified*). A Walls Engraved carinated bowl also had a rim embellished with circular punctations on the top of the lip, and a Bell Plain *var. Bell* restricted bowl had linear incisions on the top of the lip. None of the carinated or restricted bowls exhibited burnishing or sooting. Carinated and restricted bowls would probably have been used in similar ways, as they have similar performance characteristics. Their small size and restricted orifices preclude them from use as food preparation vessels, and their fine ware eliminates cooking. They may have been used as serving dishes for small amounts of food or for things like condiments or dips. Their stability and restricted orifice would provide good containment security. This and the fact that many were finely made and frequently decorated suggest that their contents may have been particularly rare, difficult to procure, or valuable. They would also have been suitable for storing small amounts of dried goods that might easily blow away. Carinated and restricted bowls were quite rare at Parchman Place, occurring primarily in early contexts.

Bottle Forms

Bottles have openings that are substantially narrower than the main vessel body and neck portions that are vertical or nearly so. According to Shepard (1956:28), "necked" vessels prevent liquids from slopping and facilitate pouring. These performance characteristics are also useful for containing small-grained things (such as seeds) that behave like liquids when poured. The relative proportions of neck to body vary widely among vessels classified as bottles. For this reason, orifice diameter is not a good predictor of bottle size or volume. However, the width of bottle necks may be indicative of vessel performance characteristics other than volume, such as containment security. Of the 58 vessels identified as bottles in the Parchman Place ceramic sample, 38 rims were sufficiently large to measure orifice diameter. A frequency histogram of bottle orifice diameters (Figure 3.7) indicates three classes of bottles based on neck width (see also Table 3.3). Most bottles (n = 30) had necks that range from 6–11 cm in diameter. I call these "standard neck bottles" (Figure 3.8) There were six "narrow neck bottles," with orifice diameters ranging from 3–5 cm (see Figure 2.5a and b). Two examples of "wide neck bottles" occurred

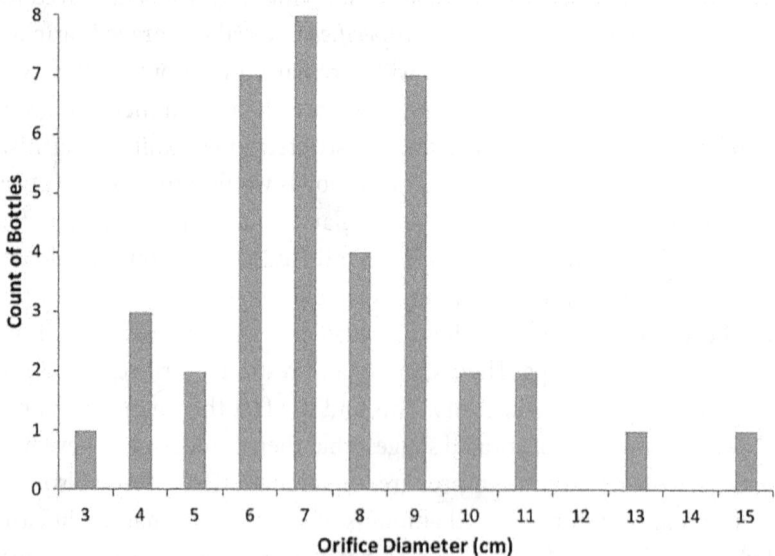

Figure 3.7. Frequency histogram of bottle orifices, indicating three possible bottle forms, including narrow neck (3–5 cm), standard neck (6–11 cm), and wide neck (13–15 cm).

Table 3.3. Types, varieties, and shapes for ceramic bottles identified at Parchman Place (22CO511)

Bottles	Narrow Neck	Standard Neck	Wide Neck	Indet. or Not Recorded	Bottle Total
Mississippi Plain *var. Neeley's Ferry*	–	8	–	3	11
Mississippi Plain *var. unspecified*	–	–	–	1	1
Leland Incised *var. unspecified*	–	–	–	1	1
Old Town Red *var. Old Town*	1	–	–	1	2
Bell Plain *var. Bell*	1	9	2	7	19
Avenue Polychrome *var. Avenue*	–	–	–	1	1
Carson Red on Buff *var. Carson*	–	–	–	1	1
Nodena Red and White *var. Nodena*	–	–	–	1	1
Old Town Red *var. Beaverdam*	1	7	–	4	12
Larto Red *var. Larto*	–	–	–	1	1
Unidentified Plain *var. unspecified*	3	6	–	–	9
Total	6	30	2	21	59

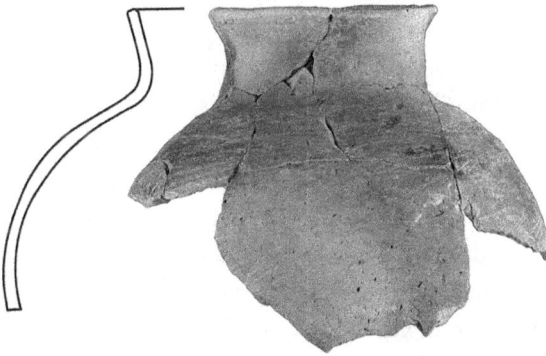

Figure 3.8. Standard neck bottle from Parchman Place (22CO511).

in the sample, with orifice diameters of 13 and 15 cm. Bottles were manufactured using both coarse and fine shell-tempered paste and were frequently decorated, most commonly by slipping or painting—more than 30% of bottles were slipped or painted with red; red and white; or red, black, and white pigments. These attributes, along with neck size may give clues about the nature of social gatherings where the bottles were used. The following section describes mechanical performance characteristics and hypothesized uses for standard, narrow neck, and wide neck bottles.

Standard Neck Bottles

Standard neck bottles had orifices ranging from 6–11 cm in diameter and were made on coarse (n = 8) and fine (n = 16) shell-tempered paste. Six bottles of unidentified plain paste also fell into this category. The only nearly whole bottle in the assemblage was an unidentified plain standard neck bottle with a slightly outflaring rim, a constricted neck and a globular body (Figure 3.8). Nearly half of fine ware standard neck bottles were decorated with an allover red slip applied prior to firing. Standard neck bottles were likely used to serve, store, and transport liquids or small-grained materials (Hally 1986:290). The presence of a neck provides high containment security and severely limits access to vessel contents. While bottle contents could have been mixed by swirling or shaking, they could only be removed by pouring. Loss of contents through evaporation or spilling would be minimal. Coarse ware vessels could plausibly have been used to heat liquid contents, though direct evidence of this is lacking. Given the relatively small size of the one nearly complete standard-neck bottle from Parchman Place, I suspect that the volume of materials contained within standard neck bottles was relatively low. While coarse ware standard neck bottles were recovered from 14th- and 15th-century mound and neighborhood contexts, they were more common in the 15th century. Fine ware standard neck bottles were present only in 15th-century contexts, though a few examples are from contexts that could not be reliably dated. Like their coarse ware counterparts, they occurred in mound and neighborhood deposits.

Narrow Neck Bottles

Six bottles fell into the narrow neck category with orifice diameters from 3–5 cm. They were manufactured on fine, coarse, and unidentified plain wares. A number of narrow neck bottles had rim portions that flare slightly and narrow neck bottles in general would have had long, slender necks, rather graceful ovular or globular bodies, and flattened or rounded bases. These bottles, often carefully decorated with painted designs, were not uncommon in the northern Yazoo, though they were more common in eastern Arkansas. None of the Parchman Place narrow neck bottles were burnished, though one fine ware and one coarse ware example were red-slipped. Narrow neck bottles would have very high containment security and were probably used to store and serve small quantities of liquids. Their rarity and the care taken in their manufacture and decoration suggests they would have been used in special, possibly ritual or elite contexts to contain liquids that were rare or valuable. Though few in number, they occur in 14th- and 15th-century mound and neighborhood contexts.

Wide Neck Bottles

Two wide neck bottles were identified in the sample with orifice diameters of 13 cm and 15 cm. Both were executed on Bell Plain paste; neither was burnished. Unfortunately, very little about their body dimensions could be determined from the rims alone, though the wider orifices of these bottles would have provided increased access to the materials held within them, while maintaining high containment security. Like standard neck bottles, wide neck bottles could have contained liquids or other pourable substances such as seeds or dried beans. Both examples were from 15th-century mound contexts.

The Parchman Place Vessel Assemblage

The functional vessel analysis resulted in the identification of 8 jar categories, 15 bowl categories, and 5 bottle categories, based primarily on combinations of vessel shape, size, and ware. A summary of these vessel classes along with their hypothesized use can be found in Table 3.4. Within the total assemblage I identified two sizes of general purpose cooking jars (small and medium coarse ware jars) made in two shapes. The assemblage

Table 3.4. Functional vessel categories for vessels from Parchman Place (22CO511) with hypothesized primary and secondary use

Vessel Type	Orifice Diameter	Count	Primary Use	Secondary Use
Jars				
Very small coarse ware jar	6–9 cm	4	Serving rare, valuable, or perishable foods	Storage of rare, valuable, or perishable foods; storage/serving of nonfood items
Very small fine ware jar	6–9 cm	1	Serving rare, valuable, or perishable foods	Storage of rare, valuable, or perishable foods; storage/serving of non-food items
Small coarse ware jar	10–18 cm	25	Cooking/boiling	Serving
Small fine ware jar	10–18 cm	2	Serving	Short-term storage
Medium coarse ware jar	20–28 cm	23	Cooking/boiling	Serving
Medium fine ware jar	20–28 cm	1	Serving	Short-term storage
Large coarse ware jar	30–40 cm	26	Storage	Cooking/Boiling
Very large coarse ware jar	45–50+ cm	10	Storage	Cooking/Boiling
Bowls				
Very small simple pinch bowl	2–6 cm	5	Serving rare, valuable, or perishable foods	
Small coarse ware simple bowl	10–23 cm	5	Serving	Food preparation (mixing, etc.); cooking/heating
Small fine ware simple bowl	10–23 cm	7	Serving	Food preparation (mixing, etc.)
Medium coarse ware simple bowl	25–38 cm	1	Serving	Food preparation (mixing, etc.); cooking/heating
Medium fine ware simple bowl	25–38 cm	2	Serving	Food preparation (mixing, etc.)

Large coarse ware simple bowl	~50 cm	1	Serving	Food preparation (mixing, etc.); cooking/heating
Small coarse ware wide shallow bowl	10–23 cm	1	Serving	Food preparation (mixing, etc.); cooking/heating
Medium coarse ware wide shallow bowl	25–28 cm	3	Serving	Food preparation (mixing, etc.); cooking/heating
Large coarse ware wide shallow bowl	~50 cm	5	Parching	Serving; food preparation (mixing, etc.)
Small coarse ware flaring rim bowl	10–23 cm	1	Serving	Heating
Small fine ware flaring rim bowl	10–23 cm	1	Serving	
Medium coarse ware flaring rim bowl	25–28 cm	3	Serving	Heating
Medium fine ware flaring rim bowl	25–28 cm	3	Serving	
Small fine ware carinated bowl	10–23 cm	2	Serving rare, valuable, or perishable foods	Storage of rare, valuable, or perishable foods; storage/serving of nonfood items
Small fine ware restricted bowl	10–23 cm	3	Serving rare, valuable, or perishable foods	Storage of rare, valuable, or perishable foods; storage/serving of nonfood items
Bottles				
Coarse ware narrow neck bottle	3–5 cm	1	Serving liquids	
Fine ware narrow neck bottle	3–5 cm	2	Serving liquids	
Coarse ware standard neck bottle	6–11 cm	8	Serving liquids	Storage of liquids and particles (e.g., seeds)
Fine ware standard neck bottle	6–11 cm	16	Serving liquids	Storage of liquids and particles (e.g., seeds)
Fine ware wide neck bottle	13–16	2	Serving liquids	Storage of liquids and particles (e.g., seeds)

also contained two (large and very large) coarse ware jars sometimes used for cooking but primarily used for storage. Also present was a very small coarse ware jar that does not seem to have been used over fire but technically could have been. Finally, very small-, small-, and medium-sized fine ware jars were made in small numbers. These were not used for cooking but may have held ingredients used for cooking or have been used to serve small to medium portions of foods or dishes once cooked. The smaller ones may have held condiments such as oil or salt water for dipping.

Like jars, bowls in the Parchman Place sample were made in multiple shapes and sizes that serve functionally different purposes. Simple and wide shallow bowls were made in sizes ranging from very small to large and were utilitarian food preparation and serving bowls. Both bowl types were manufactured on coarse and fine wares, but simple bowls were typically smaller and more often found on fine wares, whereas wide shallow bowls were more often made of coarse wares and were frequently quite large. Additionally, wide shallow bowls had thicker walls than simple bowls and the larger sizes were at least occasionally used for cooking or heating. Parching may have been an important function for large wide shallow bowls.

Flaring rim bowls were the standard food-serving vessel used at Parchman Place. Exterior sooting on one small bowl suggests they were also occasionally used for cooking or heating small amounts of food. Though they were the most common bowl form at the site, they were made in just two sizes (small and medium). Coarse and fine ware versions were identified, but many coarse ware examples were more finely made than typical coarse ware varieties. A number of flaring rim bowls were intermediate between coarse and fine shell-tempered paste and thus were classified as unidentified plain. Unlike simple and wide shallow bowls, flaring rim bowls were frequently decorated, suggesting they were used in contexts where visibility was important. Their finer ware and greater tendency toward decoration suggest a less strictly utilitarian role than that of simple and wide shallow bowls. Flaring rim bowls were common across the site in 14th- and 15th-century contexts and were more finely made as time passed. One medium flaring rim bowl may have been used to transport fire as its interior was sooted. Restricted and carinated bowls were potentially used to serve small amounts of rare or special foods (or other substances), but they did not contribute in a general way to the food practices of the Parchman Place community. Rather, they were likely used for ritual purposes or to express some kind of identity or perhaps a kinship or economic relationship with other Mississippian groups to the south.

Bottles were fairly well represented in the assemblage, though not nearly as common as jars or bowls. They occurred in low to moderate numbers in mound and neighborhood contexts throughout the occupation of Parchman Place, becoming both more numerous and more finely made in the 15th century. Bottles of all descriptions were probably used to hold small amounts of liquids or granular substances. Finely made and decorated specimens were likely used for specialized purposes.

While the functional vessel types described previously and summarized in Table 3.4 are indicative of the Parchman ceramic assemblage as a whole, they occurred with varying frequency and in different combinations throughout the site. Table 3.5 illustrates chronological trends. Vessel classes that occurred exclusively in 14th-century (Parchman I) contexts include large coarse wide shallow bowls. One example of this occurs in every context that has been dated to the 14th century, so they were ubiquitous in Parchman I contexts despite their rarity. Small restricted bowls also occurred exclusively in Parchman I contexts, and three of four carinated bowls from excavated contexts also date to Parchman I. One example of a very small coarse simple jar occurred in a Parchman I deposit. Despite small sample sizes, I believe these patterns are meaningful for reasons I discuss next.

Fine ware jars of various sizes occurred exclusively in 15th-century (Parchman II) contexts. One small carinated bowl was also associated with an early 15th-century context from Mound E. Small flaring rim bowls (one fine and one coarse) were made during Parchman II but not before. Finally, standard and wide neck fine ware bottles were only present in Parchman II contexts, following the broader trend of increasing fine ware examples of other vessel types formerly made of coarse wares (e.g., jars).

Occurring in both Parchman I and Parchman II were coarse jars of all sizes from very small to very large. Small simple bowls (fine and coarse) and medium simple bowls (fine) were present throughout both subphases, as were medium fine and coarse flaring rim bowls. Coarse standard neck bottles as well as coarse and fine ware narrow neck bottles were made during both subphases.

Table 3.5. Functional vessel types from 14th- and 15th-century deposits at Parchman Place

14th Century	14th/15th Century	15th Century
small fine ware restricted bowl	very small coarse ware jar	very small fine ware jar
large coarse ware wide shallow bowl	small coarse ware jar	small fine ware jar
	medium coarse ware jar	medium fine ware jar
	large coarse ware jar	small fine ware flaring rim bowl
	very large coarse ware jar	small coarse ware flaring rim bowl
	very small simple bowl	medium coarse ware wide shallow bowl
	small carinated bowl	standard neck fine ware bottle
	small fine ware simple bowl	wide neck fine ware bottle
	small coarse ware simple bowl	
	medium fine ware simple bowl	
	medium coarse ware flaring rim bowl	
	medium fine flaring rim bowl	
	standard neck coarse ware bottle	
	narrow neck bottle	

The results of a correspondence analysis (Figure 3.9a) distinguish between a baseline domestic assemblage and a non-domestic or special use assemblage within the Parchman Place sample. Dimension 1, which explains 32.3% of variation, essentially separates jar-dominated assemblages from bowl-dominated assemblages. That is, excavated contexts containing high relative proportions of bowls plot in a dispersed cluster to the right of the graph, while contexts that lack high relative proportions of bowls plot with cooking and storage jars in a tight cluster near the origin (Figure 3.9b). Stated another way, jar-dominated and bowl-dominated assemblages differ in their relative frequencies of vessels used primarily for cooking, serving, and storage.

Table 3.6. Counts and frequencies of ceramic cooking, serving, and storage vessels for jar-dominated assemblages from Parchman Place (22CO511)

Jar-Dominated Assemblages	MdEbase_B	N1_A	MEsum_A	MD_A	MEsw_D	AB_B	Total
Cooking	45	10	19	3	53	14	144
Serving	27	3	5	4	28	5	72
Storage	5	1	4	2	4	4	20
Total	77	14	28	9	85	23	236

The second dimension makes further distinctions among bowl-dominated assemblages based on their association with certain types of bowls, namely small restricted and carinated bowls, plotting in the top right corner, versus small (coarse) simple and wide shallow bowls, medium (coarse) flaring rim bowls, and very small pinch bowls, which plot toward the lower portion of the graph (Figure 3.9c). Thus, while bowl-dominated assemblages appear to be *functionally* similar to one another, the use of different *types* of bowls in special, non-everyday contexts may indicate one way that community members at Parchman Place made social distinctions among themselves.

Jar-dominated assemblages were associated with four mound contexts and two residential contexts at Parchman Place, while bowl-dominated assemblages were associated with two mound contexts and one residential context. A fourth residential context, designated AB_A on the correspondence analysis biplot, shares characteristics with both. Within jar-dominated assemblages, cooking vessels account for just over 60% of the total number of vessels, serving vessels for roughly 30%, and storage vessels for nearly 10% (Table 3.6). In contrast, bowl-dominated assemblages are made up of approximately 46% cooking vessels and 54% serving vessels and do not include any vessels intended for long-term storage (Table 3.7).

While these frequencies are telling, an even more compelling pattern emerges when these basic functional categories are broken down further (Table 3.8). Within jar-dominated assemblages, boiling in jars was the primary cooking method, while no vessels used for parching were identified. All serving categories are present, represented by jars and bowls used for

Table 3.7. Counts and frequencies of ceramic cooking, serving, and storage vessels for bowl-dominated assemblages from Parchman Place (22CO511)

Bowl-Dominated Assemblages	MdEbase_A	MdEsw_A	N1_B	Total
Cooking	11	11	5	27
Serving	13	10	9	32
Storage	–	–	–	–
Total	24	21	14	59

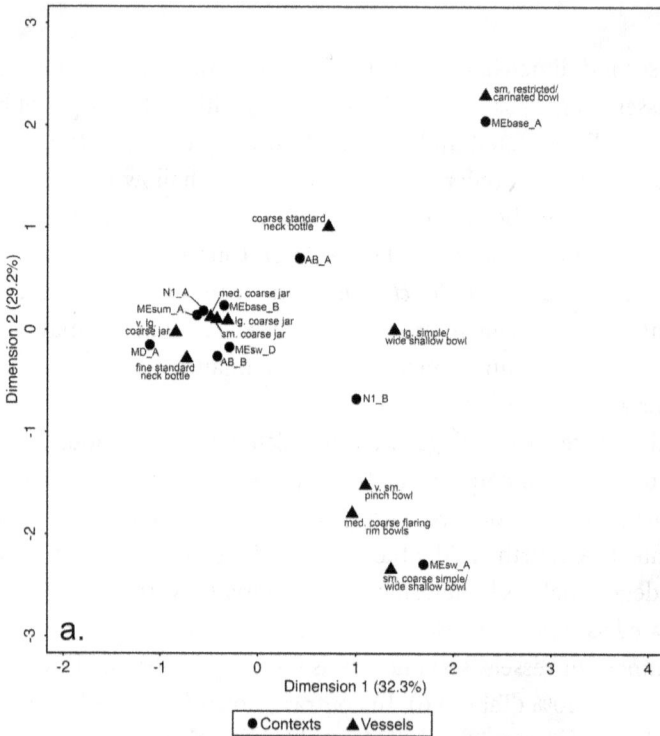

Figure 3.9. Correspondence analysis (CA) biplot showing (*a*) correspondence among ceramic functional vessel types and excavated contexts at Parchman Place (22CO511). (*b*) The same biplot highlighting two distinct clusters along the first dimension. Dimension one separates contexts characterized by high proportions of bowls (right cluster) from those that lack high proportions of bowls. (*c*) The same biplot highlighting two distinct clusters along the second dimension. Dimension two separates contexts based on differences among bowls, with small carinated and restricted bowls plotting toward the top of the graph and very small pinch bowls plotting toward the bottom. A key to context abbreviations can be found in Table 1.1.

Figure 3.9—*continued*

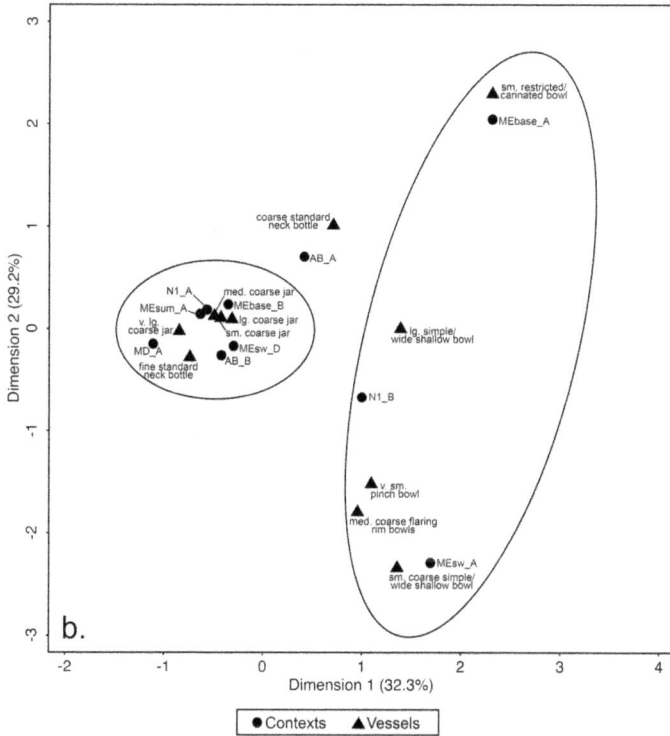

b.

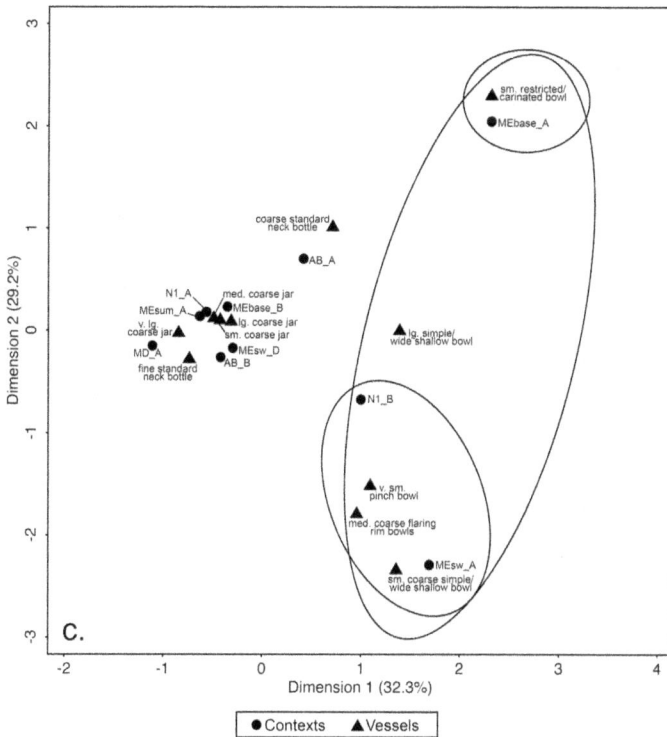

c.

Table 3.8. Jar-dominated ceramic assemblages from Parchman Place (22CO511) broken down by eight functional categories

Jar-Dominated Assemblages	MdEbase_B	N1_A	MEsum_A	MD_A	MEsw_D	AB_B	Total
Boiling	45	10	19	3	53	14	144
Parching	–	–	–	–	–	–	–
Serving	12	2	2	1	18	2	37
Serving; heating	8	1	1	1	1	1	13
Serving rare, perishable goods							
plain	1	–	–	–	–	–	1
fine	1	–	–	–	–	–	1
Serving/Storing liquids	5	–	2	2	9	2	20
Storage; cooking	2	1	3	1	3	3	13
Storage	3	–	1	1	1	1	7
Total	77	14	28	9	85	23	236

general purpose serving, bottles used to serve liquids, and small bowls/ very small jars used to serve rare, valuable, or perishable goods, though this latter function was exceedingly rare, occurring in only one out of six contexts. Finally, both storage categories are represented in jar-dominated assemblages by large and very large coarse ware jars. Because jar-dominated assemblages are ubiquitous—occurring in both Parchman I and Parchman II subphases as well as in mound and residential contexts— I argue that they represent a baseline or everyday domestic assemblage.

Bowl-dominated assemblages can be considered exceptions to the more general pattern of the all-purpose jar-dominated assemblages. While they contain coarse ware jars used for boiling, they are characterized by the presence of large coarse ware wide shallow bowls likely used for parching maize (Table 3.9). These special-use bowls occurred in all three bowl-dominated assemblages but were absent from jar-dominated assemblages. While the primary function of these bowls was parching, I suspect they were also used to serve prepared foods to large groups of people. Bowl-dominated assemblages are further characterized by the ubiquitous presence of small and very small bowls used for serving rare, valuable, or perishable goods. Finally, they are completely lacking in vessels that

Table 3.9. Bowl-dominated ceramic assemblages from Parchman Place
(22CO511) broken down by eight functional categories

Bowl-Dominated Assemblages	MdEbase_A	MdEsw_A	N1_B	Total
Boiling	10	10	4	24
Parching	1	1	1	3
Serving	7	5	6	18
Serving; heating	–	1	–	1
Serving rare, perishable goods				
plain	–	2	2	4
fine	3	–	–	3
Serving/Storing liquids	3	2	1	6
Storage; cooking	–	–	–	–
Storage	–	–	–	–
Total	24	21	14	59

could be identified as having a storage function. These characteristics of
bowl-dominated assemblages suggest that they are serving assemblages
associated with communal eating events or feasts characterized by large
quantities of food, foods cooked in nontypical ways (e.g., parching), and
foods that were rare or valuable. I argue next that these feasts are related to
the founding and continued maintenance of the community at Parchman
Place.

As indicated previously, the correspondence analysis separates bowl-
dominated contexts on the second dimension. This distinction is primarily based on differences among bowls used to serve rare, valuable, or perishable goods. Coarse ware bowls, namely very small pinch bowls, fulfill
this functional role for two of the bowl-dominated assemblages—one
mound context and one residential context that plot in the lower right
quadrant. The remaining bowl-dominated assemblage (a mound context
that plots in the upper right quadrant) is characterized by small, finely
made, carinated and restricted bowls.

The presence of restricted and carinated bowls is significant given that
neither the vessel shape nor the paste type is local to the region. These
vessels were almost certainly made by people to the south, either in the
southern portion of the Yazoo Basin or the Natchez Bluffs. Though functionally similar to vessels used elsewhere at Parchman Place, these bowls
may indicate status- or identity-based differences among groups involved

in similar activities. The presence of nonlocal fine ware vessels in certain contexts at Parchman Place could indicate a status-based difference among groups if one group had access to "exotic," nonlocal goods not available to everyone. Alternatively, they may simply indicate a kinship or trade relationship with other Mississippian groups outside the region.

In summary, I identified two major divisions in ceramic sub-assemblages at Parchman Place. Mississippian people made and used a domestic pottery assemblage consisting of jars, bowls of various kinds, and bottles that fulfilled everyday cooking, serving, and storage needs. This domestic assemblage occurred in mound and residential contexts throughout Parchman Place's history. In one instance of early activity at Parchman Place, people also brought food in their everyday pottery to a potluck-style feasting event that included the preparation and use of rare bird species, including American crow and golden eagle (Nelson et al. 2020; see also Chapter 5). More often, however, people at Parchman Place made use of a specialized serving assemblage when they gathered together as a community. Serving assemblages included specialized bowls for parching maize and serving large groups of people as well as small serving vessels used to hold rare, valuable, or perishable goods. These special-use serving assemblages occurred in the earliest deposits of Mound E, indicating that mound building and feasting were intertwined activities related to the founding of the Mississippian community at Parchman Place. Of the serving assemblages associated with early mound building, one contained coarse pinch bowls, which were rather rough and utilitarian, while another contained finely made and decorated carinated and restricted bowls of nonlocal manufacture. These vessels were not only visibly attractive but also readily conveyed a social relationship with other Mississippian groups.

A third example of a special-use serving assemblage was associated with an atypical deposit in Neighborhood 1 consisting of multiple layers of redeposited ash. Along with food serving vessels, the ash contained an abundance of faunal and botanical remains. High ratios of maize kernels to cupules within the ash deposits indicate a focus on consumption rather than processing, and high rates of burned and calcined bone suggest that faunal remains were intentionally placed in the fire, a practice that has analogs in the post-Mississippian practice of placing food offerings directly in the fire prior to consuming the remaining portion (e.g., Beverley 1705:34; Harrington 1921; Hudson 1976:368, 372; Penn 1881[1683]; Tuttle

1833; Witthoft 1949:83). Taken together, evidence for specialized food-serving vessels, consumption of maize and other late summer and fall foods, offerings of food to the fire, and the careful disposal of ash in a designated location suggests that Mississippian people at Parchman Place staged community-wide feasting events similar in nature to the annual renewal ceremonies practiced by the descendants of Mississippian people at maize harvest ceremonies such as the Busk or Green Corn Ceremony (Nelson et al. 2020; see also Chapter 4). This is but one example of the many ways people at Parchman Place took care to promote the maintenance and restoration of balance within their community and within the world.

4

Mound Building
at Parchman Place

When Mississippian people moved to Parchman Place in the first half of the 14th century, they immediately began constructing earthen mounds along the edge of the levee that marks the northern boundary of the site. These earthworks, along with the plaza and residential areas that were simultaneously established, organized the site spatially and socially (Dalan et al. 2003; Kidder 2004; Knight 1998). Like most Mississippian platform mounds, the three largest mounds at Parchman Place—Mounds A, B, and E—were constructed in multiple stages, each stage culminating in a platform upon which one or more buildings were constructed for the use of prominent community leaders. Though symbolic of the power of such leaders (Blitz and Livingood 2004; Hally 1996; Lindauer and Blitz 1997), platform mounds also symbolized the earth and the Mississippian cosmos (Knight 1986, 1989), and were frequently affiliated with individual corporate groups that constituted Mississippian towns (Knight 1998, 2010, 2016; Scarry and Steponaitis 2016). The addition of new earthen mantles encoded themes related to community and world renewal (Knight 1981) while also promoting the succession of political and religious leaders (e.g., Anderson 1994; Hally 1996). Furthermore, the act of mound building was a complex feat of technological and symbolic engineering (Sherwood and Kidder 2011). Earthen mounds of all stripes were carefully planned and executed, and builders selected materials based on the specifics of their desired properties—texture, color, or association with culturally meaningful concepts (Charles et al. 2004; Kassabaum 2019; Pauketat 2008; Purcell 2004; Sherwood and Kidder 2011). Specially chosen soils were frequently mined from well beneath the surface or transported considerable distances from their source, indicating a remarkable degree of knowledge, forethought, and consideration of appropriate materials on the part of Native American builders. Platform mounds of the Mississippi period were thus: (1) multivalent symbols, (2) constructed of culturally meaningful materials, and (3) built in stages. This combination of characteristics means that each act of mound construction was a new opportunity for the builders to negotiate the values and relationships upon which their communities were built (Pauketat 1993; Pauketat and Alt 2003). Archaeological evidence indicates that social and political negotiations were ongoing at Parchman Place, and these negotiations were reflected in and enabled by the mound-building practices of the people who lived there. In what follows, I outline the results of mound investigations at Parchman Place from 2002 to 2011. Following the excavation descriptions, I offer detailed stratigraphic interpretation to interrogate how Mississippian people used mound-building practices to promote and constrain leadership at Parchman Place.

Mound E Base Excavation

Mound excavations at Parchman Place focused extensively on Mound E to understand early mound building at the site, and to determine the stratigraphic relationship between Mound E and Mound A. An excavation placed at the southern slope of Mound E (Figure 4.1) consisted of five 1 m × 1 m units forming a 5 m × 1 m trench oriented north-south. The trench was excavated by University of Mississippi (UM) field school students in the summer of 2003 and reached approximately 280 cm at its deepest point. Two major mound construction episodes and one mound surface were identified within the excavation trench (Figure 4.2). This was one of two excavation trenches at Parchman Place that targeted the base of Mound E and thus provides an important look at the commencement of mound building and the activities that accompanied it.

The builders of Mound E began its construction by depositing basket loads of grayish brown clay ("Zone I" in Figure 4.2) on top of the natural soil horizon, described by excavators as light yellowish-brown clay ("Zone J"). The initial deposits were from 30–60 cm deep and thickest to the south, where the natural ground surface slopes down. Here, the initial fill zone was interrupted by a thin and discontinuous layer composed of

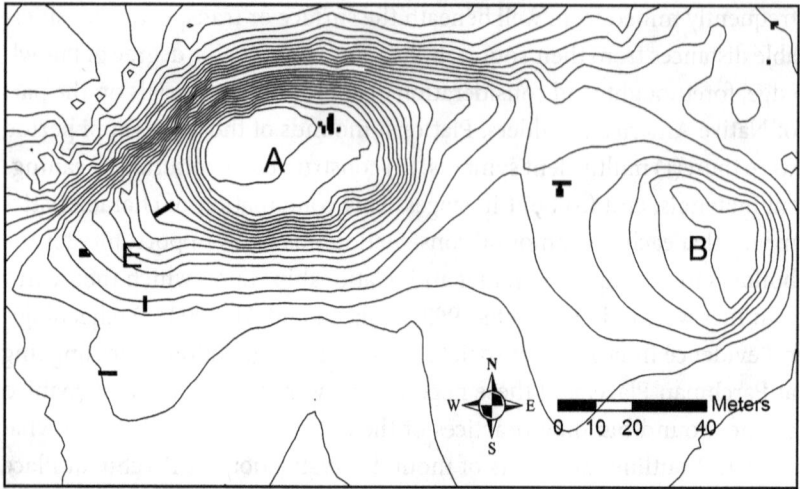

Figure 4.1. Topographic map of mound group showing location of excavations at Parchman Place (22CO511).

charcoal and white clay, then more identical fill was placed on top to create a level surface. A sample of burned cane from the base of Zone I deposits returned a date of cal 597 ± 38 BP, indicating that mound building commenced in the early to mid-14th century (Table 1.2; Figure 1.4). This dates the first episode of the construction of Mound E and is the earliest date we have for mound construction at the site.

As part of the mound's initiation, the cremated bundle burial of an adult male was placed into the initial fill zone. These remains were recorded (Wrobel 2003) and reburied, and excavation was discontinued in this area. Because excavation did not continue, it is unclear if the burial was placed on the prepared platform and fill was placed around it, or whether it intrudes into the clayey fill of Zone I. I suspect the former. Wrobel's (2003) notes as well as the excavator's indicate that there was a layer of ash (Zone H) above the burial deposit. Variously described as "a layer of ash (~1–2 cm thick)," or alternatively, as oxidized soil with ash lenses, the profile indicates that it does not extend completely over the burial. Despite some ambiguity with regard to sequence, it is clear that the burial was associated with the commencement of mound building in this location. Furthermore, the ash associated with it was placed there to mark the place as meaningful, one of multiple instances of the incorporation of special substances in mound building at Parchman Place.

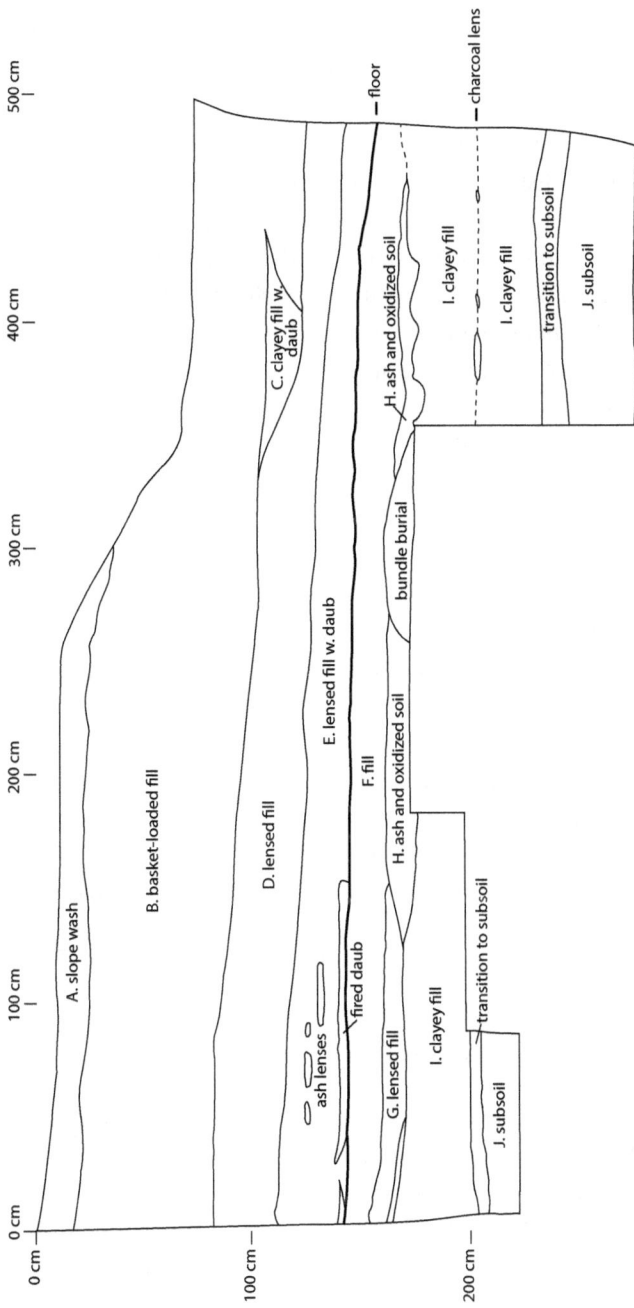

Figure 4.2. East profile wall of Mound E base trench, Parchman Place (22CO511).

Following the burial and the placement of an ashy deposit on top of it, the builders covered the area with additional fill: Zone G, a lensed clay loam, was present at the north end of the profile, and Zone F, a dark brown silt loam with daub, charcoal, and abundant artifact inclusions, capped all the underlying deposits. The surface of Zone F terminated in a living surface or floor, reddish in color and 5–6 cm thick, and representing the initial summit of Mound E. A wall trench with at least one posthole originated at this floor and was located in the southernmost unit of the trench, indicating that the bulk of the excavation trench was inside the building. However, like other buildings at Parchman Place, this one was swept clean prior to its destruction by burning and no artifacts were recovered in association with the floor. A layer composed of fired daub and thatch was in contact with the floor in the northernmost units of the trench. These materials were used in the construction of the building's walls and roof and likely fell to their present location when the building was burned.

The second major episode of mound building began after the destruction of the building on the first Mound E summit. The fired floor as well as the layer of burned daub was covered over with approximately 20 cm of fill described as "lensed" clayey silt with daub inclusions (Zone E). Some of the lenses on the north end of the trench were made of white clay and contained artifacts including bone and fish scales. Another "lensed" fill zone (Zone D) composed of clayey silt loam and containing abundant artifacts was placed on top of Zone E and differed from it in having fewer daub inclusions. Finally, the builders of Mound E constructed a 70 cm deep stage of basket-loaded fill that caps the entire mound slope. No evidence of additional mound surfaces or buildings was found. Zone A was slope wash composed of loose topsoil with daub inclusions.

Mound E Southwest Slope Excavation

An excavation block located on the southwest slope of Mound E (Figure 4.1) consisted of five 1 × 1 m units, the deepest of which reached sterile subsoil approximately 2 m below the current mound surface. This block was excavated by UM field school students in the summers of 2003 and 2004, and like the excavation just described, documented the initial building stages of Mound E (Figures 4.3 and 4.4). The original ground surface consisted of clayey sand that was variously described as an E or a B horizon in field notes. Coring from the base of the excavation indicated that

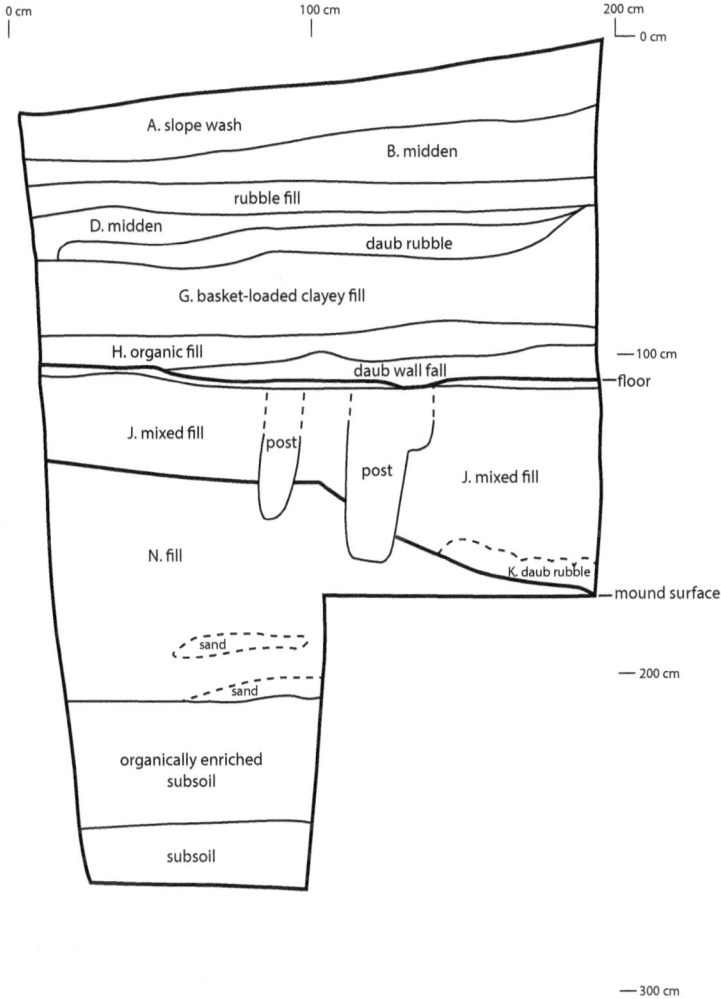

Figure 4.3. North profile wall of Mound E southwest slope trench, Parchman Place (22CO511).

this subsoil gradually transitioned to levee sand by approximately 50 cm below the excavation limits or 3 m below the surface of the mound slope in this location. The first stage of mound construction consisted of about a meter of various fill zones (Q, O, P, and N) distinguished by soil texture that terminated in the original mound summit—the same surface just described in the Mound E base excavation. This interpretation is based on their similar elevations as we do not have sufficient excavation data to link

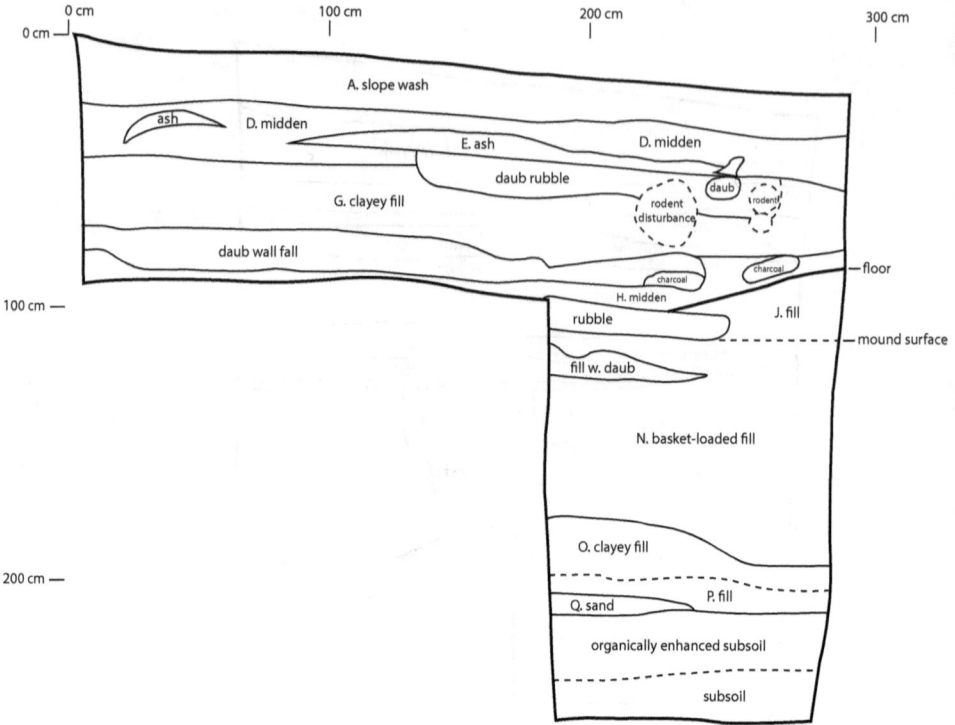

Figure 4.4. South profile wall of Mound E southwest slope trench, Parchman Place (22CO511).

the two in profile. While there were no structural remains evident in this location in the form of posts or wall trenches, the mound slope showed evidence of in situ burning and burned structural remains including charcoal and fired daub (Zone K) sat directly on its surface. Excavators also reported mussel shell sitting on the mound surface. An AMS sample of the burned material returned a date of cal 587 ± 38 BP (Table 1.2; Figure 1.4), which dates the first episode of mound summit use in this location to the early to mid-14th century.

Shortly after the burning event that took place on top of the first mound stage, the builders of Mound E began the second major stage of mound construction by adding a substantial layer of mixed mound fill (J). This fill was deposited while the mound surface was still hot, as evidenced by oxidation on either side of the interface. On top of this fill zone was a prepared floor surface (Figure 4.5), from which two lines of postholes

Figure 4.5. Fired floor located in Mound E southwest slope trench, Parchman Place (22CO511). Nahide Aydin excavates while Matt Reynolds and John Connaway look on. View south.

originated—one approximately north-south, the other approximately east-west. Like other buildings at Parchman Place, the stage 2 structure was swept out prior to its destruction by conflagration and there were no artifacts associated with its floor. The firing resulted in a hard surface of a bright orange-red color. No comparable surface was identified in the Mound E base excavation.

In some portions of the excavation block there was fired daub wall fall in direct contact with the floor. In others, excavators found burned roofing material and/or organically enhanced fill (Zone H) sandwiched between the floor and the daub rubble. An AMS sample of this material returned a date of cal 500 ± 38 BP, dating the stage 2 structure to the early 15th century (Table 1.2; Figure 1.4). Following the firing of the building, it was capped with a thick layer of clean clayey mound fill (Zone G), commencing the third stage of mound construction. A nearly complete flaring rim bowl with a scalloped and incised rim as well as interior sooting (Figure 3.6) was found sitting atop Zone G, sandwiched between the fill zone and a thick layer of daub rubble. It is unclear whether the rubble was related to a nearby structure or whether it was brought from another location and used to fill in low spots on the surface. In any case, there were no other indications of another building in this location. The remaining fill layers included a thin layer of artifact-rich midden (Zone D), followed by a white ash or kaolin surface with distinct boundaries (Zone E), followed by more of the same type of midden (Zone D). Finally, there was more midden with large quantities of daub (Zone B), as well as slope wash (Zone A) toward the surface.

Mound E Summit Excavation

An excavation trench consisting of seven 1 × 1 m units oriented roughly east-west was located on the summit of Mound E (Figure 4.1) and reached a depth of nearly 3 m at its deepest point. The trench was placed in this location to intersect a large magnetic anomaly interpreted as a burned Mississippian structure as well as to determine the stratigraphic relationship between Mounds E and A. Prior to the excavation, it was unknown whether Mound E should be considered as part of Mound A (e.g., as an "apron" or similar) or whether Mound E existed prior to the building of Mound A. The excavation was conducted in the summers of 2003 and 2004 by members of the UM field school (Nelson 2016; Stevens 2006).

Nine stages of mound construction were identified during excavation, as well as a truncation event that partially destroyed two stages and may have completely destroyed others. Six well-defined structure floors, as well as a seventh probable floor were found in association with mound surfaces (Figure 4.6). Well over 3 m of mound fill exist beyond the deepest limits of excavation, and three additional floors have been located using down-hole magnetic susceptibility (Lowe and Fogel 2007a, 2007b), though these remain unexcavated.

The earliest mound construction stage documented in this location began with a series of mound fill zones ranging in texture from silt loam to sandy silt and containing daub and charcoal in varying amounts (Zones S, T, and U). These deposits culminated in the floor of Structure 6, the earliest of the summit structures uncovered in the Mound E summit excavation (Figure 4.6). Structure 6 was a little less than 2 m higher than the initial mound summit described for the Mound E base and Mound E southwest excavations. Its floor was fired hard as a result of the burning of the building prior to abandonment. The floor had a low berm and adjacent

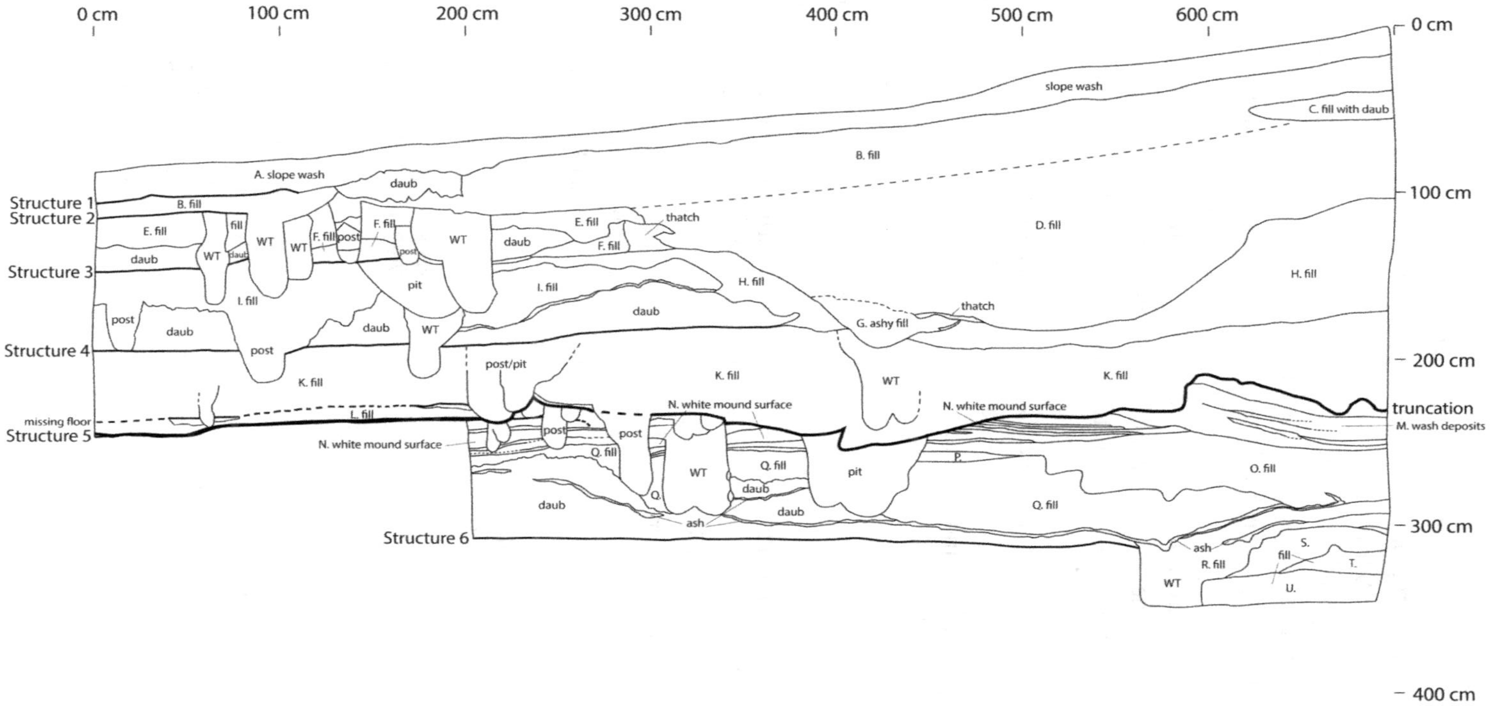

Figure 4.6. North profile wall of Mound E summit excavation at Parchman Place (22CO51l).

wall trench on its eastern edge. The next stage of mound construction began directly on top of the Structure 6 floor, with a thick layer of daub fall, representing the burning event that destroyed the building. This layer was approximately 50 cm thick at its deepest point and contained within it a layer of fine ash thought to be the result of the burning of grass fill within the walls. A sample of burned thatch associated with Structure 6 returned a radiocarbon date of cal 470 ± 40 BP, an early to mid-15th-century date (Table 1.2; Figure 1.4). The building remains were then covered over with a layer of fill (Zone Q), presumably while the structure was still smoldering, as evidenced by the oxidized nature of the soil in immediate contact with the daub rubble.

At this point, several materials, including kaolin, ash, and mussel shell, were used to construct a series of white mantles (N) over the top of the newly purified mound. As each white layer became dingy as a result of mixing with dirt, it was covered over with a new white mantle, so that at least five white layers, as well as intermediate gray ones, were visible building up to a prepared surface upon which Structure 5 was built (Figure 4.7). These white mantles were associated with a deposit of broken ceramics, including a Bell Plain *var. Bell* bottle with a perforated base. I interpret the materials used to construct the white mound surfaces as having been intentionally chosen for their aesthetic and symbolic qualities. The closest known source of kaolin is nearly 60 km away, near the present-day city of Batesville, Mississippi (Connaway, personal communication 2004). The distance required to transport the kaolin suggests that there was something significant about its use in the construction of the mound. Ash and shell had cosmological associations for Mississippian people (Baltus and Baires 2012; Hall 1997; Lankford 2004, 2007; Pauketat 2008:65). Like burning and burial, the color white has also been interpreted as symbolic of purification and renewal (Hudson 1976:226), so the use of white substances is likely a continuation of the same theme represented by the burning and burial of Structure 6.

Floor 5, the final feature associated with the second mound construction stage identified here, was built directly on top of the series of white mound surfaces. A double wall trench located at the eastern edge of the floor indicates that the structure was rebuilt. The floor was fired hard and like Structure 6, was burned. However, there was very little daub rubble on top of this floor, indicating that any wall fall was likely removed by

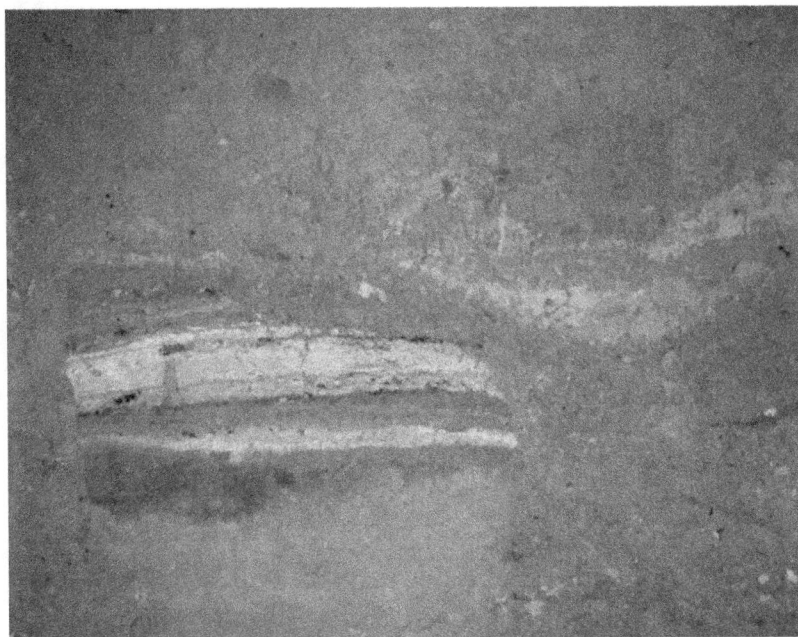

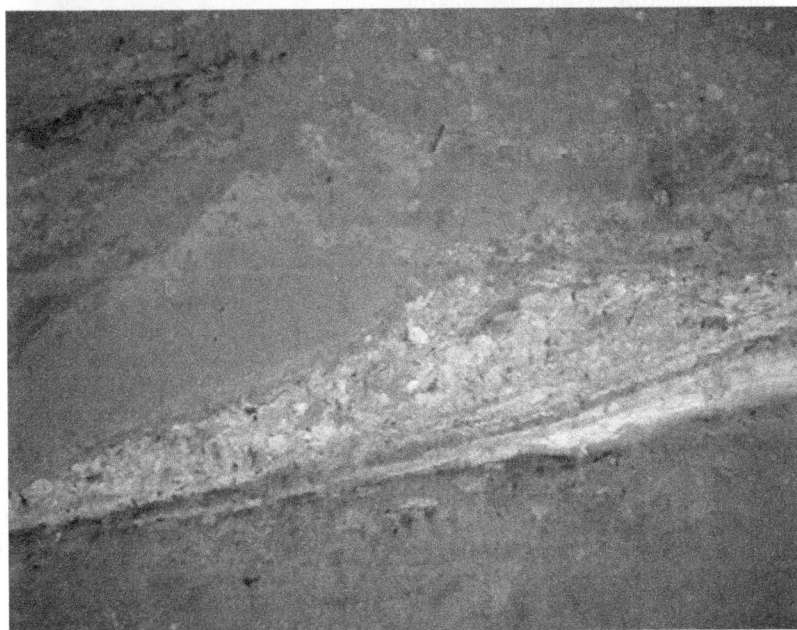

Figure 4.7. Detail photographs of white mound surface in Mound E summit excavation at Parchman Place (22CO511).

the builders. Additionally, the floor of Structure 5 was riddled with holes. Though little understood during the excavation process, close inspection of the excavation profile indicates that an unknown number of intermediate mound construction stages were removed in a truncation event that occurred sometime after Structure 5 was destroyed, explaining the appearance of its floor.

The removal of at least two mound stages was indicated by a number of features with no visible points of origin in the profile. These features included a wall trench, pit, and multiple post molds that cut into the fill below the truncation boundary, but that originated somewhere above the truncation boundary. Their lower boundaries terminate at two different depths. Additionally, a series of sloping wash deposits (M) to the far east of the profile indicated a swale between two higher points. The deposits were located as much as 28 cm higher than Floor 5 and sloped up toward the west, indicating that the truncation event destroyed a fairly large, if unknown, portion of the mound. Significantly, the deposits also sloped up toward the east, suggesting the presence of a second and separate mound—Mound A—located nearby.

The truncation itself was the next detectable event within the sequence of mound building. The interface of destruction is shown as a thick black line in Figure 4.6. To achieve this, Mississippian excavators removed the mound fill and slope wash toward the east end of the trench, leaving behind a small portion of the eastern slope. Continuing toward the west, they cut down to the white mound surface and stopped, reexposing the surface and cutting off the tops of several features belonging to missing mound stages in the process. West of the white mound surface, the excavators encountered the fired floor of Structure 5; the truncation boundary bumps along its surface for the remainder of the excavation trench, tearing it up but not completely destroying it. Subsequent to this destructive action, mound building resumed in much the same manner as before.

While not well defined, the next construction stage consisted of a relatively thin (18 cm at its thickest) deposit of mottled mound fill (L), which terminated in a flat, prepared mound surface. Small fragments of a possible floor remain intact in the western portion and can be seen on the north profile (Figure 4.6). A wall trench and pit that cut through the truncation were likely associated. This "missing" floor was not recognized during excavations and does not appear on plan maps. It is difficult to say anything conclusive about this construction stage, as evidence for it was sparse. Only a few small fragments of a floor remained and there was no structural debris on top of it. It is possible that another truncation event occurred sometime after this stage, but as there is no supporting stratigraphic evidence, this is little more than conjecture.

The next stage of mound construction resulted in a substantial increase in the height of the mound, as a thick layer of mound fill (K) was laid down, ranging from approximately 40–60 cm. This layer terminated at a flat platform or mound surface on which Structure 4 was built. This structure floor resembled Floor 6 in that it was fired extremely hard, was entirely intact, and had a small berm on its eastern edge. A wall trench with two visible posts was located at its eastern edge. Mapped in plan view as a single wall trench, in profile it appears to be two, indicating that Structure 4 was rebuilt at least once.

The destruction of Structure 4 resulted in a layer of burned daub and wall fall deposited directly on the floor surface. Like the earlier deposit created by the burning of Structure 6, this daub also contained a thin layer of fine ash, in this case running along the top of the daub fall. Two postholes were dug through the daub rubble, although it is unknown where either originated. A layer of mound fill (I) was then placed over the top of the daub rubble, while the remains of the structure were still hot enough to cause oxidation and reduction. More mound fill (H) was then added to form a prepared surface for Structure 3. The floor of Structure 3 was much like other floors, and showed evidence of burning although it was not fired quite so hard as Floors 6 and 4. The eastern boundary of Structure 3 was difficult to determine—its floor was not uniformly fired and no wall trenches could be conclusively associated with it. However, I suspect that the wall trench associated with floor 3 has been obscured by a pit-like feature that superimposes it. If this is the case, the eastern wall of Structure 3 was located about 2 m west of Structure 4, the previous mound summit structure. This appears to be a trend, as Structure 4 itself was about 2 m west of Structure 6.

Overall, this indicates a changing relationship between Mound E and Mound A to the east. The two mounds were clearly distinguished at this point, with a pronounced swale separating the two—the summit of Mound E rose approximately 55 cm above the swale and culminated in Structure 3, while Mound A rose approximately 80 cm from the same low spot, though the limits of our excavation trench prevented determining its actual height. The footprint of Mound A here was larger than in any previous stage and was beginning to encroach on the area formerly occupied by Mound E.

The next stage of construction began much like the others, with the burning of Structure 3, during which daub, ash, and burned thatch were deposited directly on top of Floor 3. A sample of the thatch returned a radiocarbon date of 390 ± 40 BP, which dates Structure 3 to the latter part of the 15th century or early 16th century (Table 1.2; Figure 1.4). After the structure burned, borrowed soil (E and F) was placed over the top of the burned remains. Additional mound fill to the east (D) was also added at this time. Significantly, Mounds E and A were no longer distinct; Mound E was completely subsumed by the western slope of Mound A, which eventually towered over the smaller mound. Finally, a surface was prepared for a new structure, and Structure 2 was built. Three separate wall trenches and at least two postholes were associated with Structure 2. While three wall trenches could represent rebuilds of the same structure, their sequence was unclear. They were located some distance from one another, indicating that the footprint of the building expanded or contracted over the course of its rebuilding.

There was no daub or wall fall covering Floor 2 so the penultimate stage of construction began with a relatively thin (approximately 6 cm in thickness) layer of soil (B) placed over the top of Structure 2, and Structure 1 was built on top. The floor of Structure 1 was not as well fired as most of the other floors and was difficult to identify during excavation. One posthole and one wall trench associated with the final structure is visible in the north profile. The final construction phase began with the burning of Structure 1 and the deposition of its wall fall on the surface of the mound outside the boundary of the building. The remains of Structure 1 were then buried with more soil (A), now disturbed by erosion and bioturbation.

To sum up, nine stages of mound construction were positively identified in the excavation. Intermediate mound stages had buildings on their summits that were swept clean at the end of their use life, as evidenced by the absence of ceramic and other artifacts in contact with their floor surfaces. The buildings were burned and then buried so quickly that in most cases the soil covering the fired structural remains was also fired to a bright orange color. Subsequent to the excavations, three additional structure floors were identified beyond the excavation's limits using down-hole magnetic susceptibility, a geophysical technique that introduces a magnetic field, then measures how easily a given material can be magnetized (Lowe and Fogel 2007a, 2007b). As the earliest of these three floors was located roughly 75 cm below the Structure 6 floor (and more than a meter above the uppermost mound surface identified in the Mound E southwest slope trench) there are likely multiple intermediate mound stages that our excavations have not yet reached. Overall, Mound E excavations and accompanying radiocarbon dates indicate that mound building at Parchman Place began in the early to mid-14th century and continued into the early decades of the 16th century.

Mound A Summit Excavation

Mound A is the largest mound at Parchman Place, recorded by the LMS at 6 or 7 m in height in 1940. It both adjoins and towers over Mound E to the west. Excavations on the summit of Mound A (Figure 4.1) were conducted by UM field school students in the summer of 2004 (Fogel 2005). The excavation block consisted of a 5 × 1 m trench placed to bisect a strongly magnetic feature, thought to be a burned mound-top structure based on its shape, size, and magnetic signature. Excavation confirmed the presence of two structures in this location (Figure 4.8). Structure 1, the later of the two, was identified based on the presence of a wall trench and the partial remnants of a structure floor (visible in the trench profile but not evident during excavation). Structure 2, which caused the strong magnetic signature, was the earlier of the two and consisted of a burned floor and associated fired debris, including wall daub and thatch. In some portions of the building the fire burned so hot as to vitrify the fallen wall material. Aside from structural debris, there were no artifacts in direct contact with the floor. Following the discovery of Structure 2, the main trench was expanded by two adjacent (.5 × 2 m and .5 × 1 m) units placed to the west to follow the contours of the floor (Fogel 2005:Figure 3.6). Four additional 1 × 1 m units were located southwest and southeast of the main trench to intersect the edges of the structure and to determine its shape. The excavation terminated on the fired floor of Structure 2, not much more than 50 cm below the current mound surface.

Excavations confirmed that the magnetic gradiometer map accurately depicted the size and shape of Structure 2—roughly 4 × 6 m and rectangular, though it may have had rounded corners. The Structure 2 floor was unusual in that it was basin-shaped. That is, it was sunken in the middle

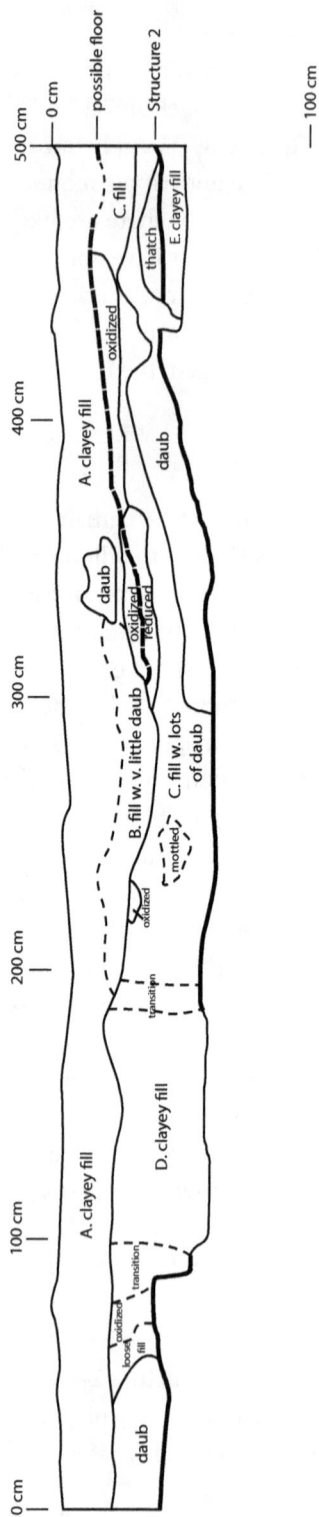

Figure 4.8. East profile of Mound A summit excavation at Parchman Place (22CO51I).

and sloped up toward the edges. Despite the disturbance interrupting the floor toward the north end of the profile, Fogel (2005:38, 71) reported that it was a continuous, sloped surface with a nearly 20 cm difference in elevation between the edges and the center of the building (Figure 4.8). Whether the observed shape represents how the floor was originally built and used or whether it is the result of subsequent destruction is unknown. Though Fogel emphasized the continuous nature of the floor, I suspect the latter scenario is more likely. If this floor *was* intentionally destroyed either before or after the building was burned, it would not be a unique occurrence at Parchman Place. At least one of the buildings on the summit of Mound E was treated in this way before it was replaced by another episode of mound building.

The deposits immediately on top of the Structure 2 floor consisted primarily of structural remains including fired daub rubble and thatch, though these were not continuous. After the daub fell to the floor, a layer of fill (C) containing abundant daub inclusions was deposited over the destroyed building remains. Unfortunately, a rather large portion of the Structure 2 floor is missing from the east profile, indicating a disturbance that destroyed part of the floor in this location. This was interpreted by Fogel (2005:37) as a possible intrusive pit.

Following the burial of Structure 2, Structure 1 was built in the same location. The remnants of its floor—fired hard and oxidized to a characteristic reddish-orange color—were visible toward the southern end of the east profile wall but did not continue throughout the rest of the excavation. A wall trench that was likely associated with these floor remains cuts through Structure 2's floor. Its north-south orientation indicates the two buildings were oriented slightly differently. A sample of charred wood from a post associated with the Structure 1 wall trench returned an AMS date of cal 350 ± 30 BP, dating the latest known Mound A summit structure to the final decades of the 15th or early decades of the 16th century (possibly later) (Table 1.2; Figure 1.4). Since most of the evidence for Structure 1 was missing, it may be that the remains of the building were removed in the same event that damaged the floor of Structure 2.

The final deposits in the Mound A building sequence included a fill zone (B) related to the burial of Structure 1. Though this fill contained very few daub fragments, there were a few large pieces of fired daub located in the same vicinity. The top 20 cm of soil in the Mound A summit excavation consisted of clayey fill (A) disturbed by plowing or other activities. Most artifacts recovered from this excavation block were from the plow zone.

Mound D Investigations

In 1940, the LMS recorded Mound D as rising 1.5 m above the ground surface at its northern extent and approximately 60 cm above the surrounding ground surface to the south (Steponaitis et al. 2002). Prior to modern investigations, however, there was still some uncertainty as to whether Mound D was constructed or alternatively was a natural rise or levee remnant that the people of Parchman Place then incorporated into the site. In June 2011, Rachel Stout-Evans, a soil scientist with the Natural Resources Conservation Service (NRCS), and I used a truck-mounted Giddings hydraulic corer to test the nature and extent of Mound D. The core contained mound fill extending for over 3 m from the present mound surface (Stout-Evans 2011b). At 3.28 m the core encountered a well-defined clay surface that caps the natural levee sands below it. Following this clay cap, Stout-Evans identified eight cultural soil horizons consisting of redeposited soils related to the Dubbs, Forestdale, and Dundee subsoil formations. The earliest four horizons consisted of approximately 1.03 m of fill ranging from silt loam to very fine sandy loam related to the Dubbs formation. There were no cultural material inclusions evident at this depth. Following this was a 25 cm deposit of silty clay related to the Dundee and Forestdale formations, which acted as a stabilizing feature within the mound (see Sherwood and Kidder 2011). Forestdale formation soils came from the earlier of the two natural levees upon which Parchman Place was built and were likely procured specifically for this purpose. The three fill horizons following the clay cap were composed of roughly 1.30 m of loam and silty clay loam related to the Dubbs and Dundee formations. The surface of these deposits culminated in a fired floor identified during excavations as Structure 2 at 38 cm below the current mound surface. No other architectural features were found. The mound fill was remarkably sterile, though Stout-Evans noted organic staining and clay films on the ped surfaces of soils located above the stabilizing clayey fill layer. Although I cannot rule out the possibility that additional structures were present within Mound D in locations not sampled by the core, it seems that the mound was constructed quickly and without intermediate surfaces.

In the summer of 2010, a 2 × 2 m unit was excavated on Mound D. Though this excavation was shallow (about 60 cm at its deepest) in comparison to the other mound excavations, we discovered the remains of two Mississippian houses associated with the Mound D summit. The earliest of the two, Structure 2, was represented by two wall trenches at right angles to one another, forming the northeast corner of a building. The wall trenches originated at a zone of burning that extended throughout most of the unit and probably represents the destruction of Structure 2 by fire, following the common practice of burning buildings at Parchman Place. In addition to the wall trenches, several posts were evident at this level, including at least one that predates and four that postdate Structure 2. A number of posts could not be correlated with any of the wall trench features, and did not resolve into a recognizable pattern. Public architecture and domestic structures at Parchman Place all utilized wall trench construction, with posts often visible within the wall trenches. These single posts probably represent a different type of construction—perhaps some of them may relate to small structures or scaffolds that postdate the mound summit buildings. Alternatively, freestanding posts may have been erected periodically for some other purpose.

A third wall trench as well as at least four of the posts postdate Structure 2. The wall trench indicates that a second building, Structure 1, was located in approximately the same place as Structure 2, though lacking any other wall trenches it is impossible to say anything about its orientation. Following the destruction of Structure 1, several large sherds belonging to a Mississippi Plain pottery vessel were placed in the base of the trench, which was then filled in with dirt and fired daub. An ashy deposit including persimmon seeds and nutshell is associated either with the second structure or possibly a later occupation. A sample of burned hickory shell submitted for AMS dating returned a date of 478 ± 38 BP, dating the ashy deposit to the first half of the 15th century (Table 1.2; Figure 1.4).

Other notable features from the Mound D summit excavations include three burned intact posts very near the surface. These posts suggest that the original height of Mound D has been reduced, likely from several years in cultivation. One of the burned posts superimposed the latest wall trench, suggesting at least three episodes of construction, though it is possible that the burned posts represent a historic intrusion.

Mound C Coring

Located on the edge of the same natural levee terrace as Mounds A and E, Mound C was originally recorded by the LMS as rising slightly more than 2 m above the remnant channel to the northwest and 1 m above the levee to the southeast (Steponaitis et al. 2002). As with Mound D, it was unclear prior to modern work if Mound C was a natural or constructed feature. In the summer of 2011, Rachel Stout-Evans and I extracted two core samples from Mound C using a truck-mounted Giddings soil-coring rig owned by the NRCS. This work determined that Mound C is cultural in origin. As the two cores revealed similar mound profiles, only one was recorded in detail (Stout-Evans 2011b). The recorded Mound C core reached a depth of 3.20 m from the current mound surface and encountered natural levee sands at approximately 2.30 m, a height pretty well in accordance with the LMS report.

At the base of the mound, the core encountered a thin buried A horizon containing an abundance of daub, suggesting that a building was located here prior to the construction of the mound. Above the buried A, 1.40 m of mound fill was deposited. Within this deposit, Stout-Evans identified two horizons consisting of fine and very fine sandy loam related to the Dubbs subsoil formation; the bottom 5 cm or so of these deposits also contained small quantities of daub. Capping this deposit was a 30 cm thick mantle of silty clay soil related to the Forestdale formation. The clayey Forestdale subsoil consisted of backswamp deposits from the earlier of the two levee formations on which Parchman Place was built and were likely procured and used for mound stabilization purposes (see Sherwood and Kidder 2011). Following the clay cap, another 30–40 cm of mound fill was deposited, this time silt loam and silty clay loam related to the Dundee formation. These deposits culminated in a fired floor surface located 33 cm below the surface. The fill immediately underneath the floor exhibited both oxidation and reduction in the signature pattern of burned structures at Parchman Place. This was the only direct evidence of building on Mound C. However, ash, charcoal, and daub occurred in small quantities throughout much of the fill.

The similarities between Mounds C and D are striking. Both mounds were relatively modest in size and more conical in appearance than the other mounds at Parchman Place, though this latter circumstance may be due to historic agricultural disturbance (LMS archaeologists recorded

Mound C as a rounded oval and Mound D as a more or less square platform). Both mounds were built using alternating layers of silty/sandy and clayey soils. The presence of a thick stabilizing layer of clayey Forestdale-like soil within each mound suggests their construction followed similar engineering conventions. Finally, both mounds were apparently built quickly and with the exception of the structural debris (daub) located underneath the first construction stage of Mound C, neither mound has evidence of structures prior to the ones at or near their current summits.

Mound B Salvage Work

According to LMS surveyors in 1940, Mound B was once a rectangular platform mound 2 m tall (Steponaitis et al. 2002). However, its height and shape have been altered since that time. Connaway (1985:2) reported that a backhoe removing fill dirt damaged the southeast edge of the mound in June 1984. Sometime prior to that, a bulldozer was used to remove a portion of the mound summit. During the 1984 demolition, Connaway noted evidence of a burned structure located on a mound surface approximately 1 m above the base of the mound. The material included a distinct layer of burned thatch with a thick layer of white ash on top of it. A sample of the burned thatch returned a radiocarbon date of 340 ± 95 BP, with a 1 s calibrated date range extending from the late 15th to early 17th centuries (Table 1.2; Figure 1.4). Other radiocarbon dates from Parchman Place suggest the likelihood that Mound B construction dates to the early part of that range. No other investigations have been conducted in Mound B.

Mound Building as Community Building

Table 1.2 and Figure 1.4 include radiocarbon dates for mound contexts at Parchman Place. These as well as the stratigraphic excavations already presented form the basis for the following discussion summarizing the history of mound building at the site. The earliest dates from mound building correspond to the initial construction stages of Mound E, and indicate that mound building was happening from the very beginning of Parchman Place's settlement, sometime in the early to mid-14th century. Unfortunately, dates are unavailable for early stages of Mounds A, B, C, and D. Given the spatial relationship between Mounds E and A, I suspect that initiation of their construction was concurrent and coincided with the founding of the Parchman Place community. I also suspect that Mound B was a contemporary of A and E. From what we know, Mound B was constructed in a manner similar to that of A and E, that is, in multiple stages with buildings located on intermediate summits. Mounds C and D, however, were constructed in relatively few stages and had no intermediate surfaces. Given the early 15th-century date associated with summit architecture on Mound D and their apparently rapid construction, it is likely that Mounds C and D were later constructions than the initial stages of Mounds A, E, and B. Dates associated with Mounds A and E extend into the late 15th or early 16th century, indicating their continual construction and use throughout the entire period of Parchman Place's occupation.

While we have ending dates for Mound A, the best evidence for mound-building practices come from Mound E. Deep trenches at the south base, on the southwest slope, and on the summit of Mound E provide evidence for at least 12 construction stages, though it is likely that there are additional stages our excavations did not reach. Within this sequence, I have identified a number of distinct mound-building practices that are relevant for understanding the mound stratigraphy in terms of the social processes that went into its building (McAnany and Hodder 2009). These include: (1) founding events, (2) mantle construction, (3) building and dismantling of summit structures, (4) veneering, (5) truncation, (6) incorporation, and (7) abandonment, each of which tells us something about the social relationships among people involved in the building.

Of these mound-building practices, we can make a distinction between those associated with "mound building as usual," and those that represent departures from the more usual pattern. Mantle construction and the building and dismantling of summit structures fall into the first category, while veneering, truncation, incorporation, and abandonment fall into the second. Founding events may be considered somewhere in between, in that they are a necessary first step in the mound-building process, but were not repeated later in the mound's history.

Founding Events

Founding events associated with mound building at Parchman Place include feasting or community eating events that included preparation and serving of large amounts of food, preparation of food in nontypical ways, and serving of rare, valuable, or perishable foods, condiments, or other substances. Early contexts from the Mound E base and Mound E southwest slope excavations were associated with serving assemblages that differ from the more typical domestic assemblages found elsewhere. Furthermore, there is evidence that multiple segments of the Parchman Place community took part in these founding feasts. While the serving assemblage in the Mound E southwest slope excavation was associated with very small plain coarse ware bowls for serving rare or valuable foods, the Mound E base serving assemblage had small carinated and restricted bowls to serve the same purpose. These differences in bowl assemblages suggest that socially distinct segments of the Parchman Place community took part in feasting events related to the founding of the mound (and, consequently, the town).

In addition to the ceramic serving assemblage, the first stage of Mound E was associated with the burial of a cremated, bundled adult male that was incorporated into the initial mound fill stage either as it was deposited or shortly after. The burial was then covered in a thick layer of ash before another layer of fill was added, which culminated in the first raised living surface of Mound E. Burials of any kind are exceedingly rare at Parchman Place, and given that mound building commenced as soon as people moved to this location, it is likely that the remains of the individual buried in the first mound construction stage were transported here from some other location. This individual may have been an important person whose physical presence at the foundation of a mound would lend legitimacy to the new town and its members.

Mound Building as Usual

Following these founding events, mound builders at Parchman Place generally followed a standard pattern of building that included mantle construction and the building and dismantling of summit structures. First, they constructed a mantle that served as a platform for a large residential building. Some mantles were constructed using redeposited midden from nearby locations; others were constructed of particular sediments chosen for their desired engineering properties. Summit buildings were wall trench structures made of wattle and daub with thatched roofs. Each building was used for a time, presumably by a leader of the lineage or house-group associated with the mound. When the building reached the end of its use life, they swept it clean of artifacts and then burned it, typically in a manner that ensured the preservation of large amounts of structural material in the form of fired or vitrified wall daub and sometimes carbonized wall posts, ceiling beams, and/or roofing material or thatch. In most cases the recently destroyed structures were immediately buried in a layer of mound fill while the building remains were still hot enough to cause oxidation and/or reduction. These mound fill episodes were relatively thick and apparently had a dual purpose—the first to bury the smoldering remains of previous structures, the second to create a level platform upon which the next structure would be built. This basic sequence of events was repeated over and over during the 14th century and the early part of the 15th century. This pattern is well documented for Mississippian sites more broadly and is frequently interpreted as a manifestation of the succession of leaders (e.g., Anderson 1994).

Exceptions to Mound Building as Usual

Sometime during the middle of the 15th century, there is evidence for a number of mound-building practices that did not follow the standard pattern of mantle construction followed by the building and destruction of summit architecture followed immediately by mantle construction, etc. These practices did not stop, but rather became punctuated and perhaps disrupted by other mound-building practices, including veneering, truncation, and the physical incorporation of one mound by another.

Veneering

The first of these was the addition of a white veneer composed of ash, crushed mussel shell, and kaolin (a fine white silty clay procured from a considerable distance) to a mound summit exposed in the Mound E summit excavation. In some places, it appears that the materials making up this deposit were mixed prior to their deposition, a preparation described by Sherwood and Kidder (2011:74). Though similar in appearance to a "zoned fill" (Sherwood and Kidder 2011:78), each layer should be understood as an individual event within a sequence, rather than as constituent parts of a single fill zone. There is evidence for at least five (and probably more) white layers, with intermediate gray layers between the pure white ones. As each surface became dirty it was renewed with additional layers of the white substances. This indicates that the white mound surface was maintained for a period of time before a new structure was built on its surface, in contrast to the previous practice, where new structures were built immediately after the burial of old ones.

Truncation

Following a period of maintenance of the white-veneered surface, at least two stages of Mound E were built in the standard manner, with each mantle supporting summit architecture that was constructed and deconstructed according to the common practice. Stratigraphy from the Mound E summit trench also suggests that Mounds A and E were separate at this time and presumably of comparable size. Following these construction stages, Mound E was truncated. That is, someone or some group of people completely removed an unknown quantity of fill from the top of the mound, all the way down to the white veneer and adjacent floor, but no farther. Recall that the floor of Structure 5, built on top of the veneer, was unusual in that any daub or structural remains associated with it were removed and that the floor exhibits many holes and other evidence of rough treatment. Wash deposits from the swale between Mounds A and B as well as posts and wall trenches associated with two buildings that postdate Structure 5 were also truncated. Given that the truncation extended to the veneered surface and no further, I consider these two unusual acts of mound building to be related. That is, the people responsible for the truncation intentionally exposed the veneered surface to reference the meanings and circumstances associated with its creation. Though unusual in the Mississippian world, aboriginal excavations in mound contexts have also been reported in the American Bottom, for example in Mound 49 at Cahokia (Pauketat 2008: 72; Pauketat et al. 2010) and the Main Street Mound at East St. Louis (Brennan 2016: 87). Much like Mound E at Parchman Place, the excavations in Cahokia's Mound 49 seem to have intentionally revealed a series of alternating light and dark mantles from an earlier stage of mound construction. According to Pauketat (2008: 75, 77), one possible goal of Native digging was to "reinspect or document the stratigraphy in the exposed profile" thereby revealing "the apparent sedimentary truths that they or their parents or grandparents had buried in the ground."

Incorporation

Following the truncation of Mound E in the mid-15th century, mound building resumed in the standard established pattern of a mound fill layer, followed by a summit structure that was destroyed and then buried. The sequence was repeated at least four times before the mound was abandoned, probably in the late 15th or early 16th century. These final construction episodes represent a return to the standard mound-building practices previously noted, with two exceptions. First, the physical relationship between Mounds E and A changed, beginning when fill from Mound A encroached on the space formerly occupied by Mound E. This spatial encroachment continued with the next stage of construction, when the swale separating the two mounds was completely filled in. Essentially, a portion of Mound E was incorporated into the now much larger Mound A, a physical relationship that continued for the rest of the site's occupation.

Second, though mantle construction and use of the Mound E summit continued after its incorporation into the Mound A side slope, the mantles were substantially thinner than previous ones. This indicates that late in the Mound E sequence less effort was put into increasing its height. It is possible that those responsible for the construction of Mound E were less able than before to marshal the labor required to build substantial mound layers. It is also possible that it was simply less important to do so. In any case, Mound E remained essentially the same height after its incorporation into Mound A. Conversely, the height of Mound A was increased substantially and rapidly after this act of incorporation, ultimately resulting in an earthen monument that towered over all other mounds at the site. It is unknown if Mound A continued to be built in punctuated increments with multiple intermediate surfaces, or alternatively, if the remaining bulk of the mound was raised in one episode. We do have evidence for two sequential buildings located on Mound A's ultimate summit, and given the late date associated with one of them, the latter scenario seems likely.

Abandonment

If we accept that mounds at Parchman Place were affiliated with corporate groups of one kind or another and that mound size was related to the relative importance of such groups, then the scenario described previously indicates a change from social relations where mound-affiliated groups were seemingly equal to a situation where one group claimed a higher status relative to others. The takeaway from this scenario, in my view, is not that increasing hierarchy was an inevitable trajectory of Mississippian societies, but rather that there was potential for social elements represented by mounds to be ranked in various ways (Crumley 1995, 2005) and that mound building was a means of negotiating these relationships. As the dramatic expansion of Mound A happened in the late 15th or early 16th century and the site was abandoned soon after, the increasingly hierarchical social relations implied by the changing physical relationship between the mounds was not in effect for very long.

In summary, mound building commenced at Parchman Place during the first half of the 14th century (Parchman I subphase) in concert with the initial occupation of the site. The founding of the Parchman Place community thus involved the founding of new mounds, which, in turn, involved feasting on the part of multiple, socially distinct segments of the community. The burial of a bundled individual in the first mound stage may also have been a critical founding event. Following the initiation of mound building, construction of Mound E (and presumably Mounds A and B) involved repeating a sequence of mantle construction followed by the building, use, and destruction of summit structures. This sequence continued throughout the late 14th century and into the 15th (Parchman II subphase). About the middle of the 15th century, this pattern was punctuated by some unusual mound-building practices, including the construction of a white veneer on Mound E's surface and the truncation of several mound construction stages in order to reexpose it. Late in the 15th century, a single mound (Mound A) was rapidly and dramatically expanded, incorporating a large portion of the adjacent Mound E and coming to physically dominate the site layout. Finally, the mounds were abandoned, probably in the early decades of the 16th century. The dissolution (or relocation?) of the Parchman Place community seems very likely to have been impacted by regional Mississippian politics, including warfare among polities to the north as well as disruptions caused by de Soto's 1539–1543 entrada, which had significant effects on Mississippian people throughout what is now the southeastern United States.

5

Spatial Practice
at Parchman Place

In this chapter, I focus on investigations in the off-mound areas of Parchman Place, with special attention to the results of near-surface geophysical survey, stratigraphic excavations, and coring in residential areas of the site. These investigations plus existing site maps produced much information regarding the physical layout of the site, the focus of the first part of this chapter. Excavations in several residential areas provided additional information regarding the nature of domestic structures, the timing and duration of occupation, and specialized activities aimed at community maintenance. In the second part of this chapter, I use this information to reconstruct an occupational history for Parchman Place and to make some inferences about the community that resided here at various scales of analysis, both spatial and temporal.

Much recent work in archaeology underlines the importance of spatial practice in community building, as "[pa]tterned layouts in the size, shape, and proximity among houses, pits, courtyards, and other elements of the built environment can be understood as generalized expressions of the prevailing social order" (Mehrer 2000:45). Knight (1998) provides a well-known Mississippian example from Moundville, where he interprets the site layout as a map or "sociogram" materializing social relations among the main corporate kin groups making up Moundville society in the 13th century (see also Wilson 2008 and Knight 2010, 2016 for updates on this general interpretation). While this example highlights the importance of mound size and location, other Mississippian scholars have focused on the organizing nature of plazas. Kidder (2004:515) points out that plazas should not be thought of as "empty spaces that developed because architecture enclosed an open area . . . but rather as one of the central design elements of community planning and intra-site spatial organization" (see also Dalan et al. 2003; Kassabaum 2019). Taking this observation as a starting point, we can think about both architecture and empty spaces as important datasets for exploring social interaction in past communities (Nelson 2014). Plazas, for instance, have a multitude of functions that have been documented archaeologically and ethnographically (Rogers et al. 1982). They are commonly regarded as a source of corporate identity— areas for inclusive ritual, games, and other social interactions (Kidder 2004; Mehrer and Collins 1995:37). Conversely, plazas are also forums for displaying social position (Kidder 2004:528), as many site layouts are designed so that the activities taking place on mound summits can be viewed from the plaza. Not unlike earthen mounds, shared communal spaces were socially meaningful and encoded various meanings simultaneously (see also Smith 2008; Robin 2002).

While monumental landscapes such as the mound and plaza complexes of the Mississippi period remain the most visible of spatial archaeological remains, near surface remote sensing and geophysical survey techniques reveal buried archaeological features, expanding our spatial knowledge of sites and regions by leaps and bounds (e.g., Conyers 2010; Conyers and Leckebusch 2010; Haley 2014; Kvamme 2003; Nelson 2014; Thompson et al. 2011; Thompson 2014). In what follows, I consider the relationship between spatial practice and social organization at Parchman Place over the course of nearly two centuries. To do this, I draw heavily on the results of geophysical explorations conducted since 2002, with particular emphasis on the organizing principles of empty space.

Flexibility of use is one aspect of spatial and material practice that is relevant for interpreting shared spaces such as plazas and courtyards. However, the actions of individuals and groups always take place within particular local and historical circumstances. When considering the possibilities for understanding these circumstances, we can look to ethnographically documented accounts of the social organization and belief systems of southeastern Indian groups. I argue that discrete residential neighborhoods at Parchman Place are analogous to the "house societies" or "house-groups" of the Muskogean-speaking descendants of Mississippian people (Brightman and Wallace 2004; Galloway and Kidwell 2004; Knight 2010, 2018; Speck 1907; Swanton 1928a, 1928c; 1931; Urban and

Jackson 2004). These house-groups were composed primarily of women and children related through the clan system, as well as unmarried male relatives and in-married males belonging to other clans. These groups of clan-related people typically shared physical spaces such as houses and the areas surrounding them as well as agricultural fields. They also shared intangible property such as naming customs and hunting territories, and were thought to share particular characteristics of personality and custom. House-groups were autonomous decision-making units at the local level, operating independently of the clan structure, and thus a salient form of community in their own right.

Towns shared similar organizing principles with one another and were typically composed of multiple house-groups (Ethridge 2003; Galloway and Kidwell 2004; Knight 1994; Swanton 1946). They were also autonomous, considered by Urban and Jackson (2004:703) to be the "minimally self-sufficient units of Muskogean social organization." Their physical manifestations include shared ceremonial facilities, though shared ceremonial *practice* rather than any physical manifestation was perhaps their defining feature (Scarry and Steponaitis 2016). Much of this ceremonial practice focused on the ongoing maintenance of social relationships among town members and with situating local communities in relation to the broader cosmos. Previously, I argued that members of the Mississippian community at Parchman Place incorporated substances with culturally meaningful associations such as ash, shell, and clay in mounds to invoke ideas related to the Mississippian cosmos. Mound building, however, was not the only forum for materializing these and related ideals. Archaeological evidence from neighborhood excavations at Parchman Place suggests that the handling and disposal of fire and its residues (including ash and carbonized food remains) was also an important communal undertaking. A multilayered metaphor, fire was at the center of social relations at every level of existence from the household to the cosmos. Maintaining the fire was a significant way of renewing the balance of the world and the social relations that exist within it. Significantly, maintenance of the fire required periodic renewal, including prescribed ways of putting the old fire to rest. Drawing on excavated data from Neighborhood 1, I argue that ash disposal was one way the people of Parchman Place renewed and renegotiated social relationships within their neighborhoods and towns.

Geophysics and Site Organization

Due to a combination of geological conditions and Mississippian cultural practices, magnetic gradiometry is an extremely successful technique for identifying buried architecture at Mississippian sites in the northern Yazoo Basin (Haley 2014; Johnson 2008; Johnson and Haley 2006; Nelson 2014). Soils high in iron prevail on the landscape, and Mississippian people used them to build wattle and daub structures, then fired the structures at high temperatures when they were no longer in use. Firing enhances the remnant magnetism of the clays such that fired structure floors and daub rubble can be identified by magnetic signatures characterized by a strong positive return (typically 20–60 nT) surrounded by a halo of strong negative return (typically -10 to -40 nT). More than 40 features with this signature have been identified in the gradiometer results, and ground-truthing indicates that they correspond well with fired buildings located from 40–60 cm below the ground surface.

Examination of the spatial relationships between magnetic features and the empty spaces they define reveals some interesting patterns. Clusters of houses separated from one another by magnetically clean areas can be understood as discrete residential districts. Three such "neighborhoods" are evident in the magnetometer data (N1, N2, and N3 in Figure 1.3; see also Figure 1.2b). While magnetic patterns on the eastern perimeter of the plaza are not so clear-cut, surface daub scatters mapped in the 1980s (Connaway 1984b) and reconstructed using GIS indicate the presence of two more (relatively diffuse) residential areas (N4 and N5 in Figure 1.3). Within neighborhoods, shared communal spaces are delineated as magnetically clean areas bounded by house features. These spaces take two forms at Parchman Place. In Neighborhoods 1 and 2, three or more houses are arranged around central spaces or courtyards that are free of magnetic features (Figure 5.1a and b). Houses in Neighborhood 4 are likely also arranged in courtyard groups. In Neighborhood 3, houses are arranged in two parallel rows with a narrow (3 m wide), magnetically clean corridor running between them (Figure 5.1c). No evidence of architecture or other archaeological features is present within this corridor.

Finally, the geophysical survey and GIS reconstruction allow us to identify a large "empty" space bounded by Neighborhoods 1, 2, 4, and 5 to the northwest, south, and east. Mounds A, B, and E delineate this space to

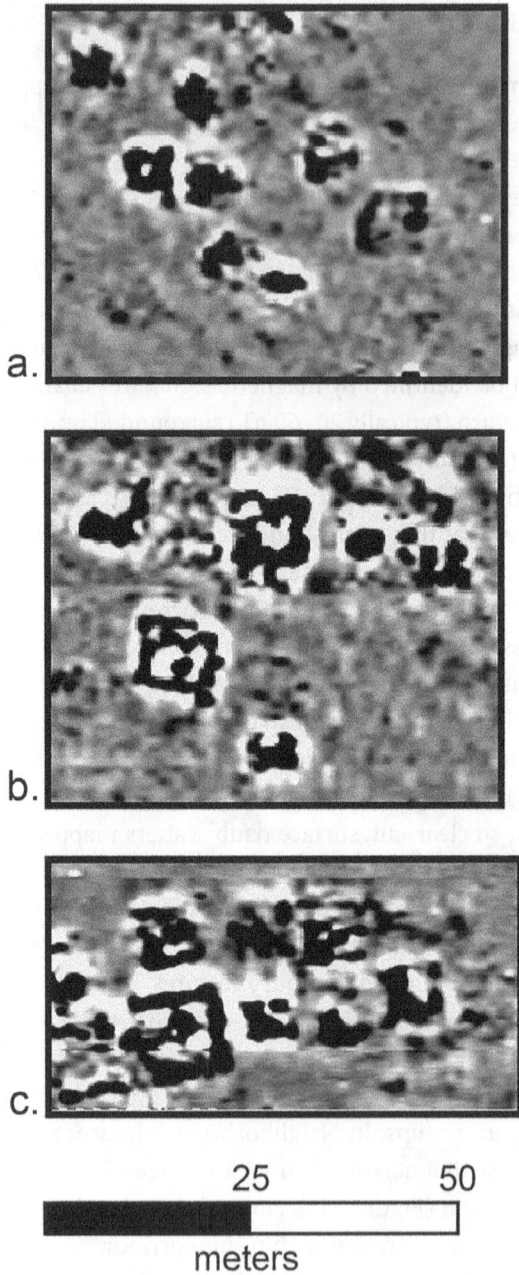

Figure 5.1. Magnetic anomalies indicate courtyard arrangements in Neighborhoods 1 (*a*) and 2 (*b*), and linear arrangement of houses separated by a path in Neighborhood 3 (*c*).

the north. While this large open area was tentatively identified as a plaza as early as the 1940s, gradiometer survey confirmed that it was kept free of habitations, and controlled surface collections indicate that there is very little refuse within it, despite decades of plowing. One possible exception to this last point is the high proportions of surface material recovered from the northeast corner of the plaza near Mound A—this area requires further investigation to interpret.

Considered together, the mound and plaza configuration, as well as houses, neighborhoods, and the shared communal spaces that structure them give us a fairly comprehensive view of site layout toward the end of Parchman Place's occupation. However, surface and near-surface features only speak to the final arrangement of community space at Parchman Place. Excavations and coring in residential areas offer a more historical view. Detailed descriptions of excavation units placed in Neighborhoods 1, 2, 3, and 4, as well as the A-B Swale can be found in Nelson 2016 and Strickland 2009 (A-B Swale only). Here, I briefly describe those findings, with special attention to community building and maintenance activities that occurred in the vicinity of Neighborhood 1 throughout the 14th and early 15th centuries (see also Nelson et al. 2020). I also consider a shift in residence from the A-B swale to Neighborhood 3 during the early 15th century that accompanied the major shift in mound-building practices discussed in the previous chapter. I argue that those responsible for the rapid enlargement of Mound A reinforced their relationship with this monument by founding a new neighborhood that was physically and socially oriented toward it. In doing so, they emphasized an increasing social distance between themselves and other members of the community.

Archaeology of Residential Areas at Parchman Place

Neighborhood 2 Investigations

In 2002, UM field school students excavated a 1 × 5 m trench in the southern plaza to intersect one of several magnetic gradiometer anomalies in Neighborhood 2 that appeared to be Mississippian structures based on their size, shape, and magnetic signature (Figure 5.2). The excavation encountered evidence of two burned structures. The earlier of the two was built directly on the original ground surface (Figure 5.3); a portion of its floor runs the length of the excavation trench, and its northern wall trench

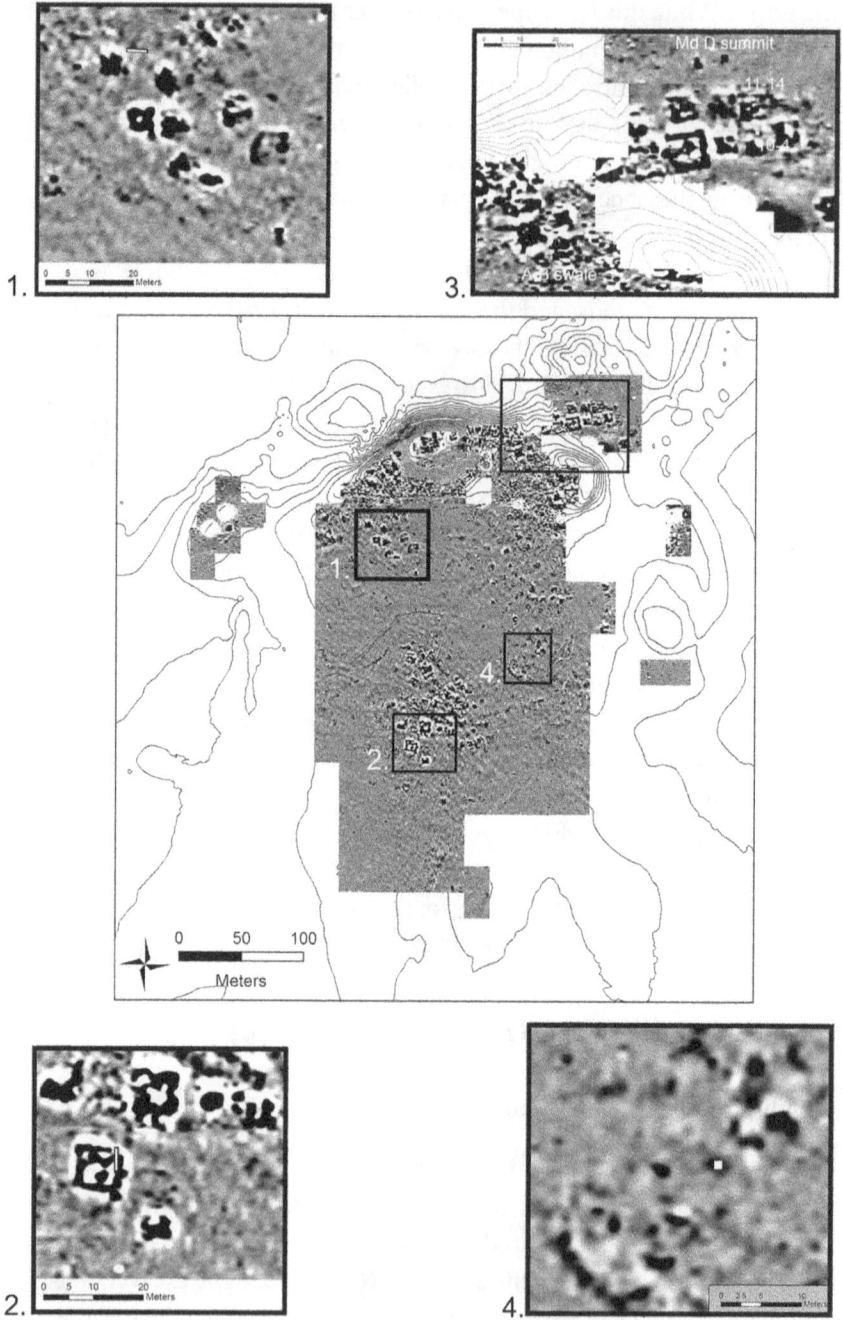

Figure 5.2. Locations of neighborhood excavations at Parchman Place (22CO511).

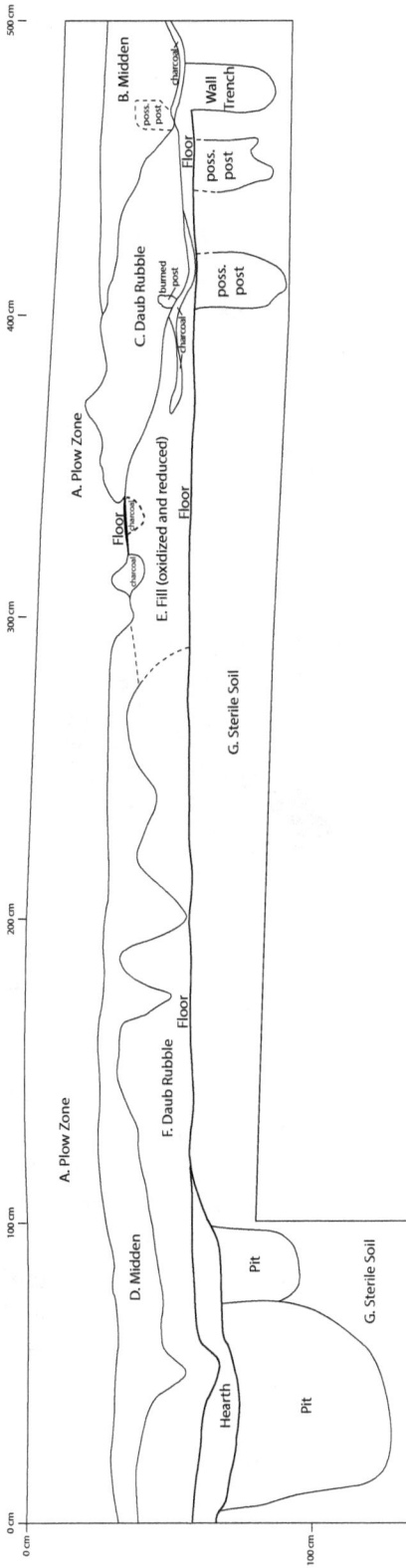

Figure 5.3. West wall profile of Neighborhood 2 excavation trench at Parchman Place (22CO511).

Figure 5.4. John Connaway surveys his work in the excavation trench in Neighborhood 2, Parchman Place (22CO511). Photograph shows fired clay hearth associated with the earlier of two structures (foreground). The wall trench visible in the center of the trench belongs to the later structure. View north.

is visible in the northernmost unit. Two superimposed pits in the southern portion of the trench predate the structure or were located within it. After infilling, the upper portions of these pits were used as a hearth, which was completely surrounded by a fired clay lining (Figure 5.4). Following its occupation, the structure was swept clean and then burned, as evidenced by burned beams, carbonized cane matting, thatch, and daub rubble in contact with the floor. A sample of the thatch submitted for AMS dating returned a date of cal 547 ± 38 BP, likely a late 14th- or early 15th-century date (Table 1.2; Figure 1.4). After the structure burned, it was immediately covered over with fill (Zone E), which was both oxidized and reduced in places. Following that, another zone of fill (Zone D) was used to create a level platform for a new construction. Most of this second structure has been destroyed by plowing, but a fragment of burned floor can be seen in the west profile (Figure 5.3). Additional evidence for this later structure included a wall trench with numerous postholes running north-south down the middle of the excavation trench (visible in Figure 5.4). The later structure was also burned following its use, at which point a thick layer of daub rubble (Zone C) was deposited on the northern slope of the raised house platform. Following the conflagration, a layer of midden fill (Zone B) was placed on top. The uppermost deposit (A) has been disturbed by plowing.

Though very few artifacts were recovered from the structures in Neighborhood 2, excavations and subsequent analysis tell us that it was likely founded in the early to mid-14th century, and that the building site was reused at least once. Given the later structure's relationship to nearby features evident in the magnetometer results (Figure 5.2), one or both buildings were part of a complex of structures organized around a central courtyard.

Neighborhood 4 Investigations

Magnetic gradiometer results along the eastern edge of the plaza were difficult to interpret. Though several buried features were highly magnetic, the data lacked the clear patterning evident in other parts of the site. The LMS map, however, shows a series of three house mounds located along the eastern perimeter of the plaza. In the fall of 2010 and again in the summer of 2011, Rachel Stout-Evans, a soil scientist with the NRCS, Metcalfe, Mississippi, branch, visited Parchman Place to conduct coring with a truck-mounted Giddings rig. We placed cores in the two northernmost house mounds recorded along the eastern edge of the plaza (HM1 and HM2) and extracted a core between HM1 and HM2 for comparison with the surrounding soil profile.

Results of the coring were mixed. Cores placed in HM1 and HM2 encountered cultural fill to depths of 90 cm and 68 cm, respectively (Stout-Evans 2011b). The fill in the HM1 core had organic staining on ped surfaces and contained both daub and charcoal. Stout-Evans identified redoximorphic features of an "olivey-yellow" color that she had previously only encountered in mound fill (Stout-Evans, personal communication 2011). She determined that the fill originated somewhere lower on the landscape, as the clay content (~30%) was too high for that particular location on the levee. Underneath the fill, a natural sandy levee soil profile extends to the terminal depth of the core, at 120 cm below the surface. The core in HM2 was composed of fill roughly similar to that of HM1, but also contained some additional cultural features, including a burned structure floor 25 cm below the surface. Roughly 40 cm of fill were deposited prior to the floor's preparation, and Stout-Evans described the upper portion of it as "greasy" in texture. At 68 cm below the surface the core encountered a 12 cm thick buried A horizon atop a natural levee soil profile that extends to the terminal depth of the core at 1.10 m below surface (Stout-Evans 2011b).

While the two cores could be interpreted as former locations of house mounds due to the nature of the fill and cultural inclusions, the core profile placed in the swale between the two is quite similar, consisting of 93 cm of redeposited fill with organic staining on ped faces, as well as daub and charcoal inclusions. There is no evidence, however, of the distinctive redoximorphic features that seem to be exclusively related to mound fill. As in the location of HM2, beneath the fill we encountered a buried A horizon on top of a buried Bt horizon representing the natural formation of levee soils (Stout-Evans 2011b).

The possible significance of olive-yellow redox features and the basic similarity of the three profiles just described leads to the possibility of two divergent interpretations. (1) House mounds mapped by the LMS are still present as buried fill zones and can be identified by their distinctive redox features. The house mounds and the swales between them have been leveled by plowing. Alternatively, (2) house mounds mapped by the LMS have been completely destroyed and the fill zones identified by coring result from some other activity, such as earthmoving intended to build up or level the plaza area of the site. Plaza modification is common for Mississippian sites and has been documented at the nearby late Mississippian Hollywood site (Haley 2014). More work is needed to determine if this was the case at Parchman Place.

Regardless, cultural inclusions in the house mound cores, surface daub scatters mapped by MDAH in 1984, and surface collections conducted in 2010 and 2011 all indicate significant habitation in this area. In 2010, we placed a 1 × 1 m test unit in Neighborhood 4 to ground-truth a geophysical anomaly we initially thought was a midden-filled pit based on its size and the strength of its magnetic signature (Figure 5.2). The test excavation did not reveal the expected pit feature, but rather a series of two superimposed living surfaces with evidence of burned Mississippian structures (Figure 5.5).

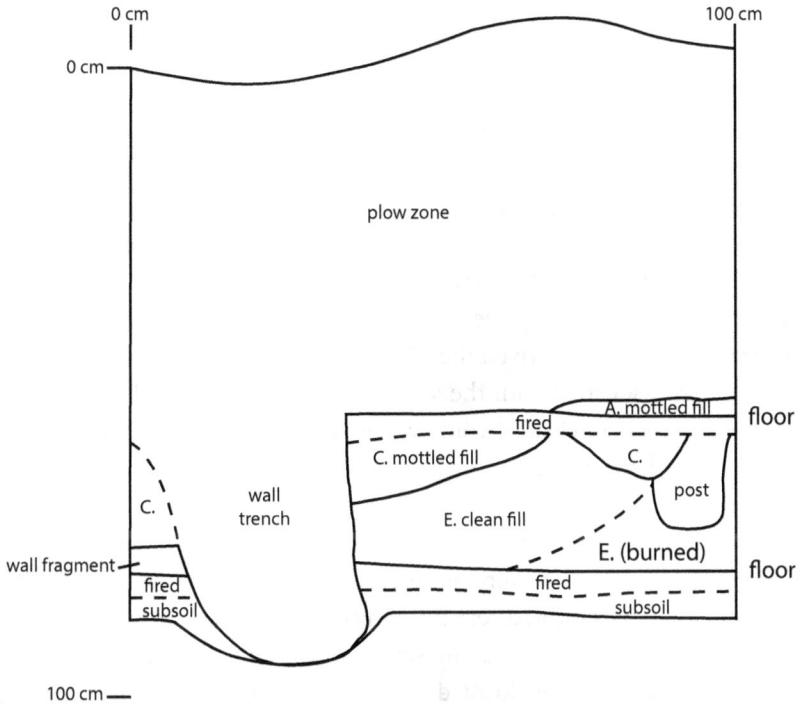

Figure 5.5. North profile of Neighborhood 4 excavation at Parchman Place (22CO511).

The earlier surface was represented by a partially fired floor and associated wall trench. Unusual for Parchman Place, this floor was roughly 15 cm lower than the sterile sandy clay subsoil located to the south, indicating that the location was prepared prior to building by removing some of the subsoil to create a level platform. The floor, located in the northern half of the unit, was fired hard toward the northeast and unfired but compacted toward the northwest. The wall trench bounded the floor on its south side, bisecting the unit on an east-west line. Though not fired as hard as many other structures at Parchman Place, the building was cleaned prior to its destruction by fire, following the familiar pattern. A small fragment of fired wall and a burned beam were found lying on the floor surface in the northwest corner. Following the deposition of these burned structural remains, two zones of clean sandy fill (Zones C and E) were placed over the top of the floor while it was still hot—both zones have evidence of oxidation and reduction where they are in contact with the floor. The surface of the later fill zone created a level platform for a new structure floor, visible in the northeast corner of the unit (Figure 5.5). A wall trench as well as a small pit feature with three zones of ashy fill were associated with it. The wall trench was well-defined and bisected the unit on a northwest-southeast line, indicating that this later structure was built without reference to the orientation of the earlier one. Though this structure was also clearly burned, there was no evidence of the fired structural remains associated with that event, which may have fallen outside the unit or been displaced by plowing. The only additional evidence of stratigraphy that survived the plow was a post that superimposed the wall trench associated with the second structure (not visible in profile). Its association is unclear. It could represent a rebuild of the structure or could be evidence of an additional construction. Very few artifacts were recovered from this unit, and it has not been firmly dated. However, the excavation provides evidence of two or more superimposed structures in Neighborhood 4 that were not identifiable as such in the gradiometer data; nor were they located very near any of the discrete surface daub scatters identified as houses by Connaway (1984b). It appears, then, that there were many more houses located along the eastern perimeter of the site (and no doubt elsewhere) than indicated by the magnetometry results.

Neighborhood 1 Investigations

Neighborhood 1 is located at the northwest edge of the plaza, just south of Mound E. The 1940s LMS map identified a large house mound in this location, and several features presumed to be burned houses were identified via magnetic gradiometry. The 2010 excavations in Neighborhood 1 targeted a small, roughly circular feature of high magnetic value that I suspected was a pit based on its size, shape, and magnetic signature (Figure 5.2). The initial 1 × 2 m excavation encountered evidence of two raised living surfaces as well as a thick layer of redeposited ash and associated features (Figure 5.6). To expose more of the ash deposit, the excavation was expanded to a 1 × 5 m trench in 2011.

The original occupation surface in Neighborhood 1 was a thick, black, anthropogenic clayey soil (Zone N), and provides evidence for some of the earliest activities at Parchman Place. Rich in artifacts and charcoal, Zone N was a natural horizon enhanced by cultural activity. Ceramic sherds pushed into the surface of Zone N are fairly large and indicate a domestic

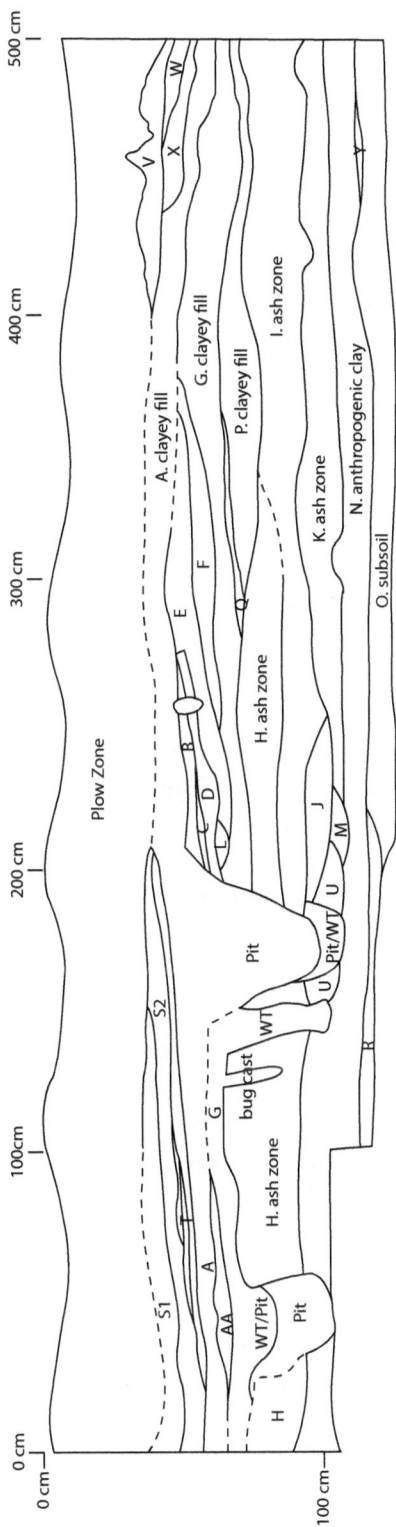

Figure 5.6. South wall profile of Neighborhood 1 excavation trench at Parchman Place (22CO511).

assemblage that includes vessels for cooking, serving, and storage (Nelson et al. 2020). This zone also contains the carbonized remains of a wide range of edible plants, including introduced and indigenous cultigens, starchy and oily seeds, fruits, nuts, and miscellaneous weeds and grasses (Melton 2013; Nelson et al. 2020). Twenty-seven animal species have been identified, including large and small mammals, birds, reptiles, fish, and shellfish. Deer bones are skewed toward high utility elements with little indication of intensive processing, and unusual aspects of the assemblage include wing elements of American Crow and Golden Eagle (Nelson et al. 2020). While both ceramics and botanical remains are suggestive of domestic consumption, these peculiarities in the faunal assemblage indicate specialized activities that my colleagues and I interpret as potluck-style feasting in the context of the founding of the Parchman Place community (Nelson et al. 2020). A sample of burned thatch from Zone N returned an AMS date of cal 640 ± 30 BP, one of the earliest dates from the site, most likely falling in the mid-14th century or perhaps a few decades earlier (Table 1.2 Figure 1.4).

Following these early feasting activities, community members deposited a large quantity of white powdery ash containing an abundance of charcoal and artifacts (Figure 5.7). The ash layers consisted of three fairly thick depositional zones (K, I, and H), none of which was a result of in situ burning. Rather, the ash was moved here from another location. All three ash zones contained broken pottery vessels and abundant food remains (Melton 2013; Nelson et al. 2020). Serving vessels dominate the ceramics assemblage, which includes large wide-shallow bowls suitable for serving large groups of people and small and very small bowls suitable for serving rare, valuable, or perishable foods or condiments. The assemblage also contains cooking vessels (36%), but storage vessels are absent. Plant species are similar to those present in Zone N. However, a high ratio of maize kernels to cupules indicates a focus on consumable plant parts as opposed to processing debris (Nelson et al. 2020). The faunal species are likewise typical for the site and region, and lack the exotic species found in Zone N. However, the faunal assemblage is unusual in that it is characterized by high rates of fragmentation, burning, and calcination. Elsewhere (Nelson et al. 2020), my colleagues and I interpret the high rates of burned and calcined bone and the disposal of edible maize as purposeful acts of deposition consistent with the common post-Mississippian practice of placing food offerings directly in the fire prior to consuming them (e.g., Beverley

Figure 5.7. Photograph of ash zone (H) in Neighborhood 1 excavation trench at Parchman Place (22CO511). View east.

1705:34; Harrington 1921; Hudson 1976:368, 372; Penn 1881[1683]; Tuttle 1833; Witthoft 1949:83). Furthermore, the disposal of ash in a designated location as well as a ceramics assemblage focused around serving vessels corroborate our interpretation of this deposit as evidence of specialized activities consistent with a community-wide feasting event similar in nature to the renewal ceremonies practiced by the descendants of Mississippian people (see Nelson et al. 2020).

The upper interface of the ashy deposits was used as a living surface. Though there is no evidence of a fired floor, a single wall trench originates at the interface of Zones H and G, as does another large wall trench or pit with two zones, located toward the east end of the excavation trench. An infant was buried in an extended position at the base of the pit or trench. The remains were well preserved, with all skeletal elements present and articulated. The infant's age is estimated at 6–9 months based on dental traits, though bone metrics gave a broader age estimate of 0–1 year (James 2012). After recording, the remains were reburied and excavation was discontinued in that area. It is unclear whether the pit was dug specifically for the purpose of burying the child or whether the remains were placed at the base of an existing wall trench. The northeastern boundary of the pit/trench terminates within the unit, but the southwestern portion extends into the excavation wall, so there was no way to determine its length. Until the burial was encountered, excavators interpreted the long, narrow dimensions of the feature as one end of a wall trench.

Following the infant burial and the occupation of the surface of the ashy deposits, the entire area was capped with clayey fill. Zones P and Q contain fired daub, likely a result of the destruction of a building indicated by the wall trench to the east. Zone G completely capped the underlying deposits, effectively burying the ash deposits and the building remains. The remaining deposits were difficult to separate during excavation but represent multiple fill episodes. A pit feature originating at the surface of Zones G and B indicates a living surface occupied for some period of time. However, there was no other evidence of a building at this point in the sequence. The pit fill contained several human skull fragments as well as a small ceramic bowl carefully placed or wedged in a small nook dug into the pit wall. The skull fragments were not recognized during excavation as the pit fill was collected in its entirety for flotation. Dale Hutchinson (personal communication, 2013) examined the fragments and determined that they belonged to an adult individual, approximately 30–50 years of age, and that there was evidence of porotic hyperostosis, which was healing at the time of death.

The next major zone (Zone A) completely capped the underlying deposits. Zone A was described by excavators as very dark grayish brown silty clay with large chunks of daub and charcoal flecks—its fill is similar to that of the underlying pit with the exception of the large chunks of daub. On top of this capping zone were a series of deposits to the west and another to the east. All of these, as well as Zone A, have been partially destroyed by plowing activity. While it is not clear what type of activity is represented by the deposits to the west, Zone T to the east shows indications of in situ burning, with oxidized, charcoal-rich, and ashy layers. A number of pottery sherds were lying flat on the surface of Zone T, and are covered by Zone S, a series of dark gray clayey deposits with daub and charcoal inclusions. The flat sherds sandwiched between Zones T and S may indicate another living surface in this location. A sample of carbonized cane from Zone T returned an AMS date of cal 482 ± 38 BP, an early to mid-15th-century date (Table 1.2; Figure 1.4). Finally, on top of Zone S was a mixed plow zone containing an abundance of ceramic and other artifacts; a pit or large post with two (possibly three) zones originated in the plow zone and extended nearly all the way through the buried ashy zones.

Overall, excavations in Neighborhood 1 offer significant insights into practices related to the founding and continued maintenance of the Parchman Place community. "Potluck-style" feasting was coincident with early mound building and the establishment of residential neighborhoods in the early to mid-14th century, a time when social relationships were first codified in spatial practice. Though not distinguished by special foods, wing portions of American Crow and Golden Eagle indicate a ritual or ceremonial component to these founding events. Some decades later, the deposition of large quantities of ash containing offerings of first fruits to the fire indicate an ongoing attention to the ceremonial upkeep of the community, not unlike yearly renewal ceremonies such as the Busk or Green Corn Ceremony practiced by the descendants of Mississippian groups. The excavations also offer insight into variation in 14th and 15th-century burial practices, as these isolated instances of burial do not fit the pattern of burial established at nearby contemporaneous sites such as Carson (James 2010; 2015). Each of the Neighborhood 1 burials, for instance, was associated with a living surface that postdates the earlier ash deposits. Perhaps the burials were intended to mark the continued significance of this location.

A-B Swale Investigations

On the 1940s LMS map, the swale between Mounds A and B appeared as a flat area that is slightly higher than the surrounding topography. In 2004 and 2005 UM field school students excavated a trench placed to investigate one of several geophysical anomalies in this location interpreted as burned Mississippian structures (Figure 5.2). The results of the A-B Swale excavation were the subject of an MA thesis by Glenn Strickland (2009), and portions of his analysis are included here, though my interpretations of the stratigraphy differ slightly from his (see Strickland 2009: 116–119 for comparison). A profile map of the main excavation trench is reproduced as Figure 5.8.

Excavation in this area confirmed that the raised, flat area between Mounds A and B is cultural in origin. This low platform sits atop undisturbed natural levee deposits (Strickland 2009:116) and was constructed of fill variously described in excavation notes as "mound fill" or "midden" (Zone G). It is very likely basket-loaded fill, as some portions of it are artifact rich, while other portions have low artifact density. An AMS sample of carbonized pecan shell from this zone returned a date of 609 ± 39 BP, a 14th-century date and one of the earliest reported for Parchman Place (Table 1.2; Figure 1.4).

Following the first stage of platform construction, multiple layers of clayey fill were deposited (Zones H, I, F, and E), effectively raising the ground surface about 70 cm above the surface of the underlying fill. Strickland (2009:116) interpreted this as the building of a house mound, though it may have been part of the raised platform. The clayey fill layers can be divided into at least two depositional events, as evidenced by an ashy deposit and a number of pottery sherds lying on the surface of Zone F. Though difficult to discern, a probable post also originated at the surface of Zone F; excavation notes described the feature fill as rich in fish and small animal bones as well as small pottery sherds. I interpret Zones H and F to be stratigraphically equivalent and likely composed of the same fill (cf. Strickland 2009:Figure 3.4A).

The addition of fill (Zone E) in the western portion of the profile resulted in a raised area or platform in that portion of the unit, while the adjacent area to the east remained at a lower elevation. This low area was the location of some interesting and difficult-to-interpret activity that resulted in a series of thin stratified deposits (jointly designated Zone D). Some deposits were ashy, while others had discrete deposits of ceramics and/or mussel shell. Unfortunately, these deposits were not described by excavators, though plan and profile maps indicate the complicated nature of the stratigraphy. I cannot help but think these deposits are the result of some of the same meaningful depositional practices noted elsewhere at Parchman Place and that I have interpreted as acts of placemaking that were integral in constituting the community. According to Strickland

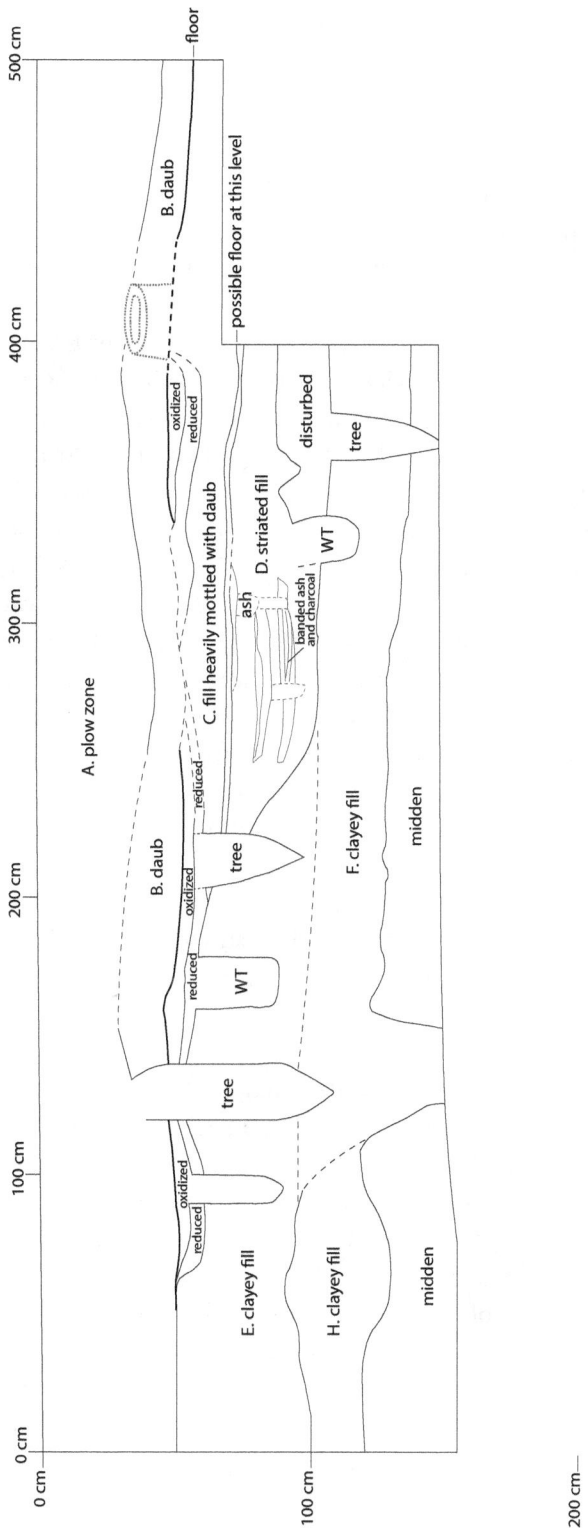

Figure 5.8. North wall profile of A-B swale excavation trench at Parchman Place (22CO511).

(2009:116), a structure was built on top of these deposits and later burned, though again, there is no record of a structure in the excavation level forms, nor does it appear on plan or profile maps. The only possible indication of this structure that *was* recorded is a post or wall trench mapped in profile within Zone D. Although its upper boundaries could not be identified, it must have originated within or at the surface of the series of striated deposits.

Atop this presumed structure, the next fill zone (Zone C) consisted of 10–20 cm of clayey soil heavily mottled with daub, forming a platform upon which a second structure was built. The remains of this structure consist of a floor surface that was fired hard upon its destruction along with interior structural features, including a post with a clay "collar" or reinforcement at its base. This reinforcement consisted of a thickness of clay, approximately 17 cm tall and 25 cm in diameter, molded around an interior post. Both the collar and the portion of the post that was set into the floor were preserved when the building was fired. Other structural remains include "a series of wall trenches" (Strickland 2009:117), at least one of which is visible in the north profile though it was not identified as such in the excavation notes. In a departure from most episodes of house destruction at Parchman Place, a nearly complete but smashed Mississippi Plain jar was found in direct contact with the floor, left behind when the building was destroyed. Strickland (2009:117) also reports evidence of woven matting on the floor. Presumably, this evidence consists of cane impressions pushed directly into the floor surface, though the cane itself was not preserved. A sample from the burned post associated with the structure returned an AMS date of cal 570 ± 60 BP, an early to mid-14th-century date (Table 1.2; Figure 1.4).

As a result of the later house's destruction, the structure floor as well as the post collar were fired hard and a characteristic pattern of oxidation and reduction of the floor is visible in profile. Additionally, a thick layer of fired daub (Zone B) was deposited on the floor surface, smashing the aforementioned Mississippi Plain jar and surrounding the clay post collar. This was the last discernible cultural stratum in the sequence, as the overlying 30–50 cm of fill have been disturbed by plowing.

Though the excavation revealed as many as six episodes of construction, it was necessary to collapse these for the purposes of ceramics analysis due to small sample sizes and inadvertent mixing of deposits. Fill Zones G, H, I, F, and E represent as many as three building episodes. In combination, they contained what I have identified as an "intermediate" ceramics assemblage—having characteristics of both domestic and serving assemblages distinguished by the correspondence analysis (Figure 3.9b). The striated fill designated Zone D and the mottled fill overlying it (Zone C) were also combined, though they represent two distinct stages of construction, possibly separated by an episode of house construction. This combined sample contained a domestic ceramics assemblage of cooking, serving, and storage vessels (assemblage AB_B in Table 3.8).

Though the combined ceramic samples are less useful than those that represent discrete deposits, they do suggest that the inhabitants of the A-B Swale participated in both domestic and non-domestic activities within their neighborhood. It is no surprise that ceramics used primarily for non-domestic purposes occur in the earlier part of the sequence as these assemblages are associated with community founding events in other parts of the site, and the early date from the platform fill confirms that earthmoving activities in this area are among the earliest at Parchman Place. The date from the final structure is also early in the overall chronology. I argue next that this neighborhood was abandoned by the early 15th century and that its inhabitants founded a new neighborhood to the northeast.

Neighborhood 3 Investigations

As described previously, Neighborhood 3 was the only residential area at Parchman Place that was not plaza-adjacent. Located east of Mound A and north of Mound B, its inhabitants would have been physically and visually separated from other community members. Furthermore, its constituent buildings were arranged not in courtyard groups, but on either side of a corridor oriented toward Mound A. In 2010 and 2011, I, along with volunteers from UM and the University of North Carolina, excavated two test units in Neighborhood 3 (Figure 5.2). In the first of these, a 1 × 1 m unit (Unit 10-4), excavators uncovered at least five sequential occupations (Figure 5.9).

The earliest occupation was represented by a fill zone (EE) and three posts (not visible in the profile) that originated at its upper surface. The line of posts was oriented roughly east-west. Though no wall trench was identified, one likely existed here. Burned structural remains deposited on the northern slope of the platform indicate the building on its summit was

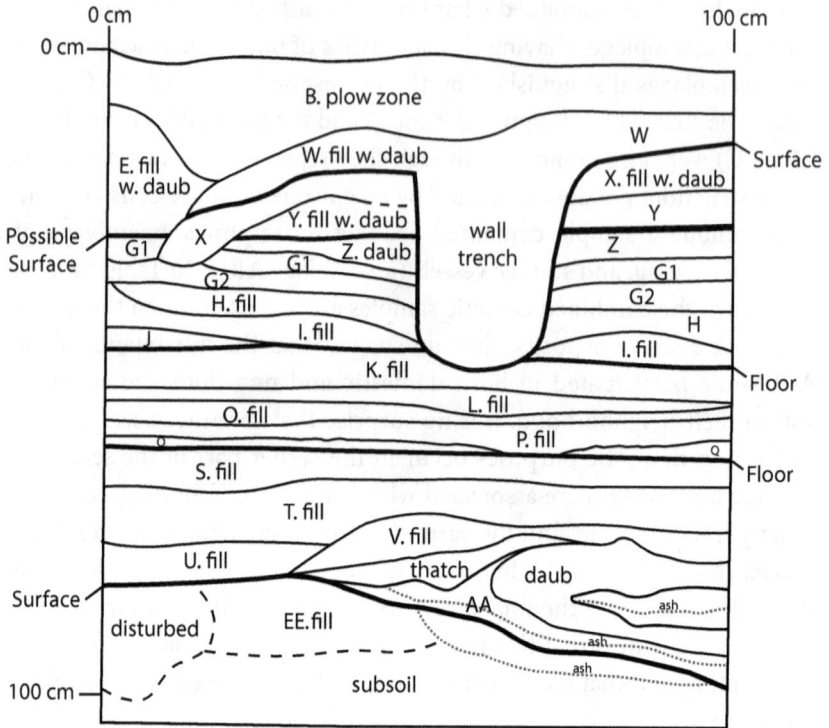

Figure 5.9. West profile of Neighborhood 3 (Unit 10-4) excavation at Parchman Place (22CO511).

destroyed by fire and the remains left where they fell or possibly pushed over the edge. A sample of carbonized thatch returned an AMS date of cal 505 ± 38 BP, an early 15th-century date (Table 1.2; Figure 1.4). The burned structure was covered with a layer of fill (Zones U and V) exhibiting a pattern of oxidation and reduction typical for fills used to cover still-smoldering structures. More fill (Zones T and S) was then placed on top to increase the height of the platform. The surface of this fill zone is a prepared floor, though it was unfired and there were no structural remains associated with it. Another episode of zoned fill (Zones Q, P, O, L, and K) lay on the surface of the floor and terminated in a third floor surface (top of Zone K) similar to the previous one in that it was unfired and unassociated with structural remains. It was, however, slightly oxidized on its upper surface, perhaps indicating a low-temperature firing.

The next construction episode consisted of another series of zoned fills (J, I, H, G), the upper limits of which may represent a fourth living surface. Two posts originated at this surface, both located in the southeast quadrant of the unit. A deposit of daub rubble (Zone Z) was located on the sloped surface, probably representing burned construction material from a building located on the platform to the south.

Zones Y, X, E, W, and B, all containing large quantities of fired daub, were deposited next. Though these zones were all disturbed by plowing, there appears to have been another surface corresponding with the upper limit of Zone X, indicated by a wall trench that originated at the top of the zone. Altogether, then, there were five sequential living surfaces identified in this location.

The second excavation in Neighborhood 3, Unit 11-13, was placed over a deposit of large pot sherds discovered protruding from a plow ridge (Figure 5.2). The original 1 × 1 m unit was excavated to a depth of nearly 120 cm to obtain information about stratigraphy and additional subsurface features (Figure 5.10), while two additional units to the south and east were excavated to a depth sufficient to recover what turned out to be three reconstructible pottery vessels as well as fragments of additional vessels located between 20 and 35 cm from the surface.

The stratigraphy in Unit 11-13 was less complicated than Unit 10-4. While there was no direct evidence of a building or living surface at the base of the excavation unit, there was evidence of structures nearby. Though not visible in the profile, a layer of daub rubble fell or was pushed into the southwestern portion of the unit—stratigraphically, it comes after Zone J, a thin zone of fill with charcoal and small daub inclusions. If similar to the pattern seen elsewhere at Parchman Place, the daub likely fell from a nearby structure that was burned and then quickly buried. This makes sense given the unit's proximity to a highly magnetic feature to the southwest. Approximately 60 cm of mottled fill (Zones G, E, D, and N) were then deposited. The top of Zone N terminated in a floor or other surface. While the surface was difficult to identify during excavation, a single post located in the southwest corner of the unit originated at this level. If the post belonged to a structure, it was either unfired or located outside the limits of the excavation.

Following this apparent construction, additional mottled fill (Zones L, M, and B) was deposited to cover it. The top of Zone B represents the third occupational surface located within the unit, identified by an abundance

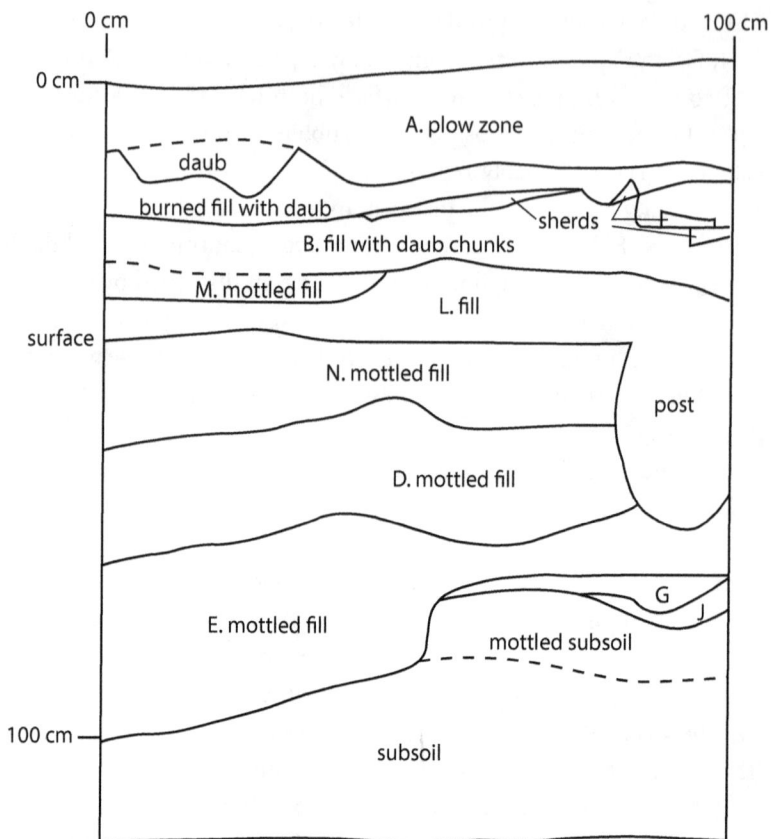

Figure 5.10. East profile of Neighborhood 3 (Unit 11-13) excavation at Parchman Place (22CO511).

of sherds lying on its surface. The sherds from this unit as well as those to the south and east refit into three nearly complete vessels, including one bottle (Figure 3.8) and two jars, as well as fragments of additional vessels. These vessels were likely crushed as a burning building located to the south collapsed, though it was not clear if they were sitting outside the building in a storage or work space adjacent to the house or if perhaps they fell from the rafters. Sherds belonging to the uppermost layer of the largest vessel were lying with exterior faces up, while those belonging to the lower level were lying with exterior faces down; a thin layer of soil separated the upper pieces from the lower. Thatch as well as fired daub rubble was located underneath, around, and over the sherds. A sample of carbonized maize associated with this burning event returned an AMS date of 446 ± 38 BP, a mid-15th-century date, and the latest from any neighborhood context at Parchman Place (Table 1.2; Figure 1.4).

The earliest radiocarbon sample taken from Neighborhood 3 dates its founding to the first half of the 15th century, around the time when the A-B swale neighborhood was abandoned. Given its late founding date relative to other neighborhoods, it is perhaps surprising that excavation should have revealed five sequential occupations, more than any other non-mound context. However, the latest radiocarbon date suggests Neighborhood 3 may have been occupied later than other neighborhoods, that is, occupation continued in this part of the site after other neighborhoods had been abandoned. A higher-than-average proportion of painted polychrome pottery recovered from surface collections supports this interpretation. Other circumstances distinguish Neighborhood 3 as well, including its planned orientation toward Mound A, as well as the recovery of two gourd-shaped ceramic rattles during controlled surface collections. All of this is suggestive of special activities taking place in Neighborhood 3, though more excavation is required to understand the nature of those activities.

Residential Occupation at Parchman Place

Gradiometer survey, supplemented by controlled surface collections, the LMS plane-table map, and the MDAH survey, gives us a general picture of off-mound residential areas on or near the surface at Parchman Place, including six relatively discrete residential areas or neighborhoods, and as many as eight house mounds. Figure 1.3 shows the locations of house features identified in the geophysical data as well as those reconstructed by plotting surface daub scatters in ArcGIS. Radiocarbon dates from excavated neighborhood contexts are presented in Table 1.2 and Figure 1.4.

Drawing on these data, I have identified a number of residential practices that speak to issues of identity and community-building activities that were ongoing at Parchman Place. These include the arrangement of space within neighborhoods and within the site as a whole, as well as an unusual deposit in Neighborhood 1 consisting of large quantities of ash. Of the six residential neighborhoods identified at Parchman Place, four are similar in that the houses and other buildings are arranged around central courtyards and the neighborhoods are arranged around a large open plaza. Neighborhood 3 differs significantly in that it is located well away from the central plaza, and its buildings are arranged on either side of a 3 m wide avenue or path. When overlaid on a topographic map (Figure 1.3b), it is apparent that the path in Neighborhood 3 was oriented directly toward a ramp extending from the Mound A summit. These spatial arrangements have several implications for understanding how people living at Parchman Place organized their community.

First, courtyard groups probably represented distinct subgroups of the community that may be akin to the "house-groups" of the Chickasaw and Choctaw. If so, these groups were probably composed of related women and their husbands and children. They likely made autonomous decisions at the household level about daily activities such as tending crops, gathering and hunting activities, cooking, maintenance of the household, etc. Many such tasks would have taken place within the shared space of the courtyard. Daily interaction and shared practice, then, were common and indicate that courtyards were group-focused, but at a fairly intimate scale.

Stepping back to look at the site as a whole, the notion of a central space was repeated in the plaza, a roughly five-hectare area that was both free of built architectural features and low in surface artifact density. Neighborhoods 1, 2, 4, and 5 were all located near the plaza, indicating shared use of the space by families or lineages residing in multiple courtyard groups. As with courtyard groups, the arrangement of neighborhoods around a shared public plaza also suggests a community-focused ideology, with residents facing inward and toward other community members.

Thus far, the mound-and-plaza site plan described previously, with residential areas flanking the plaza, is a fairly expected pattern for a Mississippian settlement and has analogs among the towns of Muskogean-speaking descendants of Mississippian people, wherein multiple clan-based lineages resided together. Recall, however, that the defining feature of a town is shared ceremonial practice, rather than shared physical space. In addition to certain mound-building practices discussed in Chapter 4, the ashy deposits located in the Neighborhood 1 excavation constitute evidence of shared ceremonial practice among community members at Parchman Place. In particular, the deposition of large quantities of ash in a single location bears a resemblance to the cleaning and treatment of ash during community renewal ceremonies practiced annually by numerous post-contact Native communities. The maintenance of sacred fire and proper disposal of its residues was and is a significant way of restoring balance in the world and within the community for many southeastern

Indians, and the collection and disposal of large quantities of ash in Neighborhood 1 suggests that this was important for community members at Parchman Place as well.

Returning to the idea of spatial practice, it is clear that Neighborhood 3 does not fit the pattern described for other neighborhoods. First, its location is unexpected in that it lies outside the mound-and-plaza configuration typical for the time period. By building in this area, residents differentiated themselves spatially and visually from the rest of the community. Second, Neighborhood 3 differs from the others in its internal organization. Rather than being arranged around a shared central space, houses here were organized in tightly spaced rows, with a 3 m wide corridor running between them. The association of Neighborhood 3 and Mound A via the path that connects them suggests that residents of Neighborhood 3 were primarily oriented visually and physically toward monumental architecture, rather than toward the rest of the community. I suggest that this orientation was social as well.

While these observations regarding spatial practice are based primarily on near-surface (i.e., late) features, evidence from excavations within residential areas suggest that these spatial patterns were of significant duration, and I now turn to a chronological reconstruction of neighborhood occupation at Parchman Place.

Parchman I (14th century)

Radiocarbon dates from residential contexts indicate that plaza-adjacent neighborhoods (including houses in Neighborhoods 1, 2, 4, and 5) were initially founded in the early to mid-14th century, contemporaneous with early mound building. Houses in the A-B swale were also early, and while their location on an elevated platform sets them apart, they also can be considered plaza-adjacent. Multiple stacked houses in many of the neighborhoods indicate that occupation continued throughout the Parchman I subphase. Dates from the A-B swale excavation suggest that occupation in this area of the site may have ended during the latter part of Parchman I. In addition to the establishment of the mound and plaza complex and the residential areas that make up Parchman Place, founding community members organized and took part in inclusive social events such as the potluck feasting activities evident in Neighborhood 1.

Parchman II (15th century)

Occupation of neighborhoods surrounding the plaza continued into the Parchman II subphase, and we can infer that courtyard organization was in effect at this time, if not from the very beginning. At the same time the occupation of the A-B swale was ending, however, Neighborhood 3 was founded. I suggest, therefore, that the occupants of the A-B swale shifted their residence at this time to a location that was removed from the rest of the community. Excavations in Neighborhood 3 suggest that its internal organization and thus, the orientation of its central path toward Mound A, was established at its founding. Conversely, the ash deposits in Neighborhood 1 also date to the early Parchman II subphase, indicating the importance of community-based renewal rituals at this time. On the one hand, one subgroup of people emphasized social distinctions between themselves and others by physically separating themselves from the rest of the community. On the other hand, many or perhaps all segments of the population also participated in world-renewal ceremonies focused on maintaining and restoring balance within the community.

Overall, the occupation at Parchman Place spans a relatively short period, roughly 200 years, and Neighborhoods 1, 2, and 3 were occupied simultaneously for much of that time. However, the late date from Neighborhood 3 and a higher frequency of late ceramic types (notably painted polychrome vessels) in surface collections suggest that occupation in Neighborhood 3 may have continued after other neighborhoods had been abandoned. If this scenario is true, the ongoing social negotiations documented in 15th-century mound building, ceremonial, and spatial practice seem to have resulted in some portions of the community moving entirely, while others remained.

6

The Mississippian Community at Parchman Place

In Chapter 2, I proposed splitting Phillips' (1970:939–940) Parchman phase into two subphases based on differing frequencies of ceramic types, attributes, and functional vessel classes found in 14th- and 15th-century contexts at Parchman Place. Though ceramic phases do not usually coincide perfectly with other archaeological indicators of cultural change, they offer convenient frameworks within which to discuss how sites and the social groups that inhabited them developed over time. Radiocarbon dates from Parchman Place (Table 1.2; Figure 1.4) also separate roughly into two clusters—those from the 14th century and those from the 15th century—though some of the latest dates from mound summits extend into the early 16th century. Within this temporal framework, I offer a brief social history of the Mississippian town at Parchman Place, with particular attention to the ways Mississippian people continually created their community in place.

Parchman I

The Parchman I subphase corresponds roughly to the 14th century. During the early part of this period Mississippian people first moved to Parchman Place. This initial settlement, I argue, represents the relocation of a town, perhaps from a nearby site such as Salomon. The environmental setting included an oxbow lake created by one or more prior channels of the Mississippi River, as well as smaller active streams such as Mill Creek, presently located west of the site. People no doubt chose this location to

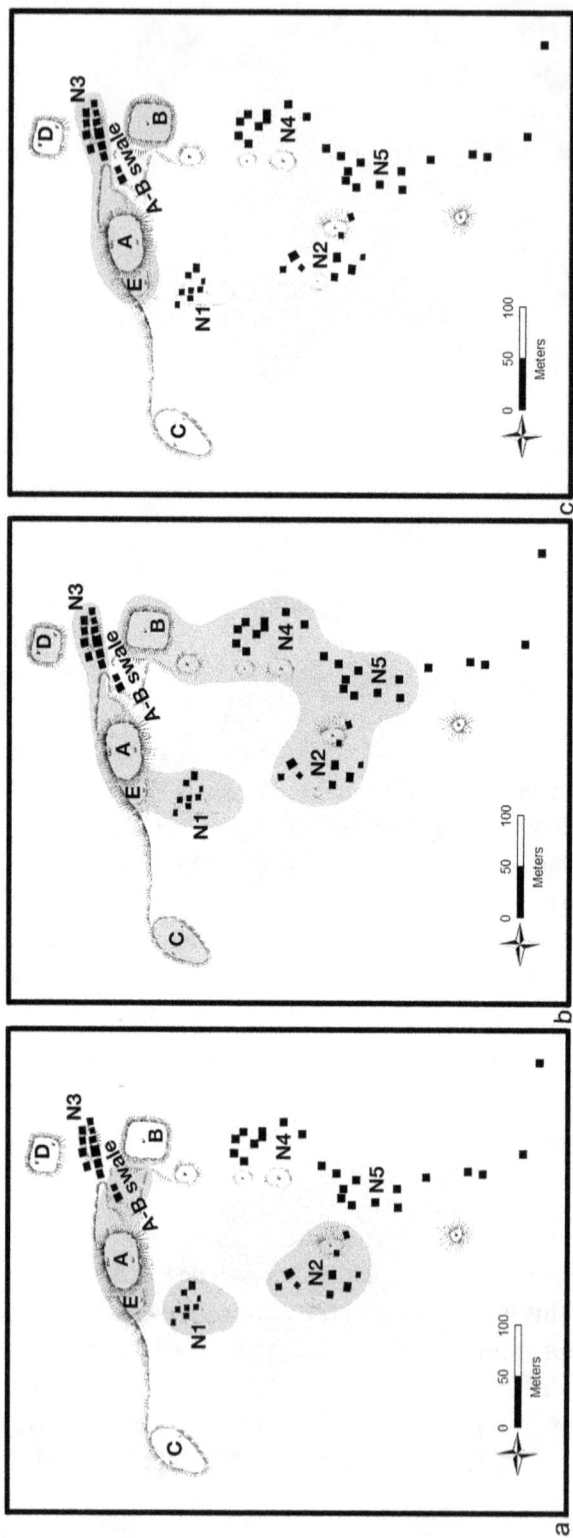

Figure 6.1. Locations of activity during the Parchman I subphase (*a*), the Parchman II subphase (*b*), and the terminal Parchman II subphase (*c*).

take advantage of the vicinity's rich terrestrial and aquatic resources. Additionally, the site would have been ideal for the cultivation of maize and other crops due to the flood-enriched soil.

As soon as people moved to Parchman Place, they laid out a site plan that included a series of low earthen platform mounds built along the edge of the natural levee to the north, as well as a large open plaza around which community members established their households. Areas of the town for which we have direct evidence (in the form of C14 dates) of early settlement are shaded in Figure 6.1a. Each neighborhood or house-group at Parchman Place probably belonged to a clan-based matrilineage, each one affiliated with one of the small mounds at the site. Founding the community also involved large feasting events that happened in concert with mound building. From ceramic evidence we know these feasts were characterized by consumption of large quantities of food cooked in nontypical ways, foods that may have been rare or valuable. Some participants used specialized nonlocal serving vessels, drawing attention to their connection with Mississippian people in the southern Yazoo Basin or Natchez Bluffs region.

Once mounds were established, leaders of the community (presumably affiliated with the various matrilineages) resided in large houses atop the mound summits. When these houses were no longer occupied, they were cleaned out, burned, and immediately buried, after which a new mound mantle was added and a new building constructed. Residences in off-mound areas of the site were also treated in this way. Throughout much of Parchman I, individual mounds were roughly equivalent in size, indicating that no one leader or corporate group had more authority than any other, or perhaps that different types of authority were balanced among them. Ceremonial activity during Parchman I also emphasized balance, as the ash heap deposits in Neighborhood 1 are likely related to community and world-renewal rites.

Parchman II

Activities associated with both mound and neighborhood areas continued into the Parchman II subphase, which largely coincides with the 15th century (Figure 6.1b). However, houses in the A-B swale were abandoned during the terminal Parchman I subphase, and Neighborhood 3 was founded soon after. It seems that those living in the A-B swale moved their neighborhood to a new location, one removed from the plaza and therefore isolated from other neighborhoods and those residing in them. Neighborhoods adjacent to the plaza continued to be occupied and we can infer from the geophysical data that the courtyard arrangement that characterizes these neighborhoods was in effect at this time. Given the sequential nature of buildings within each residential area, this neighborhood organizational scheme probably continued from Parchman I. In any case, during the 15th century, people living in Neighborhoods 1, 2, and perhaps 4 and 5 arranged their living spaces around shared central courtyards, while those living in Neighborhood 3 arranged their houses in tightly spaced rows separated by an avenue or path.

While mound-building practices in Mound E proceeded as usual for much of Parchman II, activities occurring near the middle of the 15th century indicate a significant disruption or reorientation related to mound building and its goals. First, the builders of Mound E added a veneer made from layers of ash, mussel shell, and white kaolin that they maintained or renewed for some time before mound building resumed. Second, the builders truncated the mound, removing a number of mound stages and reducing its height to that of the white veneer. I have argued that these events may coincide with a time of political instability at Parchman Place, perhaps one or more contested chiefly successions, and that the creation of the white veneer and its reexposure reflect efforts of some community members to balance authority with community-focused values. Subsequent to this truncation, mound building continued as it had before, with a sequence of mound construction episodes associated with summit architecture.

Up until this point, Mounds E and A were separate structures, presumably of comparable size. However, the end of Parchman II (Figure 6.1c), sometime in the late 15th or early 16th century, witnessed an incorporation of Mound E by the rapid and dramatic expansion of Mound A. By this time, if not before, the people living in Neighborhood 3 affirmed a spatial relationship with Mound A by orienting the path separating their houses toward a ramp leading to the Mound A summit, a social as well as physical reorientation. I suspect that many if not all the other neighborhoods were abandoned around this time. In any case, the site was entirely abandoned sometime in the early to middle part of the 16th century, so the increasingly hierarchical social relations implied by the dramatic expansion of Mound A were not in effect for very long.

Parchman Place was occupied for a relatively short period of time, roughly 200 years. Mound-building practices and town and neighborhood organization both suggest ongoing social negotiations at Parchman Place throughout its occupation, with a dramatic change in the relationships among corporate groups that made up the community during the latter half of the 15th century. Abandonment of the site in the first half of the 16th century can be understood as a continuation of these negotiations. Just as the inhabitants of Parchman Place moved here as a group in the early 14th century, they may have relocated in the 16th century to another one of the many sites in the northern Yazoo Basin.

Considering Scale in Community Studies

In Chapters 4 and 5, I presented excavation data from mound and residential contexts at Parchman Place, as well as spatial data based on the results of geophysical survey, mapping, excavation, coring, and surface collecting activities at the site. I argued that many principles of kinship, social structure, and patterns of residence among colonial period Southeastern Indian groups have relevance for understanding late prehistoric communities in the northern Yazoo Basin. Here, I draw on these data to address the following question: What was it like to live in a Mississippian community in the 14th- and 15th-century Yazoo Basin? Because community building takes place at multiple scales, I begin this section with the most intimate of spatial and social locations considered thus far, the neighborhood, and work my way through progressively broader loci of interaction, ending with a consideration of how the residents of Parchman Place located themselves physically and socially within a broadly shared Mississippian worldview.

Mississippian Neighborhoods at Parchman Place

I argued in Chapter 5 that neighborhoods at Parchman Place can be understood as house-groups akin to those of the colonial period Chickasaw and Choctaw. If we accept this analogy, we can make some informed speculations regarding the social makeup of neighborhoods. Most nearby historic Indian groups were matrilineal, marriage was typically clan-exogamous, and residence was matrilocal. If this was also the case for people at Parchman Place, then the core of the social group associated with each courtyard group was comprised of related women belonging to the same clan. Also resident were children of these women and their unmarried male relatives, members of the same matrilineage (and clan). Married men (with different clan affiliations) residing with their wives would be considered unrelated. In this scenario women likely had a lot of decision-making authority over day-to-day goings-on at the neighborhood level. This may be one context in which women (perhaps especially older women) exercised as much or more influence than men. As Sullivan (2006) and others have pointed out, Mississippian scholars have tended to privilege male leadership in their interpretations, though women had considerable political influence among many historic period groups (e.g., Perdue 1999).

Most house-groups at Parchman Place were organized around shared, central spaces—individual houses around courtyards, and house-groups around a central plaza. This suggests that community members valued, at least outwardly, shared practice and cooperative decision making. Courtyards, for instance, were shared workspaces where daily activities such as food processing, cooking, pottery making, and other types of craft production took place. They were also social spaces, places where people shared food and gossip, told stories, planned their days, and instructed their children and grandchildren. They were literally and figuratively the center of social life for small groups. As domestic spaces, they were designed and maintained by members of the house-group, who negotiated the terms of their use with one another. Though these negotiations were likely shaped by individual experiences based on gender, age, work, and status differences, the daily activities of people sharing courtyard space were necessarily intertwined (Robin 2002:257).

Neighborhood 3 may also represent a house-group, as the concept does not seem to have been tied to any particular arrangement of houses. However, the building of houses in rows with intervening corridors or paths does imply different possibilities for interaction at the local level. While courtyards and plazas are center spaces that promote the gathering of people, paths promote mobility. Snead et al. (2009:xv) tell us that "trails, paths, and roads are the manifestation of human movement throughout the landscape and are central to an understanding of movement at multiple scales." In addition to enabling physical movement by linking people with places and things, I suggest the path in Neighborhood 3 symbolizes the upward social mobility of those associated with it.

The orientation of the path is significant. Unlike other neighborhoods at Parchman, there is no evidence for shared central workspace that could serve as a focal point for social life. Indeed, the size and shape of the path suggest a different primary function. For those living in Neighborhood 3, the path spatially oriented and connected residents to an earthen monument that dwarfed all others on the site. Anyone walking the path had a direct line of sight west toward the mound summit and any activities taking place there. Significantly, the path also represents a social orientation, pointing to the locus of communal activity for people living in this part of the site. The focal point of people living here was not inward, toward courtyards, as with other social groups living at the site, but toward monumental architecture and the various meanings people associated with it.

A Mississippian Town in the Northern Yazoo

Changing the scale to look at the site as a whole, we can think of the community at Parchman Place as similar in many ways to historic-period Indian towns. Evidence for mound-building activities, spatial organization at the site level, and shared ceremonial practice supports this interpretation.

Radiocarbon dates indicate that mound building and residential activities first took place in the early part of the 14th century and that they were concurrent. Bowl-dominated ceramics assemblages associated with the earliest mound-building stages further suggest that activities related to the initiation of mound building involved large-scale feasting on the part of community members. Furthermore, differences in types of bowls used for serving in different contexts indicate that multiple distinct segments of the population took part in the feasting events. Use of nonlocal carinated and restricted bowls by one of these segments suggests that they had social ties to Mississippian groups in the southern Yazoo Basin or Natchez Bluffs region, perhaps based on kinship or trade relationships. Finally, inclusion of a bundle burial in the early stages of mound building can be interpreted as a founding event. Burials are rare at Parchman

Place, and this one happened at the very outset of the town's settlement. These bundled remains may well have been transported from elsewhere for burial at Parchman Place as part of the founding of the community. All of this suggests that mound building and the activities associated with it are related to the founding of a town *in a particular place.*

The arrangement of constituent parts of the community around a central space appears to have been an equally important component of the establishment of the Mississippian town at Parchman Place. Early dates from residential areas of the site indicate occupation in Neighborhoods 1 and 2 as well as the A-B swale at the beginning of Parchman Place's occupational history, and Neighborhoods 4 and 5 were probably founded at this time. Thus, from the beginning of Parchman Place's occupation, the overall site plan was analogous to the organization of historic period towns, wherein a number of distinct house-groups maintained a shared ceremonial practice (Lewis et al. 1998). House-groups occupied spatially discrete locations, but their arrangement referenced site features such as mounds and, particularly, the plaza. This "package deal" suggests that the town may have existed prior to relocating to this place. We know the identity of a town is *not* defined by physical space but rather is composed of individuals and their shared practice. However, acts of feasting and mound building, as well as the establishment of a plaza, suggest that *place making* is an important process of community-building at this scale.

If the analogy between Parchman Place and historic-period Indian towns can be relied on, then we can infer that the population at Parchman Place consisted of multiple lineages with different clan affiliations. While clans (and their more localized manifestations, house-groups) operated as autonomous social entities, we also know they had distinct and complementary ritual roles and were ranked with respect to one another, rankings that were continually negotiated (Knight 1990).

Evidence for shared ceremonial practice at Parchman Place comes in a number of forms. In addition to community-wide feasting events associated with the initiation of mound building, the practice of mound building was embedded within community values related to wholeness and balance, as evidenced by the inclusion of special substances such as ash, kaolin, and mussel shell in mound construction stages. Additionally, I interpret the layers of redeposited ash adjacent to Neighborhood 1 in terms of community and world renewal ceremonialism related to the proper treatment of old fire in preparation for the new fire. These interpretations suggest that individuals at Parchman Place participated in shared ritual action that was community-wide in scope.

Finally, manipulation of the site plan late in Parchman Place's history suggests that the inclusive ideals expressed by founding events and other ceremonial practices were not shared by everyone or that they were downplayed in certain situations. One group in particular distinguished themselves from others by building away from the plaza and orienting their neighborhood toward monumental architecture. This happened sometime *after* the town was founded and suggests that the cooperative ideals espoused in the rest of the site plan were not shared by everyone and that spatial practice could be used to manipulate or challenge these ideals. Abandonment of the site soon afterward suggests that this manipulation was not to everyone's liking.

Authority and Autonomy at Parchman Place

In Chapter 4, I presented data on mound excavations to investigate how acts of mound building and associated activities reveal ways that leadership and authority were enacted at Parchman Place. One hallmark of Mississippian societies is the presence of hereditary leaders whose association with mounds, and especially mound summits, is well established. As at many other Mississippian sites, leaders of the Parchman Place community were physically and symbolically elevated above others by virtue of their residence on mound summits. Certain aspects of the mound-building sequence provide clues about the long-term trajectory of changing power relations over the course of the 14th and 15th centuries. Others reveal a process of negotiation that accompanied mound building and the worldview within which these processes took place. In addition to the founding events discussed previously, mound building at Parchman Place included acts of mantle construction, building and dismantling of summit structures, veneering, truncation, and incorporation, all of which indicate some of the ways in which power and authority were enabled and constrained.

I have argued that individual mounds at Parchman Place were associated with particular subgroups of the population—in effect, that lineages associated with each house-group built and maintained their own mound. The builders of Mound E followed a repeating pattern of mantle construction alternating with the erection and use of summit structures. Destruction and burial of these structures after a period of use initiated the next episode of mantle construction. The repeated sequence of construction, use, destruction, and burial of mound top buildings on Mound E (and probably Mounds A and B) indicates a remarkable degree of continuity through time. In social terms, the rules regarding succession of lineage leaders were well established and happened smoothly throughout Parchman Place's early history. Additionally, early in the site's history, the comparable sizes of individual mounds suggests that leaders from several matrilineages may have shared power equally, or perhaps had different but equally esteemed forms of authority. This observation accords with Knight's (2010:365) claim that mound building, mound-summit activities, and burial practices are indicative of the "pervasive sharedness of authority" at Moundville. Only later did one resident lineage at Parchman Place assert a dominant leadership role by dramatically increasing the size of their mound.

While these circumstances indicate some ways leadership was enabled by mound-building traditions, others suggest that authority was also constrained by actions that emphasized community values related to wholeness and balance. In a number of instances, special substances such as white clay, ash, and mussel shell were incorporated into the mounds at Parchman Place, sometimes deposited on mound surfaces and sometimes as mound fills or facings. A thick layer of ash, for instance, was placed above the bundled burial of an adult male located at the base of Mound A. Loaded ash and white sediment was also used as fill in an intermediate mound stage revealed in the Mound E southwest slope trench. Mussel shell was found on the initial surface of Mound E and in a number of other locations. Kaolin, a white fine silty clay, was used (along with ash) in the final stage of mound construction, identified in the Mound E southwest slope trench, and was the main component (along with both ash and mussel shell) of the white veneer maintained for some time on an intermediate surface of Mound E.

Like the burning and burial of mound-top structures, the white mound veneer and other instances of special inclusions can be interpreted as ritually significant. For many southeastern Indian groups, the color white has associations with purification and renewal, as well as peace, wisdom, breath, sky, and purity (Hudson 1976:226; Knight 1986:678; Pursell

2004:147). The use of this color in the form of clay sediments, redeposited ash, and crushed mussel shell may therefore represent an extension of the burning/burial phenomenon common at Parchman Place and other Mississippian sites. However, when considering Mississippian beliefs about the nature of the cosmos, the substances themselves and their depositional relationships to one another take on additional significance. Drawing on Lankford's (2004, 2007) interpretation of Mississippian shell gorgets as cosmograms, we can understand each component of the white mound surface as referencing one of the three divisions of the Mississippian cosmos: ash, with similar connective and communicative properties as smoke (Jackson 2003), references a connection between This World and the Above World. Crushed mussel shell references the Beneath World. By extension, clay is the representation of This World. When gathered together, or bundled (Bradley 1990, 1998; Mills 2008; Pauketat 2013a, 2013b; Zedeño 2008), these substances were more than the sum of their parts. Mound building at Parchman Place was a matter of world building.

The unusual nature of the white veneer as well as its continued maintenance may correspond to some particularly trying event for the Parchman Place community, perhaps a contested succession. This circumstance was counteracted by an extended focus on community purification and renewal during which some members of the Parchman Place community emphasized values related to wholeness and balance between complementary parts. Furthermore, those responsible for the truncation of Mound E intentionally removed a portion of the mound summit to reexpose the surface, or, at the very least, halted their cutting activities once it was reached. This is undoubtedly significant and reinforces the importance of the white mound surface and the meanings it held for those who created it. If maintenance of a white mound surface can be interpreted in terms of corporate group values related to balance, wholeness, renewal, and autonomy, then reexposing the surface at a later date implies a desire on the part of those responsible to return to those values.

Northern Yazoo Basin Mississippians

Until considerably more work is done in the northern Yazoo Basin, interpretations regarding how the residents of Parchman Place interacted with those of nearby towns must remain largely speculative. With that caveat,

I offer some preliminary suppositions. According to Phillips (1970), the Parchman phase consists of some 15 sites that are roughly contemporary, based on surface-collected ceramics assemblages. Unfortunately, for many sites, the early surface collections upon which the phase was defined still represent the total of our archaeological information on them. Exceptions include Wilsford (Connaway 1984a); Carson (Butz 2015; Carpenter 2013; Connaway n.d.; James 2010, 2015; Lansdell 2009, McLeod 2015; Mehta 2015; Mehta et al. 2012); West (Buchner 1996, 2002; Dye and Buchner 1998); Salomon (Connaway 1983; Johnson et al. 2016); and Barbee (Walling and Chapman 1999). Here I consider Parchman Place's relationship to two of these—Salomon, located approximately 6.5 km to the northeast, and Carson, roughly 10.5 km to the southwest.

LMS records indicate that Salomon and Parchman Place are structurally similar. Salomon had four large earthen platform mounds and a number of smaller mounds surrounding a plaza. Additionally, LMS surveyors reported house sites in the plowed field, which Brown (1978) and Connaway (1983) also observed, describing the plaza as circled by large concentrations of daub. Limited test excavations conducted by UM in 2014 indicate that Mound A at Salomon is a Mississippi period construction atop a Woodland period midden (Johnson et al. 2016). A radiocarbon sample from mound fill returned a 13th-century date, surprisingly early for a Parchman phase site. Preliminary ceramics analyses suggest that the Mississippian component predates the earliest occupation at Parchman Place (Jay Johnson, personal communication 2015). All of this begins to answer a long-standing question about the contemporaneity of closely spaced Parchman phase sites in the northern Yazoo. Rather than contemporaneous occupations, Salomon and Parchman Place may have been occupied sequentially. I suggest that the structural similarities between the two sites, their physical proximity, and their sequential ceramics assemblages and radiocarbon dates indicate a population shift from Salomon to Parchman Place around the beginning of the 14th century, a situation perhaps analogous to the wholesale relocation of post-Mississippian towns. This pattern of movement may have been typical for the region, given the number of similarly sized adjacent sites.

While Salomon is structurally similar to Parchman Place, Carson is categorically different. The largest site in the region by an order of magnitude, the Carson site stretches for more than a mile and once had seven large earthen mounds, 80 smaller house mounds, and an earthen embankment. Unlike many Parchman phase sites, Carson was occupied throughout the Mississippi period, beginning around AD 1200 or a little earlier. At that time, people living at Carson were interacting with Mississippian people from the American Bottom, as evidenced by a Cahokia microlith technology utilizing Burlington chert from eastern Missouri, as well as semi-subterranean architecture (unique in the Yazoo Basin) and pottery indicative of the late Lohmann phase in the American Bottom (Butz 2015; Johnson 1987; Johnson and Connaway 2019; Lansdell 2009; McLeod 2015). Mound building at Carson also began around this time (Butz 2015; Carpenter 2013; Mehta et al. 2012; Mehta 2015). This interaction sparked significant social change in the region, though there is little to no evidence of Cahokia contact in the northern Yazoo Basin outside of Carson (but see Williams and Brain 1983:375–376; 409–412). Carson must certainly figure in a regional understanding of Parchman phase sites; the question is how.

One clue may come from off-mound investigations at Carson, especially from the area surrounding Mound A once enclosed by an earthen embankment. In this part of the site, archaeologists have discovered houses, palisade walls, large storage pits, and evidence of elaborate mortuary ritual in the form of charnal houses and communal burial pits (James 2010, 2015; Johnson and Connaway 2019; McLeod 2015). Mortuary facilities stratigraphically superimpose earlier domestic features and are considered to date to the late Mississippi period, after AD 1400. James (2010) interpreted the secondary burial of individuals at Carson as emphasizing the social importance of corporate groups, rather than some other form of social differentiation (based on status, age, etc.). Given the relative lack of burials found at Parchman Place, the elaborate mortuary program at Carson may indicate one way in which the sites were connected. If people from the surrounding region were buried at Carson, that would indicate significant social integration and interaction among late Mississippian communities in the northern Yazoo.

Living in the Mississippian World

There is good evidence that Mississippian people in the northern Yazoo Basin were aware of and connected with the greater Mississippian world. Lithic tools and raw materials, pottery, and architectural styles link the early Mississippian population at Carson with people from the American

Bottom. Carinated and restricted bowls found in 14th-century contexts at Parchman Place indicate a connection with Mississippian centers in the southern Yazoo. And decorative styles on pottery common in the northeast Arkansas and the Memphis region became increasingly prevalent in Parchman phase assemblages during the 15th century. These social connections can be considered both "real" and "ideological," in the sense that the people in question shared not only material goods and practices but also a worldview within which their actions were meaningful.

Mound building was an important way that people at Parchman Place materialized their views about leadership, the community, and the Mississippian cosmos. Special substances such as ash, shell, and clay "recreated" the cosmos locally, in effect, *locating* the community within the cosmos. Acts of cleaning, burning, and burial are all related to ideas about cleansing, purification, and renewal in Southeastern Indian belief systems (Hudson 1976:126; Knight 1986:687). Additionally, smoke has sentient properties for Southeastern people, including the ability to communicate between the human and spirit worlds (Jackson 2003:74). Large quantities of smoke would be a significant, if fleeting, by-product of the firing of mound top buildings and can be understood as an effort to communicate with Above World spirits about earthly happenings. Production of smoke therefore may have been as important as the cleansing destruction and burial of carbonized and fired structural remains.

Excavations from Neighborhood 1 suggest that ritual action in off-mound areas is also relevant for understanding the relationship between local communities and the Mississippian cosmos. In Chapter 5 I described a series of ash deposits containing an abundance of charcoal, food remains, and pottery. This ash was clearly redeposited, not the result of burning in place. I interpreted these deposits as the remains of one or more cooking and eating events, possibly from individual household cooking hearths or from the remains of one or more larger gatherings. However, given the importance of ash generally and practices related to its disposal in particular, the act of disposing of large quantities of ash in a designated location is as significant or more so than the remains of the food-related activities contained within it.

The ash deposits in Neighborhood 1 recall historic and modern accounts related to extinguishing the old fire in preparation for the renewal of sacred fire during the annual Busk or Green Corn Ceremony (e.g., Jackson 2003:198). I suggest that these remains represent the remains of sacred fire—that is, the hearth scrapings of households and other contexts within the community, gathered and deposited together in a specially designated location, perhaps analogous to the "ash heaps" shown on a number of Swanton's (1928c) maps of Muskogee Creek square grounds in Oklahoma. From this conceptual perspective, a deposit that archaeologists might typically consider only as incidental "trash" takes on far greater significance (Colwell-Chanthaphonh and Ferguson 2006). This was the first step in an annual rite intended, literally, to restore balance within the community and within the world.

Conclusions

There are many questions yet to be answered regarding Mississippian communities in the northern Yazoo Basin. What were their origins? What was the nature of interactions among them? And ultimately, what happened to them in the 16th century, when we lose their traces in the archaeological record? One tangible result of this study, then, is that it offers a refinement of the late Mississippi period chronology of the surrounding region, a basis on which to build our understanding of the relationships, spatial, chronological, and social, of the Mississippian people who lived here. Beyond that, I offer an approach to Mississippian community studies based on a consideration of the material practices of placemaking at a single site and an examination of the fit between those practices and what we know of the social organization, beliefs, ritual, and everyday practices of Mississippian people and their Muskogean-speaking descendants. How successful I have been is for the reader to determine. For my part, I believe it to be a powerful combination of theory and method. This approach allows us to move beyond using geophysical data simply to reconstruct spatial patterns, and to consider more fully what those spatial patterns can tell us about the identities, daily interactions, and relationships of the people who lived in those houses, neighborhoods, and towns. It allows us to understand atypical depositional practices in the context of a worldview within which substances can effect social change, and in which wholeness and balance are critically important and constantly sought. Not least of all, it allows us to consider the ways in which cross-cutting social identities were brought to bear on the histories of particular Mississippian communities, and ultimately, to rethink our essentializing characterizations of these communities as hierarchical on the one hand and unstable or prone to fission on the other. Though hierarchy may characterize Mississippian societies, equally characteristic are those tendencies toward mediating and subverting hierarchy that were guided by an ethos of autonomy inherent in the structure of Mississippian towns. Though Mississippian polities may have been vulnerable to collapse, Mississippian towns could and did persist beyond the rise and fall of polities, just as the communities, towns, and nations of Mississippian descendants persist in the face of relentless colonialism. This study has considered a single Mississippian community residing in a single place, but the approach I have taken invites us to consider the ways Mississippian people everywhere *made* and *remade* their communities in the image of a whole and balanced world.

References Cited

Anderson, David G.
1994   *The Savannah River Chiefdoms: Political Change in the Late Prehistoric Southeast*. University of Alabama Press, Tuscaloosa.

Appadurai, Arjun
1981   Gastro-politics in Hindu South Asia. *American Ethnologist* 8(3):494–511.

Ashmore, Wendy, and A. Bernard Knapp
1999   *Archaeologies of Landscape: Contemporary Perspectives*. Blackwell Publishers, Oxford.

Baires, Sarah E., and Melissa R. Baltus
2017   Matter, Places, and Persons in Cahokian Depositional Acts. *Journal of Archaeological Method and Theory* 24:974–997.

Baltus, Melissa R.
2018   Vessels of Change: Everyday Relationality in the Rise and Fall of Cahokia. In *Relational Engagements of the Indigenous Americas: Alterity, Ontology, and Shifting Paradigms*, edited by Melissa R. Baltus and Sarah E. Baires, pp. 63–85. Lexington Books, Lanham, Maryland.

Baltus, Melissa R., and Sarah E. Baires
2012   Elements of Ancient Power in the Cahokian World. *Journal of Social Archaeology* 12(2):167–192.

2016   *Relational Engagements of the Indigenous Americas: Alterity, Ontology, and Shifting Paradigms*. Lexington Books, Lanham, Maryland.

Barth, Fredrik
1969   *Ethnic Groups and Boundaries: The Social Organization of Culture Difference*. Little Brown and Company, Boston.

Belmont, John S.
1961   The Peabody Excavations Coahoma County, Mississippi 1901–1902. Unpublished Bachelor's thesis, Department of Anthropology, Harvard University, Cambridge, Massachusetts.

Bennett, Jane
2010   *Vibrant Matter: A Political Ecology of Things*. Duke University Press, Durham, North Carolina.

Beverley, Robert

1705   *The History and Present State of Virginia, in Four Parts*. R. Parker, London.

Blitz, John H.

1993a   *Ancient Chiefdoms of the Tombigbee*. University of Alabama Press, Tuscaloosa.

1993b   Big Pots for Big Shots: Feasting and Storage in a Mississippian Community. *American Antiquity* 58(1):80–96.

1999   Mississippian Chiefdoms and the Fission-Fusion Process. *American Antiquity* 64(4):577–592.

2010   New Perspectives in Mississippian Archaeology. *Journal of Archaeological Research* 18(1):1–39.

Blitz, John H., and Patrick Livingood

2004   Sociopolitical Implications of Mississippian Mound Volume. *American Antiquity* 69(2):291–301.

Boudreaux, Edmond A.

2007   *The Archaeology of Town Creek*. University of Alabama Press, Tuscaloosa.

Bourdieu, Pierre

1977   *Outline of a Theory of Practice*. Cambridge University Press, Cambridge.

Bradley, Richard

1990   *The Passage of Arms: An Archaeological Analysis of Prehistoric Hoards and Votive Deposits*. Cambridge University Press, Cambridge.

1998   *The Significance of Monuments: On the Shaping of Human Experience in the Neolithic and Bronze Age*. Routledge, London.

Brain, Jeffrey P.

1978   Late Prehistoric Settlement Patterning in the Yazoo Basin and Natchez Bluffs Regions of the Lower Mississippi Valley. In *Mississippian Settlement Patterns*, edited by Bruce D. Smith, pp. 331–368. Academic Press, New York.

1988   *Tunica Archaeology*. Harvard University Press, Cambridge, Massachusetts.

1989   *Winterville: Late Prehistoric Culture Contact in the Lower Mississippi Valley*. Mississippi Department of Archives and History, Jackson.

Brain, Jeffrey P., Ian W. Brown, and Vincas P. Steponaitis

1995   Archaeology of the Natchez Bluffs. Manuscript on file, Research Laboratories of Archaeology, University of North Carolina, Chapel Hill.

Braun, David P.

1980   Experimental Interpretation of Ceramic Vessel Use on the Basis of Rim and Neck Formal Attributes. In *The Navajo Project*, edited by D. C. Fiero, R. W. Munson, M. T. McClain, S. M. Wilson, and A. H. Zier, pp. 171–231. Research Paper 11. Museum of North Arizona, Flagstaff.

1983   Pots as Tools. In *Archaeological Hammers and Theories*, edited by J. A. Moore and A. S. Keene, pp. 107–134. Academic Press, New York.

Brennan, Tamira K. (editor)

2016   Main Street Mound: A Ridgetop Monument at the East St. Louis Mound Complex. With contributions by Steven L. Boles, Tamira K. Brennan, Kristin M. Hedman, Michael F. Kolb, and Lenna M. Nash. Research Report 36. Illinois State Archaeological Survey Prairie Research Institute, University of Illinois at Urbana-Champaign.

Briggs, Rachel V.

2015   The Hominy Foodway of the Historic Native Eastern Woodlands. *Native South* 8:112–146.

2016   The Civil Cooking Pot: Hominy and the Mississippian Standard Jar in the Black Warrior Valley, Alabama. *American Antiquity* 81(2):316–332.

Brightman, Robert A., and Pamela S. Wallace

2004   Chickasaw. In *Southeast*, edited by Raymond D. Fogelson, pp. 478–495. Handbook of North American Indians, Vol. 14, William C. Sturtevant, general editor, Smithsonian Institution, Washington, DC.

Bronk Ramsay, Christopher

2013   OxCal v4.2.3. http//c14.arch.ox.ac.uk, accessed May 24, 2019.

Brown, Calvin S.

1926   *Archeology of Mississippi.* Mississippi Geological Survey, University, Mississippi.

Brown, Ian

1978   An Archaeological Survey of Mississippi Period Sites in Coahoma County Mississippi. Final Report submitted to Cottonlandia Museum, Greenwood, Mississippi. Peabody Museum of Archaeology and Ethnology, Harvard University, Cambridge, Massachusetts.

2008   Culture Contact along the I-69 Corridor: Protohistoric and Historic Use of the Northern Yazoo Basin, Mississippi. In *Time's River: Archaeological Syntheses from the Lower Mississippi River Valley*, edited by Evan Peacock and Janet Rafferty, pp. 357–394. University of Alabama Press, Tuscaloosa.

Brown, James A.

2010   Cosmological Layouts of Secondary Burials as Political Instruments. In *Mississippian Mortuary Practices: Beyond Hierarchy and the Representationist Perspective*, edited by Lynne P. Sullivan and Robert C. Mainfort Jr., pp. 30–53. University Press of Florida, Gainesville.

Brown, Teresa Lynn

2005   *Ceramic Variability within the Parkin Phase: A Whole Vessel Metric Analysis from Northeast Arkansas.* Arkansas Archeological Survey, Fayetteville.

Buchanan, Meghan E., and B. Jacob Skousen (editors)

2015   *Tracing the Relational: The Archaeology of Worlds, Spirits, and Temporalities.* University of Utah Press, Salt Lake City.

Buchner, C. Andrew

1996   Mound A Excavations at the West Mounds Site, Tunica County, Mississippi. In *Mounds, Embankments, and Ceremonialism in the* Midsouth, edited by Robert C. Mainfort and Richard Walling, pp. 78–86. Arkansas Archaeological Survey Research Series No. 46, Fayetteville.

2002   The West Mounds Chiefdom and Late Protohistoric Ethnicity in Tunica County, Mississippi. In *Ethnicity in Archaeology*. Proceedings of the 21st

Mid-South Archaeological Conference. Panamerican Consultants, Special Publication No. 2, Memphis, Tennessee.

Butz, Samuel Henri
2015   Excavations of Mound B: A Ridge-top Mound at the Carson Site, A Mississippian Mound Center in the Northern Yazoo Basin. Unpublished Master's thesis, Department of Sociology and Anthropology, University of Mississippi, Oxford.

Canuto, Marcello A., and Jason Yaeger
2000   *The Archaeology of Communities: A New World Perspective.* Routledge, London.

Carpenter, Erika
2013   Examination of Architectural Features on Mound C of the Carson Mound Group, Coahoma County, Mississippi. Unpublished Master's thesis, Department of Sociology and Anthropology, University of Mississippi, Oxford.

Charles, Douglas K., Julieann Van Nest, and Jane E. Buikstra
2004   From the Earth: Minerals and Meaning in the Hopewellian World. In *Soils, Stones, and Symbols: Cultural Perceptions of the Mineral World,* edited by Nicole Boivin and Mary A. Owoc, pp. 43–70. Cavendish, Portland, Oregon.

Childress, Mitchell R.
1992   Mortuary Vessels and Comparative Ceramic Analysis: An Example from the Chucalissa Site. *Southeastern Archaeology* 11:31–50.

Cobb, Charles
2003   Mississippian Chiefdoms: How Complex? *Annual Review of Anthropology* 32:63–84.

Colwell-Chanthaphonh, Chip, and T. J. Ferguson
2006   Memory Pieces and Footprints: Multivocality and the Meanings of Ancient Times and Ancestral Places among the Zuni and Hopi. *American Anthropologist* 108(1):148–162.

Connaway, John M.
1983   National Register of Historic Places Inventory—Nomination Form for the Salomon Site (22-Co-504). Mississippi Department of Archives and History, Jackson.
1984a   *The Wilsford Site (22-Co-516) Coahoma County, Mississippi: A Late Mississippi Period Settlement in the Northern Yazoo Basin of Mississippi.* Mississippi Department of Archives and History, Jackson.
1984b   Parchman 4-7-84. Field notes on file, Mississippi Department of Archives and History, Clarksdale, Mississippi.
1985   Recent Radiocarbon Date Announcement. In *Mississippi Archaeological Association Newsletter.* Mississippi Archaeological Association, Jackson, Mississippi.
n.d.   127 Years of Archaeological Research at the Carson Mounds, 22-CO-518, Coahoma County, Mississippi: A Summary. Manuscript on file with Mississippi Department of Archives and History, Clarksdale.

Connaway, John M., and Samuel O. McGahey
1970   Archaeological Survey and Salvage in the Yazoo-Mississippi Delta and in Hinds County: November 1, 1968–December 31, 1969. Mississippi Archaeological Survey, Preliminary Report, Mississippi Department of Archives and History, Jackson.

Conyers, Lawrence B.
2010   Ground-Penetrating Radar for Anthropological Research. *Antiquity* 84:175–184.

Conyers, Lawrence B., and Juerg Leckebusch
2010   Geoarchaeology Research Agendas for the Future: Some Ground-Penetrating Radar Examples. *Archaeological Prospection* 17:117–123.

Crawford, Jessica
2015   Parchman Site and My Road to the Archaeological Conservancy. The Archaeological Conservancy. Electronic document, https://www.archaeologicalconservancy.org/parchman/, accessed August 26, 2018.

Cruciotti, Eric, Rita Fisher-Caroll, Robert C. Mainfort, Charles H. McNutt, and David H. Dye
2006   An Experiment in Ceramic Description: Upper Nodena. *Southeastern Archaeology* 25(1):78–88.

Crumley, Carole L.
1995   Heterarchy and the Analysis of Complex Societies. In *Heterarchy and the Analysis of Complex Societies*, edited by Robert M. Ehrenreich, Carole L. Crumley, and Janet E. Levy. Archaeological Papers of the American Anthropological Association no. 6, pp. 1–5. American Anthropological Association, Washington, DC.

2005   Remember How to Organize: Heterarchy Across Disciplines. In *Nonlinear Models for Archaeology and Anthropology*, edited by Christopher S. Beekman and William S. Baden, pp. 35–50. Ashgate Press, Aldershot, United Kingdom.

Dalan, Rinita A., George R. Holley, William I. Woods, Harold W. Watters Jr., and John A. Koepke
2003   *Envisioning Cahokia: A Landscape Perspective.* Northern Illinois University Press, DeKalb.

David, Bruno, and Julian Thomas (editors)
2008   *Handbook of Landscape Archaeology.* Left Coast Press, Walnut Creek, California.

Díaz-Andreu, Margarita, Sam Lucy, Staša Babiæ, and David N. Edwards
2005   *The Archaeology of Identity: Approaches to Gender, Age, Status, Ethnicity and Religion.* Routledge, New York.

Diaz-Granados, Carol, Jan Simek, George Sabo III, and Mark Wagner
2018   *Transforming the Landscape: Rock Art and the Mississippian Cosmos.* Oxbow Books, Oxford.

Dietler, Michael, and Brian Hayden (editors)
2001   *Feasts: Archaeological and Ethnographic Perspectives on Food, Politics, and Power.* Smithsonian Institution Press, Washington, DC.

Dobres, Marcia-Anne
2000   *Technology and Social Agency: Outlining a Practice Framework for Archaeology.* Blackwell Publishers, Oxford.

Dunnell, Robert C.
1985   Archaeological Survey in the Lower Mississippi Alluvial Valley, 1940–1947: A Landmark Study in American Archaeology. *American Antiquity* 50(2):297–300.

Dye, David H.
1993   Reconstruction of the de Soto Expedition Route in Arkansas: The Mississippi Alluvial Plain. In *The Expedition of Hernando de Soto West of the Mississippi, 1541–1543: Proceedings of the de Soto Symposia, 1988 and 1990,* edited by Gloria A. Young and Michael P. Hoffman, pp. 36–57. University of Arkansas Press, Fayetteville.

Dye, David H., and Andrew Buchner
1998   Preliminary Archaeological Investigations of the West Mounds (22-Tu-520), Tunica County, Mississippi. *Mississippi Archaeology* 23(2):64–75.

Dye, David H, and Cheryl Anne Cox (editors)
1990   *Towns and Temples along the Mississippi.* University of Alabama Press, Tuscaloosa.

Ethridge, Robbie
2003   *Creek Country: The Creek Indians and Their World.* University of North Carolina Press, Chapel Hill.

Finger, Michael
2003   An Investigation of Parchman Place Mounds Reveals the Expected and the Unexpected. *American Archaeology* 7(1):20–25.

Fisk, Harold N.
1944   *Geological Investigation of the Alluvial Valley of the Lower Mississippi River.* U.S. Army Corps of Engineers, Mississippi River Commission Publication, No. 52, Vicksburg, Mississippi.

Fogel, Aaron S.
2005   Investigating a Mississippian Mound Top Structure Utilizing Archaeogeophysics and Archaeology: A Three-Dimensional Application of Down-Hole Magnetic Susceptibility Technology. Unpublished Master's thesis, Department of Sociology and Anthropology, University of Mississippi, University.

Fowler, Chris
2013   *The Emergent Past: A Relational Realist Archaeology of Early Bronze Age Mortuary Practices.* Oxford University Press, Oxford.

Galloway, Patricia, and Clara Sue Kidwell
2004   Choctaw in the East. In *Southeast* edited by Raymond Fogelson, pp. 499–519. Handbook of North American Indians, William C. Sturtevant, general editor, Smithsonian Institution, Washington, DC.

Giddens, Anthony

1979 *Central Problems in Social Theory: Action, Structure, and Contradiction in Social Analysis*. University of California Press, Berkeley.

1984 *The Constitution of Society: Introduction of the Theory of Structuration*. University of California Press, Berkeley.

Haag, William

1950 Field notes and map on file. Mississippi Site File, Mississippi Department of Archives and History, Jackson.

Haley, Bryan S.

2014 The Big Picture at Hollywood: Geophysical and Archaeological Investigations at a Mississippian Mound Center. *Archaeological Prospection* 21:39–47.

Hall, Robert

1997 *An Archaeology of the Soul: North American Indian Belief and Ritual*. University of Illinois Press, Urbana.

Hally, David J.

1972 The Plaquemine and Mississippian Occupations of the Upper Tensas Basin, Louisiana. Unpublished PhD dissertation. Department of Anthropology, Harvard University, Cambridge.

1983a The Interpretive Potential of Pottery from Domestic Contexts. *Midcontinental Journal of Archaeology* 8(2):163–196.

1983b Use Alteration of Pottery Vessel Surfaces: An Important Source of Evidence in the Identification of Vessel Function. *North American Archaeologist* 4(1):3–26.

1984 Vessel Assemblages and Food Habits: A Comparison of Two Aboriginal Southeastern Vessel Assemblages. *Southeastern Archaeology* 31:46–64.

1986 The Identification of Vessel Function: A Case Study from Northwest Georgia. *American Antiquity* 51(2):267–295.

1993 The Territorial Size of Mississippian Chiefdoms. In *Archaeology of Eastern North America: Papers in Honor of Stephen Williams*, edited by James B. Stoltman, pp. 143–168. Mississippi Department of Archives and History Archaeological Report 25. Mississippi Department of Archives and History, Jackson.

1996 Platform-Mound Construction and the Instability of Mississippian Chiefdoms. In *Political Structure and Change in the Prehistoric Southeastern United States*, edited by John F. Scarry, pp. 92–127. University Press of Florida, Gainesville.

1999 The Settlement Pattern of Mississippian Chiefdoms in Northern Georgia. In *Settlement Pattern Studies in the Americas: Fifty Years Since Virú*, edited by Brian R. Billman and Gary M. Feinman, pp. 96–115. Smithsonian Institution Press, Washington, DC.

2008 *King: The Social Archaeology of a Late Mississippian Town in Northwestern Georgia*. University of Alabama Press, Tuscaloosa.

Harrington, Mark Raymond

1921 Religion and Ceremonies of the Lenape. Indian Notes and Monographs, Miscellaneous, No. 19. Museum of the American Indian, New York.

Harris, Oliver J. T.

2013 Relational Communities in Prehistoric Britain. In *Relational Archaeologies: Humans, Animals, Things*, edited by Christopher Watts, pp. 173–189. Routledge, London.

2014 (Re)assembling Communities. *Journal of Archaeological Method and Theory* 21:76–97.

Harrison-Buck, Eleanor, and Julia A. Hendon (editors)

2018 *Relational Identities and Other-Than-Human Agency in Archaeology.* University Press of Colorado, Louisville.

Henrickson, Elizabeth R., and M. McDonald

1983 Ceramic Form and Function: An Ethnographic Search and an Archaeological Application. *American Anthropologist* 85(3):630–643.

House, John H.

1991 Monitoring Mississippian Dynamics: Time, Settlement and Ceramic Variation in the Kent Phase, Eastern Arkansas. Unpublished PhD dissertation. Department of Anthropology, Southern Illinois University, Carbondale.

1993 Dating the Kent Phase. *Southeastern Archaeology* 12:21–32.

1996 East-Central Arkansas. In *Prehistory of the Central Mississippi Valley*, edited by Charles H. McNutt, pp. 137–154. University of Alabama Press, Tuscaloosa.

Hudson, Charles M.

1976 *The Southeastern Indians.* University of Tennessee Press, Knoxville.

1997 *Knights of Spain, Warriors of the Sun: Hernando De Soto and the South's Ancient Chiefdoms.* University of Georgia Press, Athens.

Hudson, Charles M., Marvin T. Smith, and Chester B. DePratter

1990 The Hernando de Soto Expedition: From Mabila to the Mississippi River. In *Towns and Temples along the Mississippi*, edited by David H. Dye and Cheryl Anne Cox, pp. 181–207. University of Alabama Press, Tuscaloosa.

Hunt, Elizabeth Kay

2017 Austin (22TU549): Mississippian Emergence in the Northern Yazoo Basin. Unpublished Master's thesis, Department of Anthropology and Sociology, University of Southern Mississippi, Hattiesburg.

Ingold, Tim

2007 Materials Against Materiality. *Archaeological Dialogues* 14(1):1–16.

Jackson, Jason Baird

2003 *Yuchi Ceremonial Life: Performance, Meaning, and Tradition in a Contemporary American Indian Community.* University of Nebraska Press, Lincoln.

James, Jenna

2010 Modeling Mortuary Behavior Based on Secondary Burial Data from Carson Mound Group, Coahoma County, Mississippi. Unpublished Master's thesis, Department of Anthropology, University of Mississippi, Oxford.

2012   Parchman Infant Osteological Analysis. Notes on file at Research Laboratories of Archaeology, University of North Carolina, Chapel Hill.

2015   Social Houses at Carson Mounds, 22-CO-518, as Evidenced by Dental Morphological Analysis. Unpublished PhD dissertation, Department of Anthropology, University of Alabama, Tuscaloosa.

Johnson, Jay K.

1987   Cahokia Core Technology in Mississippi: The View from the South. In *The Organization of Core Technology*, edited by Jay K. Johnson and Carol A. Morrow, pp. 187–205. Westview Press, London.

2003   Cyclic Changes in the Structural Organization of Mississippian Mound Sites in the Yazoo Basin. Paper presented at the 20th Annual Visiting Scholar Conference, Center for Archaeological Investigations, Southern Illinois University, Carbondale.

2008   Archaeological Remote Sensing Research in the Yazoo Basin: A History and Evaluation. In *Time's River: Archaeological Syntheses from the Lower Mississippi River Valley,* edited by Janet Rafferty and Evan Peacock, pp. 344–356. University of Alabama Press, Tuscaloosa.

Johnson, Jay K., and John M. Connaway

2019   Carson and Cahokia. In *Cahokia in Context: Hegemony and Diaspora,* edited by Charles H. McNutt and Ryan M. Parish. University Press of Florida, Gainesville.

Johnson, Jay K., and Bryan S. Haley

2006   A Cost-Benefit Analysis of Remote Sensing Applications in Cultural Resource Management Archaeology. In *Remote Sensing in Archaeology: An Explicitly North American Perspective,* edited by Jay K Johnson, pp. 33–46. University of Alabama Press, Tuscaloosa.

Johnson, Jay K., Bryan S. Haley, Stephen Harris, Erika Carpenter, and Travis Cureton

2016   Mississippi Mound Trail, Northern Region: Phase II Investigations. Report submitted to Mississippi Department of Archives and History, Jackson.

Jones, Siân

1997   *The Archaeology of Ethnicity: Reconstructing Identities in the Past and Present.* Routledge, London.

Kassabaum, Megan C.

2014   Feasting and Communal Ritual in the Lower Mississippi Valley, AD 700–1000. Unpublished PhD dissertation. Department of Anthropology, University of North Carolina, Chapel Hill.

2019   Early Platforms, Early Plazas: Exploring the Precursors to Mississippian Mound-and-Plaza Centers. *Journal of Archaeological Research* 27:187–247.

Kidder, Tristram R.

1998   Mississippi Period Mound Groups and Communities in the Lower Mississippi Valley. In *Mississippian Towns and Sacred Spaces: Searching for an Architectural Grammar,* edited by R. Barry Lewis and Charles Stout, pp. 123–150. University of Alabama Press, Tuscaloosa.

2004   Plazas as Architecture: An Example from the Raffman Site, Northeast Louisiana. *American Antiquity* 69(3):514–532.

King, Adam

2003   *Etowah: The Political History of a Chiefdom Capital.* University of Alabama Press, Tuscaloosa.

2006   The Historic Period Transformation of Mississippian Societies. In *Light on the Path: The Anthropology and History of the Southeastern Indians*, edited by Thomas J. Pluckhahn and Robbie Ethridge, pp. 179–195. University of Alabama Press, Tuscaloosa.

2007   *Southeastern Ceremonial Complex: Chronology, Content, Context.* University of Alabama Press, Tuscaloosa.

Knight, Vernon James, Jr.

1981   Mississippian Ritual. Unpublished PhD dissertation. Department of Anthropology, University of Florida, Gainesville.

1986   The Institutional Organization of Mississippian Religion. *American Antiquity* 51(4):675–687.

1989   Symbolism of Mississippian Mounds. In *Powhatan's Mantle: Indians in the Colonial Southeast*, edited by Peter H. Wood, Gregory A. Waselkov and M. Thomas Hatley, pp. 279–291. University of Nebraska Press, Lincoln.

1990   Social Organization and the Evolution of Hierarchy in Southeastern Chiefdoms. *Journal of Anthropological Research* 46(1):1–23.

1994   The Formation of the Creeks. In *The Forgotten Centuries: Indians and Europeans in the American South, 1521–1704*, edited by Charles Hudson and Carmen Chaves Tessar, pp. 373–392. University of Georgia Press, Athens.

1998   Moundville as a Diagramatic Center. In *Archaeology of the Moundville Chiefdom*, edited by Vernon James Knight Jr., and Vincas P. Steponaitis, pp. 44–62. Smithsonian Institution Press, Washington, DC.

2001   Feasting and the Emergence of Mound Ceremonialism in Eastern North America. In *Feasts: Archaeological and Ethnographic Perspectives on Food, Politics, and Power*, edited by Michael Dietler and Brian Hayden, pp. 311–333. Smithsonian Institution Press, Washington, DC.

2010   *Mound Excavations at Moundville: Architecture, Elites, and Social Order.* University of Alabama Press, Tuscaloosa.

2013   *Iconographic Method in New World Prehistory.* Cambridge University Press, Cambridge.

2016   Social Archaeology of Monumental Spaces at Moundville. In *Rethinking Moundville and Its Hinterland*, edited by Vincas P. Steponaitis and C. Margaret Scarry, pp. 23–43. University Press of Florida, Gainesville.

2018   Puzzles of Creek Social Organization in the Eighteenth and Nineteenth Centuries. *Ethnohistory* 65(3):373–389.

Knight, Vernon J, and Vincas P. Steponaitis

1998   *Archaeology of the Moundville Chiefdom.* Smithsonian Institution Press, Washington, DC.

Kowalski, Jessica A.

2019   Hierarchy, Scale, and Complexity: Arcola Mounds (22WS500) Mississippian Ceremonialism in the Southern Yazoo Basin. Unpublished PhD dissertation, Department of Anthropology, University of Alabama, Tuscaloosa.

Kvamme, Kenneth L.

2003   Geophysical Surveys as Landscape Archaeology. *American Antiquity* 68(3):435–457.

Lankford, George E.

2004   World on a String: Some Cosmological Components of the Southeastern Ceremonial Complex. In *Hero, Hawk, and Open Hand: American Indian Art of the Midwest and South*, edited by Richard F. Townsend and Robert V. Sharp, pp. 207–218. Art Institute of Chicago in Association with Yale University Press, New Haven, Connecticut.

2007   Some Cosmological Motifs in the Southeastern Ceremonial Complex. In *Ancient Objects and Sacred Realms: Interpretations of Mississippian Iconography*, edited by F. Kent Riley, III, and James Garber, pp. 8–38. University of Texas Press, Austin.

Lankford, George E., F. Kent Reilly III, and James F. Garber (editors)

2011   *Visualizing the Sacred: Cosmic Visions, Regionalism, and the Art of the Mississippian World*. University of Texas Press, Austin.

Lansdell, Brent

2009   A Chronological Assessment of the Carson Mound Group Stovall, Mississippi. Unpublished Master's thesis. Department of Sociology and Anthropology, University of Mississippi, Oxford.

Latour, Bruno

1993   We Have Never Been Modern. Harvard University Press, Cambridge, Massachusetts.

2005   Reassembling the Social: An Introduction to Actor-Network Theory. Oxford University Press, Oxford.

Lewis, R. Barry, and Charles B. Stout

1998   *Mississippian Towns and Sacred Spaces: Searching for an Architectural Grammar*. University of Alabama Press, Tuscaloosa.

Lewis, R. Barry, Charles Stout, and Cameron B. Wesson

1998   The Design of Mississippian Towns. In *Mississippian Towns and Sacred Spaces: Searching for an Architectural Grammar*, edited by R. Barry Lewis and Charles B. Stout, pp. 1–21. University of Alabama Press, Tuscaloosa.

Lindauer, Owen, and John H. Blitz

1997   Higher Ground: The Archaeology of North American Platform Mounds. *Journal of Archaeological Research* 5(2):169–207.

Lowe, Kelsey M.

2006   Evaluating Paleochannels Using Interdisciplinary Methods in the Yazoo Basin of Northwest Mississippi. *Digital Discovery: Exploring New Frontiers in Human Heritage*. Proceedings of the 34th Conference on Computer Applications and Quantitative Methods in Archaeology (CAA), Fargo, North Dakota.

Lowe, Kelsey M., and Aaron S. Fogel

2007a Geophysical Anomaly Testing with Down-Hole Magnetic Susceptibility. Poster presented at the 72nd Annual Meeting of the Society for American Archaeology, Austin, Texas.

2007b Testing Mississippian Mound Structures with Down-hole Magnetic Susceptibility. Paper presented at the Mid-South Archaeological Conference, Memphis, Tennessee.

Lucy, Sam

2005 Ethnic and Cultural Identities. In *The Archaeology of Identity: Approaches to Gender, Age, Status, Ethnicity and Religion*, edited by Margarita Díaz-Andreu, Sam Lucy, Babic Stasa, and David N. Edwards, pp. 86–109. Routledge, London.

Lumb, Lisa Cutts, and Charles H. McNutt

1988 *Chucalissa: Excavations in Units 2 and 6, 1959–1967*. Memphis State University Anthropological Research Center Occasional Papers 15, Memphis State University, Memphis.

Mainfort, Robert C., Jr.

1999 Late Period Phases in the Central Mississippi Valley: A Multivariate Approach. In *Arkansas Archaeology: Essays in Honor of Dan and Phyllis Morse*, edited by Robert C. Mainfort Jr., and Marvin D. Jeter, pp. 143–168. University of Arkansas Press, Fayetteville.

2003 Late Period Ceramic Rim Attribute Variation in the Central Mississippi Valley. *Southeastern Archaeology* 22(1):33–46.

2004 An Ordination Approach to Assessing Late Period Phases in the Central Mississippi Valley. *Southeastern Archaeology* 22(2):176–184.

2005 A *K*-Means Analysis of Late Period Ceramic Variation in the Central Mississippi Valley. *Southeastern Archaeology* 24(1):59–69.

Mainfort, Robert C., Jr., and Marvin D. Jeter (editors)

1999 *Arkansas Archaeology: Essays in Honor of Dan and Phyllis Morse*. University of Arkansas Press, Fayetteville.

Marcoux, Jon Bernard

2008 Cherokee Households and Communities in the English Contact Period, A.D. 1670–1740. Unpublished PhD dissertation. Department of Anthropology, University of North Carolina, Chapel Hill.

Marcus, Joyce

2000 Toward an Archaeology of Communities. In *The Archaeology of Communities: A New World Perspective*, edited by Marcello A. Canuto and Jason Yaeger, pp. 231–242. Routledge, London.

McAnany, Patricia A., and Ian Hodder

2009 Thinking about Stratigraphic Sequence in Social Terms. *Archaeological Dialogues* 16(1):1–22.

McLeod, Todd B.

2015   Developing an Architectural Sequence for a Portion of the Mound A Enclosure at the Carson Mound Group, Coahoma County, Mississippi. Unpublished Master's thesis, Department of Sociology and Anthropology, University of Mississippi, Oxford.

McNutt, Charles H.

1996a   *Prehistory of the Central Mississippi Valley*. University of Alabama Press, Tuscaloosa.

1996b   The Upper Yazoo Basin in Northwest Mississippi. In *Prehistory of the Central Mississippi Valley*, edited by Charles H McNutt, pp. 155–185. University of Alabama Press, Tuscaloosa.

2008   Late Mississippian Phases in the Central Mississippi Valley: A Commentary. *Southeastern Archaeology* 27(1):122–143.

Mehrer, Mark W.

2000   Heterarchy and Hierarchy: The Community Plan as Institution in Cahokia's Polity. In *The Archaeology of Communities: A New World* Perspective, edited by Marcello A. Canuto and Jason Yaeger, pp. 44–58. Routledge, London.

Mehrer, Mark W., and James M. Collins

1995   Household Archaeology at Cahokia and in its Hinterlands. In *Mississippian Communities and Households*, edited by J. Daniel Rogers and Bruce D. Smith, pp. 32–57. University of Alabama Press, Tuscaloosa.

Mehta, Jayur Madhusudan

2015   Native American Monuments and Landscape in the Lower Mississippi Valley. Unpublished PhD dissertation. Department of Anthropology, Tulane University, New Orleans, Louisiana.

Mehta, Jayur Madhusudan, Kelsey M. Lowe, Rachel Stout-Evans, and John Connaway

2012   Moving Earth and Building Monuments at the Carson Mounds Site, Coahoma County, Mississippi. *Journal of Anthropology* 2012:1–21.

Mehta, Jayur Madhusudan, Rachel Stout Evans, and Zhixiong Shen

2017   Mississippian Monumentality in the Yazoo Basin: Recent Investigations at the Carson Site (22CO505), Northwestern Mississippi. *Southeastern Archaeology* 36(1):14–33.

Melton, Mallory A.

2013   Analysis, Contextualization, and Conceptualization of Macrobotanical Remains Recovered from Parchman Place (22CO511). Unpublished manuscript on file at Center for Archaeological Studies, University of South Alabama, Mobile.

Miller, Jay

2015   *Ancestral Mounds: Vitality and Volatility of Native America*. University of Nebraska Press, Lincoln.

Mills, Barbara J.

2008   Remembering While Forgetting: Depositional Practices and Social Memory at Chaco. In *Memory Work: Archaeologies of Material Practice*, edited by

Barbara J. Mills and William H. Walker, pp. 88–108. School for Advanced Research Press, Santa Fe, New Mexico.

Mitchem, Jeffrey M.

1996   Investigations of the Possible Remains of de Soto's Cross at Parkin. *Arkansas Archaeologist* 35:87–95.

Morse, Dan F.

1990   The Nodena Phase. In *Towns and Temples along the Mississippi*, edited by David H. Dye and Cheryl Anne Cox, pp. 69–97. University of Alabama Press, Tuscaloosa.

Morse, Dan F, and Phyllis A. Morse

1983   *Archaeology of the Central Mississippi Valley*. University of Alabama Press, Tuscaloosa.

Morse, Phyllis A.

1981   *Parkin: The 1978–1979 Archaeological Investigations of Cross County, Arkansas Site*. Arkansas Archaeological Survey Research Series 13. Arkansas Archaeological Survey, Fayetteville.

1990   The Parkin Site and the Parkin Phase. In *Towns and Temples Along the Mississippi*, 118–134. University of Alabama Press, Tuscaloosa.

Murdock, George Peter

1949   *Social Structure*. Macmillan, New York.

Nelson, Erin Stevens

2014   Intimate Landscapes: The Social Nature of the Spaces Between. *Archaeological Prospection* 21(1):49–57.

2016   Community Identity in the Late Prehistoric Yazoo Basin: The Archaeology of Parchman Place, Coahoma County, Mississippi. Unpublished PhD dissertation, Department of Anthropology, University of North Carolina at Chapel Hill, Chapel Hill, North Carolina.

2020   Negotiating Community at Parchman Place, a Mississippian Town in the Northern Yazoo Basin. In *Reconsidering Mississippian Communities and Households*, edited by Elizabeth Watts Malouchos and Alleen Betzenhauser, in press.

Nelson, Erin Stevens, Ashley Peles, and Mallory A. Melton

2020   Foodways and Community at the Late Mississippian Site of Parchman Place. *Southeastern Archaeology*, in press.

O'Brien, Michael J., and R. Lee Lyman

1998   *James A. Ford and the Growth of Americanist Archaeology*. University of Missouri Press, Columbia.

Pauketat, Timothy R.

1987   A Functional Consideration of a Mississippian Domestic Assemblage. *Southeastern Archaeology* 6(1):1–15.

1993   Temples for Cahokia Lords: Preston Holder's 1955–1956 Excavations of Kunnemann Mound. Memoirs No. 26. Museum of Anthropology, University of Michigan, Ann Arbor.

2003   Resettled Farmers and the Making of a Mississippian Polity. *American Antiquity* 68(1):39–66.

2007   *Chiefdoms and Other Archaeological Delusions.* AltaMira Press, Lanham, Maryland.

2008   Founders' Cults and the Archaeology of Wa-kan-da. In *Memory Work: The Archaeologies of Material Practice*, edited by Barbara J. Mills and William H. Walker, pp. 61–81. School for Advanced Research Press, Santa Fe, New Mexico.

2013a   *An Archaeology of the Cosmos: Rethinking Agency and Religion in Ancient America.* Routledge, New York.

2013b   Bundles in/of/as Time. In *Big Histories, Human Lives: Tackling Problems of Scale in Archaeology*, edited by John Robb and Timothy R. Pauketat, pp. 35–56. School for Advanced Research Press, Santa Fe, New Mexico.

Pauketat, Timothy R., and Susan M. Alt

2003   Mounds, Memory, and Contested Mississippian History. In *Archaeologies of Memory*, edited by Susan E Alcock and Ruth Van Dyke, pp. 151–179. Blackwell, Malden, Massachusetts.

2005   Agency in a Postmold? Physicality and the Archaeology of Culture-Making. *Journal of Archaeological Method and Theory* 12:213–236.

Pauketat, Timothy R., and Thomas E. Emerson

1991   The Ideology of Authority and the Power of the Pot. *American Anthropologist* 93(4):919–941.

Pauketat, Timothy R., Mark A. Rees, Amber M. VanDerwarker, and Kathryn E. Parker

2010   Excavations into Cahokia's Mound 49. *Illinois Archaeology* 22(2):397–436.

Penn, William

1881[1683] Letter from William Penn, Proprietary and Governour of Pennsylvania in America, to the Committee of the Free Society of Traders of that Province, residing in London. Reprinted by James Coleman, London.

Perdue, Theda

1999   *Cherokee Women: Gender and Culture Change, 1700–1835.* University of Nebraska Press, Lincoln.

Phillips, Philip

1970   *Archaeological Survey in the Lower Yazoo Basin, Mississippi, 1949–1955.* Papers of the Peabody Museum of American Archaeology and Ethnology, Vol. 60. Harvard University, Cambridge, Massachusetts.

Phillips, Philip, James A. Ford, and James B. Griffin

1951   *Archaeological Survey in the Lower Mississippi Alluvial Valley, 1940–1947.* Papers of the Peabody Museum of American Archaeology and Ethnology, Vol. 25. Harvard University, Cambridge, Massachusetts.

Pollard, Joshua

2008   Deposition and Materian Agency in the Early Neolithic of Great Britain. In *Memory Work: Archaeologies of Material Practice*, edited by Barbara J. Mills and William H. Walker, pp. 41–60. School for Advanced Research Press, Santa Fe, New Mexico.

Pursell, Corin C.

2004   Geographic Distribution and Symbolism of Colored Mound Architecture in the Mississippian Southeast. Unpublished Master's thesis. Department of Anthropology, Southern Illinois University, Carbondale.

Rafferty, Janet, and Evan Peacock

2008   *Time's River: Archaeological Syntheses from the Lower Mississippi River Valley.* University of Alabama Press, Tuscaloosa.

Reilly, F. Kent, III, and James F. Garber

2007   *Ancient Objects and Sacred Realms: Interpretations of Mississippian Iconography.* University of Texas Press, Austin.

Reimer, Paula J., Edouard Bard, Alex Bayliss, et al.

2013   IntCal13 and Marine13 Radiocarbon Age Calibration Curves 0–50,000 Years cal BP. *Radiocarbon* 55(4):1869–1887.

Riser, George M.

2009   The Patterned Rise and Fall of Water in the Lower Mississippi Valley: A Proposed Origin for Phillips' Green Line—The Linear Transect Across the Valley Connecting Greenville and Greenwood. Paper presented at the Joint Meeting of the Mississippi Archaeological Association and the Louisiana Archaeological Association, Natchez, Mississippi.

Robin, Cynthia

2002   Outside of Houses: The Practice of Everyday Life at Chan Nòohol, Belize. *Journal of Social Archaeology* 2:245–268.

Rogers, J. Daniel, Michael C. Moore, and Rusty Greaves

1982   *Spiro Archaeology: The Plaza.* Studies in Oklahoma's Past, No. 10. Oklahoma Archaeological Survey, Norman.

Rogers, J. Daniel, and Bruce D. Smith

1995   *Mississippian Communities and Households.* University of Alabama Press, Tuscaloosa.

Saucier, Roger T.

1994   *Geomorphology and Quaternary Geologic History of the Lower Mississippi Valley.* U.S. Army Corps of Engineers, Vicksburg, Mississippi.

Scarry, C. Margaret, and Vincas P. Steponaitis

1997   Between Farmstead and Center: The Natural and Social Landscape of Moundville. In *People, Plants, and Landscapes: Studies in Paleoethnobotany,* edited by Kristen J. Gremillion, 107–122. University of Alabama Press, Tuscaloosa.

2016   Moundville as a Ceremonial Ground. In *Rethinking Moundville and Its Hinterland,* edited by Vincas P. Steponaitis and C. Margaret Scarry, pp. 255–268. University Press of Florida, Gainesville.

Shepard, Anna O.

1956   *Ceramics for the Archaeologist.* Carnegie Institution of Washington, Washington, DC.

Sherwood, Sarah C., and Tristram R. Kidder
2011   The DaVincis of Dirt: Geoarchaeological Perspectives on Native American Mound Building in the Mississippi River Basin. *Journal of Anthropological Archaeology* 30(1):69–87.

Skousen, Jacob
2012   Posts, Places, Ancestors, and Worlds: Dividual Personhood in the American Bottom Region. *Southeastern Archaeology* 31:57–69.

Smith, Gerald P.
1969   Ceramic Handle Styles and Cultural Variation in the Northern Sector of the Mississippi Alluvial Valley. Memphis State University Anthropological Research Center Occasional Papers, No. 3, Memphis, Tennessee.
1990   The Walls Phase and Its Neighbors. In *Towns and Temples along the Mississippi*, edited by David H. Dye and Cheryl Anne Cox, pp.135–169. University of Alabama Press, Tuscaloosa.

Smith, Monica L.
2008   Urban Empty Spaces: Contentious Places for Consensus-Building. *Archaeological Dialogues* 15(2):216–231.

Snead, James E., Clark L. Erickson, and J. Andrew Darling
2009   *Landscapes of Movement: Trails, Paths, and Roads in Anthropological Perspective.* University of Pennsylvania Press, Philadelphia.

Speck, Frank G.
1907   Notes on Chickasaw Ethnology and Folk-lore. *Journal of American Folk-lore* 20(76):50–58.

Stark, Miriam T.
1998   Technical Choices and Social Boundaries in Material Culture Patterning: An Introduction. In *The Archaeology of Social Boundaries*, edited by Miriam T. Stark, pp. 1–11. Smithsonian Institution Press, Washington, DC.

Starr, Mary Evelyn
1984   Parchman Phase in the Northern Yazoo Basin. In *The Wilsford Site (22-Co-516) Coahoma County, Mississippi: A Late Mississippi Period Settlement in the Northern Yazoo Basin of Mississippi*, by John M. Connaway, pp. 163–222. Mississippi Department of Archives and History, Jackson.

Steponaitis, Vincas P.
1978   Location Theory and Complex Chiefdoms: A Mississippian Example. In *Mississippian Settlement Patterns*, ed. Bruce D Smith, pp. 417–453. Academic Press, New York.
1983   *Ceramics, Chronology, and Community Patterns: An Archaeological Study at Moundville.* University of Alabama Press, Tuscaloosa.
1984   Technological Studies in the Prehistoric Pottery of Alabama: Physical Properties and Vessel Function. In *The Many Dimensions of Pottery*, ed. Sander L. van der Leeuw and A. Pritchard, pp. 81–127. Amsterdam.

Steponaitis, Vincas P., Stephen Williams, R. P. Stephen Davis, Ian W. Brown, Tristram R Kidder, and Melissa Salvanish
2002   LMS Archives Online. http://www.rla.unc.edu/lms, accessed 3-13-09.

Stevens, Erin L.

2006   The Making of Monument: Investigating Mound Stratigraphy in the Yazoo Basin. Unpublished Master's thesis. Department of Sociology and Anthropology, University of Mississippi, Oxford.

2008   Late Prehistoric Social Dynamics in the Northern Yazoo Basin. Unpublished Fourth Semester Paper. Department of Anthropology, University of North Carolina, Chapel Hill.

Stout-Evans, Rachel

2011a   Parchman Geomorphology. Manuscript on file at Center for Archaeological Studies, University of South Alabama, Mobile.

2011b   Parchman coring notes. Field notes on file at Center for Archaeological Studies, University of South Alabama, Mobile.

Strickland, Glenn D.

2009   Multidimensional Visual Testing of a Mississippian Mound. Unpublished Master's thesis. Department of Sociology and Anthropology, University of Mississippi, Oxford.

Sullivan, Lynne P.

2006   Gendered Contexts of Mississippian Leadership in Southern Appalachia. In *Leadership and Polity in Mississippian Society,* edited by Paul Welch and Brian Butler, pp. 264–285. Southern Illinois University Press, Carbondale.

Swanton, John R.

1928a   Chickasaw Society and Religion. In *Forty-second Annual Report of the United States Bureau of American Ethnology.* United States Government Printing Office, Washington, DC.

1928b   The Interpretation of Aboriginal Mounds by Means of Creek Indian Customs. In *Smithsonian Institution, Annual Report for 1927*, Government Printing Office, Washington, DC.

1928c   Social Organization and Social Usages of the Indians of the Creek Confederacy. In *Forty-second Annual Report of the Bureau of American Ethnology.* Government Printing Office, Washington, DC.

1928d   Sun Worship in the Southeast. *American Anthropologist* 30(2):206–213.

1931   Source Material for the Social and Ceremonial Life of the Choctaw Indians. Smithsonian Institution Bureau of American Ethnology Bulletin 103. United States Government Printing Office, Washington, DC.

1946   *The Indians of the Southeastern United States.* Smithsonian Institution Press, Washington, DC.

Thomas, Cyrus

1894   *Report on the Mound Explorations of the Bureau of Ethnology for the Years 1890–1891.* 12th Annual Report to the Bureau of American Ethnology, pp. 17–730. Smithsonian Institution, Washington, DC.

Thompson, Victor D. (editor)

2014   Exploring the Space Between: Remote Sensing, Monuments, Households and Broader Landscape in the American Southeast. *Archaeological Prospection,* special issue 21(1).

Thompson, Victor D., Phillip J. Arnold III, Thomas J. Pluckhahn, and Amber M. Vanderwarker
2011   Situating Remote Sensing in Anthropological Archaeology. *Archaeological
        Prospection* 18:195–213.
Townsend, Robert F., and Robert V. Sharp (editors)
2004   *Hero, Hawk, and Open Hand: American Indian Art of the Ancient Midwest
        and South.* Art Institute of Chicago in association with Yale University Press,
        New Haven, Connecticut.
Tuttle, Sarah
1833   *Letters and Conversations on the Cherokee Mission.* 2nd ed. Massachusetts
        Sabbath School Society, Boston.
Twiss, Katherine C.
2007   We Are What We Eat. In *The Archaeology of Food and Identity*, edited by
        Katherine C. Twiss, pp. 1–15. Center for Archaeological Investigations,
        Southern Illinois University, Carbondale.
Urban, Greg, and Jason Baird Jackson
2004   Social Organization. In *Southeast*, edited by Raymond Fogelson, pp. 697–
        706. Handbook of North American Indians, Vol. 14, William C. Sturtevant,
        general editor, Smithsonian Institution, Washington, DC.
Van der Veen, Marijke
2003   When Is Food a Luxury? *World Archaeology* 43(3):408–427.
VanDerwarker, Amber M., Gregory D. Wilson, and Dana N. Bardolph
2013   Maize Adoption and Intensification in the Central Illinois River Valley: An
        Analysis of Archaeobotanical Data from the Late Woodland through Early
        Mississippian Periods (AD 600–1200). *Southeastern Archaeology* 32(2):147–
        168.
Vermeulan, Hans, and Cora Govers
1994   *The Anthropology of Ethnicity: Beyond "Ethnic Groups and Boundaries."* Spi-
        nhuis, Amsterdam.
Walling, Richard, and S. Chapman
1999   *Archaeological Data Recovery at the McNight Site (22CO560), Coahoma
        County, Mississippi.* Submitted to the Mississippi Department of Transpor-
        tation. Panamerican Consultants, Memphis, Tennessee.
Watts, Christopher (editor)
2013   *Relational Archaeologies: Humans, Animals, Things.* Routledge, London.
Watts, Vanessa
2013   Indigenous Place-thought and Agency Amongst Humans and Non-humans
        (First Woman and Sky Woman go on a European World Tour!). *Decoloniza-
        tion: Indigeneity, Education & Society* 2(1):20–34.
Weinstein, Richard, Susan B. deFrance, and David B. Kelley
1985   *Cultural Resources Survey in the Vicinity of Sunflower Landing: Investigations
        related to the Rena Lara Landside Berm, Item L-628*, Coahoma County, Mis-
        sissippi. Contract report submitted to U.S. Army Corps of Engineers, Mem-
        phis District. Coastal Environments, Baton Rouge.

Welch, Paul D., and C. Margaret Scarry
1995   Status Related Variation in Foodways in the Moundville Chiefdom. *American Antiquity* 60:397–419.

Whallon, Robert
1969   Rim Diameter, Vessel Volume, and Economic Prehistory. *Michigan Academician* 11(2):89–98.

Willey, Gordon R., and Philip Phillips
1958   *Method and Theory in American Archaeology*. University of Chicago Press, Chicago.

Williams, Stephen, and Jeffrey P. Brain
1983   *Excavations at the Lake George Site, Yazoo County, Mississippi, 1958–1960*. Papers of the Peabody Museum of Archaeology and Ethnology, Vol. 74. Peabody Museum, Harvard University, Cambridge, Massachusetts.

Wilson, Gregory D.
2008   *The Archaeology of Everyday Life at Early Moundville*. University of Alabama Press, Tuscaloosa.

Wilson, Gregory D., and Christopher B. Rodning
2002   Boiling, Baking, and Pottery Breaking: A Functional Analysis of Ceramic Vessels from Coweta Creek. *Southeastern Archaeology* 21(1):29–35.

Witthoft, John
1949   Green Corn Ceremonialism in the Eastern Woodlands. Occasional Contributions from the Museum of Anthropology of the University of Michigan, No. 13. University of Michigan Press, Ann Arbor.

Wrobel, Gabriel
2003   Field notes from 01 August 2003. Field notes on file at Center for Archaeological Studies, University of South Alabama, Mobile.

Yaeger, Jason, and Marcello A. Canuto
2000   Introducing an Archaeology of Communities. In *The Archaeology of Communities: A New World Perspective*, edited by Marcello A. Canuto and Jason Yaeger, pp. 1–15. Routledge, London.

Zedeño, María Nieves
2008   Bundled Worlds: The Roles and Interactions of Complex Objects from the North American Plains. *Journal of Archaeological Method and Theory* 15:362–378.

2013   Methodological and Analytical Challenges in Relational Archaeologies: A View from the Hunting Ground. In *Relational Archaeologies: Humans, Animals, Things*, edited by Christopher Watts, pp. 117–134. Routledge, London.

Index

ERIN S. NELSON is associate professor of anthropology at the University of South Alabama and a specialist in southeastern prehistory.

RIPLEY P. BULLEN SERIES

Florida Museum of Natural History
Edited by Neill J. Wallis, Charles R. Cobb, and Kitty F. Emery

Tacachale: Essays on the Indians of Florida and Southeastern Georgia during the Historic Period, edited by Jerald T. Milanich and Samuel Proctor (1978)

Aboriginal Subsistence Technology on the Southeastern Coastal Plain during the Late Prehistoric Period, by Lewis H. Larson (1980)

Cemochechobee: Archaeology of a Mississippian Ceremonial Center on the Chattahoochee River, by Frank T. Schnell, Vernon J. Knight Jr., and Gail S. Schnell (1981)

Fort Center: An Archaeological Site in the Lake Okeechobee Basin, by William H. Sears, with contributions by Elsie O'R. Sears and Karl T. Steinen (1982)

Perspectives on Gulf Coast Prehistory, edited by Dave D. Davis (1984)

Archaeology of Aboriginal Culture Change in the Interior Southeast: Depopulation during the Early Historic Period, by Marvin T. Smith (1987)

Apalachee: The Land between the Rivers, by John H. Hann (1988)

Key Marco's Buried Treasure: Archaeology and Adventure in the Nineteenth Century, by Marion Spjut Gilliland (1989)

First Encounters: Spanish Explorations in the Caribbean and the United States, 1492–1570, edited by Jerald T. Milanich and Susan Milbrath (1989)

Missions to the Calusa, edited and translated by John H. Hann, with an introduction by William H. Marquardt (1991; first paperback edition 2024)

Excavations on the Franciscan Frontier: Archaeology at the Fig Springs Mission, by Brent Richards Weisman (1992)

The People Who Discovered Columbus: The Prehistory of the Bahamas, by William F. Keegan (1992)

Hernando de Soto and the Indians of Florida, by Jerald T. Milanich and Charles Hudson (1992)

Foraging and Farming in the Eastern Woodlands, edited by C. Margaret Scarry (1993)

Puerto Real: The Archaeology of a Sixteenth-Century Spanish Town in Hispaniola, edited by Kathleen Deagan (1995)

Political Structure and Change in the Prehistoric Southeastern United States, edited by John F. Scarry (1996)

Bioarchaeology of Native American Adaptation in the Spanish Borderlands, edited by Brenda J. Baker and Lisa Kealhofer (1996)

A History of the Timucua Indians and Missions, by John H. Hann (1996)

Archaeology of the Mid-Holocene Southeast, edited by Kenneth E. Sassaman and David G. Anderson (1996)

The Indigenous People of the Caribbean, edited by Samuel M. Wilson (1997; first paperback edition, 1999)

Hernando de Soto among the Apalachee: The Archaeology of the First Winter Encampment, by Charles R. Ewen and John H. Hann (1998)

The Timucuan Chiefdoms of Spanish Florida, by John E. Worth: vol. 1, *Assimilation*; vol. 2, *Resistance and Destruction* (1998; first paperback edition, 2020)

Ancient Earthen Enclosures of the Eastern Woodlands, edited by Robert C. Mainfort Jr. and Lynne P. Sullivan (1998)

An Environmental History of Northeast Florida, by James J. Miller (1998)

Precolumbian Architecture in Eastern North America, by William N. Morgan (1999)

Archaeology of Colonial Pensacola, edited by Judith A. Bense (1999)

Grit-Tempered: Early Women Archaeologists in the Southeastern United States, edited by Nancy Marie White, Lynne P. Sullivan, and Rochelle A. Marrinan (1999; first paperback edition, 2001)

Coosa: The Rise and Fall of a Southeastern Mississippian Chiefdom, by Marvin T. Smith (2000)

Religion, Power, and Politics in Colonial St. Augustine, by Robert L. Kapitzke (2001)

Bioarchaeology of Spanish Florida: The Impact of Colonialism, edited by Clark Spencer Larsen (2001)

Archaeological Studies of Gender in the Southeastern United States, edited by Jane M. Eastman and Christopher B. Rodning (2001)

The Archaeology of Traditions: Agency and History Before and After Columbus, edited by Timothy R. Pauketat (2001)

Foraging, Farming, and Coastal Biocultural Adaptation in Late Prehistoric North Carolina, by Dale L. Hutchinson (2002)

Windover: Multidisciplinary Investigations of an Early Archaic Florida Cemetery, edited by Glen H. Doran (2002)

Archaeology of the Everglades, by John W. Griffin (2002; first paperback edition, 2017)

Pioneer in Space and Time: John Mann Goggin and the Development of Florida Archaeology, by Brent Richards Weisman (2002)

Indians of Central and South Florida, 1513–1763, by John H. Hann (2003)

Presidio Santa María de Galve: A Struggle for Survival in Colonial Spanish Pensacola, edited by Judith A. Bense (2003)

Bioarchaeology of the Florida Gulf Coast: Adaptation, Conflict, and Change, by Dale L. Hutchinson (2004; first paperback edition, 2020)

The Myth of Syphilis: The Natural History of Treponematosis in North America, edited by Mary Lucas Powell and Della Collins Cook (2005)

The Florida Journals of Frank Hamilton Cushing, edited by Phyllis E. Kolianos and Brent R. Weisman (2005)

The Lost Florida Manuscript of Frank Hamilton Cushing, edited by Phyllis E. Kolianos and Brent R. Weisman (2005)

The Native American World Beyond Apalachee: West Florida and the Chattahoochee Valley, by John H. Hann (2006)

Tatham Mound and the Bioarchaeology of European Contact: Disease and Depopulation in Central Gulf Coast Florida, by Dale L. Hutchinson (2007)

Taíno Indian Myth and Practice: The Arrival of the Stranger King, by William F. Keegan (2007; first paperback edition, 2022)

An Archaeology of Black Markets: Local Ceramics and Economies in Eighteenth-Century Jamaica, by Mark W. Hauser (2008; first paperback edition, 2013)

Mississippian Mortuary Practices: Beyond Hierarchy and the Representationist Perspective, edited by Lynne P. Sullivan and Robert C. Mainfort Jr. (2010; first paperback edition, 2012)

Bioarchaeology of Ethnogenesis in the Colonial Southeast, by Christopher M. Stojanowski (2010; first paperback edition, 2013)

French Colonial Archaeology in the Southeast and Caribbean, edited by Kenneth G. Kelly and Meredith D. Hardy (2011; first paperback edition, 2015)

Late Prehistoric Florida: Archaeology at the Edge of the Mississippian World, edited by Keith Ashley and Nancy Marie White (2012; first paperback edition, 2015)

Early and Middle Woodland Landscapes of the Southeast, edited by Alice P. Wright and Edward R. Henry (2013; first paperback edition, 2019)

Trends and Traditions in Southeastern Zooarchaeology, edited by Tanya M. Peres (2014)

New Histories of Pre-Columbian Florida, edited by Neill J. Wallis and Asa R. Randall (2014; first paperback edition, 2016)

Discovering Florida: First-Contact Narratives from Spanish Expeditions along the Lower Gulf Coast, edited and translated by John E. Worth (2014; first paperback edition, 2016)

Constructing Histories: Archaic Freshwater Shell Mounds and Social Landscapes of the St. Johns River, Florida, by Asa R. Randall (2015)

Archaeology of Early Colonial Interaction at El Chorro de Maíta, Cuba, by Roberto Valcárcel Rojas (2016)

Fort San Juan and the Limits of Empire: Colonialism and Household Practice at the Berry Site, edited by Robin A. Beck, Christopher B. Rodning, and David G. Moore (2016)

Rethinking Moundville and Its Hinterland, edited by Vincas P. Steponaitis and C. Margaret Scarry (2016; first paperback edition, 2019)

The Historical Turn in Southeastern Archaeology, edited by Robbie Ethridge and Eric E. Bowne (2020)

Falls of the Ohio Archaeology: Archaeology of Native American Settlement, edited by David Pollack, Anne Tobbe Bader, and Justin N. Carlson (2021)

A History of Platform Mound Ceremonialism: Finding Meaning in Elevated Ground, by Megan C. Kassabaum (2021)

New Methods and Theories for Analyzing Mississippian Imagery, edited by Bretton T. Giles and Shawn P. Lambert (2021)

Methods, Mounds, and Missions: New Contributions to Florida Archaeology, edited by Ann S. Cordell and Jeffrey M. Mitchem (2021)

Unearthing the Missions of Spanish Florida, edited by Tanya M. Peres and Rochelle A. Marrinan (2021)

Presidios of Spanish West Florida, by Judith A. Bense (2022)

En Bas Saline: A Taíno Town before and after Columbus, by Kathleen Deagan (2023)

Mississippian Women, edited by Rachel V. Briggs, Michaelyn Harle, and Lynne P. Sullivan (2024)

www.ingramcontent.com/pod-product-compliance
Lightning Source LLC
Chambersburg PA
CBHW071103280326
41928CB00051B/2774